FAMILY ACTIVISM

LATINIDAD

Transnational Cultures in the United States

This series publishes books that deepen and expand our knowledge and understanding of the various Latina/o populations in the United States in the context of their transnational relationships with cultures of the broader Americas. The focus is on the history and analysis of Latino cultural systems and practices in national and transnational spheres of influence from the nineteenth century to the present. The series is open to scholarship in political science, economics, anthropology, linguistics, history, cinema and television, literary and cultural studies, and popular culture and encourages interdisciplinary approaches, methods, and theories. The series grew out of discussions with faculty at the School of Transborder Studies at Arizona State University, where an interdisciplinary emphasis is being placed on transborder and transnational dynamics.

Matthew Garcia, Series Editor, School of Historical, Philosophical, and Religious Studies and Director of Comparative Border Studies

For a list of titles in the series, see the last page of the book.

FAMILY ACTIVISM

Immigrant Struggles and the Politics of Noncitizenship

AMALIA PALLARES

RUTGERS UNIVERSITY PRESS
New Brunswick, New Jersey, and London

Library of Congress Cataloging-in-Publication Data
Pallares, Amalia, 1965–
    Family activism : immigrant struggles and the politics of noncitizenship / Amalia
Pallares.
        pages cm — (Latinidad: transnational cultures in the United States.)
    Includes bibliographical references and index.
    ISBN 978-0-8135-6457-9 (hardback) — ISBN 978-0-8135-6456-2 (pbk.) —
ISBN 978-0-8135-6458-6 (e-book)
    1. Immigrant families—United States. 2. Families—Political aspects—United
States. 3. United States—Emigration and immigration. 4. United States—Emigration
and immigration—Government policy. 5. Immigrants—United States—Social
conditions. 6. Immigrant families—Illinois—Chicago. 7. Immigrants—Illinois—
Chicago—Social conditions. 8. Chicago (Ill.)—Emigration and immigration. I. Title.
    JV6456.P35 2014
    325.73—dc23
                                                                    2014014277

A British Cataloging-in-Publication record for this book is available from the British
Library.

Visit our website: http://rutgerspress.rutgers.edu

Manufactured in the United States of America

To Elvira, Flor, Rosi, Fanny, and
all the families in the struggle

CONTENTS

PREFACE

As I reflect on eight years of fieldwork and the hundreds of people I have met in the process of researching and writing this book, I return to the images of four undocumented mothers whose different circumstances have deeply informed my quest for understanding what the immigrant movement seeks, and what would be considered socially just outcomes in a context of diverse and differentiated claims.

Elvira Arellano, who motivated me to embark on this project, was a twenty-eight-year-old activist from Michoacán and the mother of seven-year-old citizen Saul when she sought sanctuary in a Methodist church in 2006, stating that it was inhumane to separate a mother and child and that deporting her was like deporting her son. One year later she was deported after leaving the church on a tour of different sanctuary churches throughout the country. Today Elvira is an activist in Mexico, working for the rights of Central American and Mexican immigrants and deportees.

Flor Crisóstomo was twenty-nine years old when she followed in Elvira's footsteps and sought sanctuary in the same church in January 1998. An activist with Centro Sin Fronteras (CSF) and a factory worker of Zapotec origin, she was a single mother of three small children in Mexico when she decided to migrate alone in order to support her children. While she had no citizen children, she linked her claim to remain in the United States to her economic displacement as an indigenous woman in Mexico as a consequence of the North American Free Trade Agreement (NAFTA). Flor left sanctuary in October 2008 and remains in the United States.

Rosi Carrasco, fifty-four, works in a Chicago social service organization and has deep ties to several immigrant rights organizations. She has lived in the United States for seventeen years, since she and her daughters followed her husband, who had a job and the promise of legalization by an employer, which never came to fruition. She is a member of an entirely undocumented family with an extensive trajectory of activism. Her husband, Martín, is the founder of a workers' organization, and her daughters, Tania and Ireri, are founding members of the Immigrant Youth Justice League (IYJL). All four family members have lobbied; organized marches, protests, and rallies; and personally participated in acts of civil disobedience. In recent years, Rosi has supported the youth movement and worked intensively with parents of young activists engaging in civil disobedience. She has recently founded an organization of undocumented immigrants and allies of many ages.

Fanny López is a twenty-five-year-old activist who came to the United States as a child. The recent recipient of a master's degree from the University of Chicago, Fanny has been active in two youth organizations, Latino Action Youth League (LOYAL) and IYJL, and is now a founding member of the West Suburban Immigrant Collective (SWIC). She has participated in coming-out events and engaged in civil disobedience. Married to David Martinez, a U.S. citizen who is a veteran of the Afghan war, she had baby David in October 2012 and is currently working for a large immigrant rights organization.

All of these undocumented mothers have different claims of belonging that are based on or strengthened by their motherhood. State practices of categorizing and differentiating among immigrants lead to decisions that indicate that some people, and some mothers, are more worthy than others. If you believe only mothers of U.S. citizens should be have the right to remain in the United States, that means that Elvira and Fanny would qualify, and that Flor and Rosi should be excluded. If you consider extended length of time in the United States as your criterion, Rosi and Fanny would remain, and Flor and Elvira would be excluded. If you believe that only those immigrants who were brought here as children should remain, only Fanny would fall under this description. But to what extent do these categorizations make sense, and which ones should be used? Can they be questioned altogether? Are any of these mothers more "deserving" than the others?

This book explores how different immigrant movement activists and organizers have constructed and reinforced but also challenged and redefined existing distinctions and categorizations of families facing separation due to deportation. I look at the malleability and flexibility of the notion of family as it comes to represent and express different ideologies, goals, and strategies in the movement. Elvira, Flor, Rosi, and Fanny, and thousands like them, have all participated in the creation of some form of family activism while simultaneously struggling for political recognition and agency in a context in which the political voices of the undocumented have been muffled.

While they share the marginality of status, their narratives and claims are different, relying on different ideological bases and strategies, and expressing different positionalities. Their voices and political actions, and those of others like them, have taught me many lessons about the complicated relationship between activism, meaning, and political outcome. They have also taught me through their own lives about the polyvalence of family as a lived experience and symbolic representation. My hope is that through the window of the family claim, this book offers readers an opportunity to reflect on the dynamic relationship between meaning and political action, between mainstream understandings and activists' interruptions and reinterpretations of those understandings, and between the restraints on citizenship and the potential of undocumented political agency.

As I reflect on my biography in relationship to the project, I must start by stating that while I did have a research and personal background that facilitated my interest in this research, I have also been transformed by it. I am an immigrant from Ecuador who is somewhere between being a first-generation immigrant and 1.5er. Due to changing family circumstances, while I first came to the United States as a ten-month-old infant, I returned to live in Ecuador on at least three separate occasions. An imperfect but close description would be that I attended most of elementary school in Houston, Texas; junior high in Ponce, Puerto Rico; and some elementary and all of high school in Guayaquil, Ecuador. All the years I was in high school we experienced family separation. My father, despite being a skilled surgeon with postdoctoral training in Baylor College of Medicine, was never able to find solid employment in Ecuador because he came from a working-class background, and did not have the necessary personal connections to land a job in a clinic or hospital that would enable him to afford his most basic dreams for his children. By the time I was a teenager, my mother, after years of being a homemaker in three different states in the United States and Puerto Rico, was mentally and emotionally exhausted and longed for her family and friends in Ecuador. Back in Houston in 1978, we kids were unable to make new friends after bouncing around, and were feeling a bit ostracized in our new schools (being new, brown, and perceived as Mexican or Puerto Rican—the only two options before the terms "Hispanic" or "Latino" became prevalent—was not a recipe for popularity in the Texas we experienced in the late 1970s). Returning to Ecuador was a comfort for my mother and us kids, but my father remained working in the United States. Although he visited us briefly every one or two months and we joined him in Houston some summers, the separation took its toll, and I became familiar with the feeling of having a parent who was mostly absent and the dynamic of being a family split between two countries.

Although my family reunited in the mid-1980s, the feeling of being split between two countries continued through my adult years back in the United States. Although I have lived consistently in this country since the age of seventeen, my desire to not lose my connection to Ecuador has shaped my career as a Latin Americanist and Latino studies scholar as well as my changing legal status. A legal permanent resident since childhood, I did not become a citizen until 1998, once Ecuador allowed dual citizenship. However, the change in Ecuadoran law was not the only reason. While still in graduate school I followed the Proposition 187 movement in California and the 1996 federal immigration bill and witnessed the bill's immediate effects on permanent residents who lost access to medical benefits and risked being deported if they had been convicted of certain felonies. I saw how citizenship became more privileged, while other statuses such as legal permanent resident (LPR) and undocumented status became diminished and ever more vulnerable. Fortunately for me, this was a vulnerability that I could escape by applying for citizenship—however, I also became acutely aware of how many did not have this option.

By 2006, after years of increased deportation and vulnerability, the environment in Chicago and the country was characterized by increasing efforts to mobilize, as immigrants and their supporters intensified the struggle against enforcement and repression. With a long history of labor, community, and Latino and immigrant organizing, Chicago is a site of many different types of immigrant advocacy organizations and groups of different ideological orientations and the site of the first massive immigrant march on March 10, 2006. Faculty and graduate students at the University of Illinois at Chicago (UIC), moved by what we were witnessing, created a collective research project focusing on the 2006 and 2007 marches and on the social movement activism that had made them possible. Out of this effort came *Marcha* (2010), a book I coedited with Nilda Flores-Gonzalez, which analyzed the many different organizing efforts that coalesced in the historical moment of the megamarches. As I conducted my research and worked very closely with undocumented mothers Elvira Arellano and Flor Crisóstomo, I met many other activists and families, some mixed-status, some entirely undocumented. In the process, I became more aware of key differences and similarities between their lives and mine. I had the privilege to have residency status—and later citizenship—and a class background that enabled me to pursue a graduate degree. By contrast, many of the people I met during my field research had multiple life possibilities barred to them because of their status, and they depended on limited, tenuous, and often temporary job opportunities. People with advanced degrees in their country of origin could not even dream of pursuing their professions here. Youths finishing high school or college were faced with dire prospects. What we did share was a history of migration, a language, and the belief that everyday political actions and multiple strategies of resistance could have an impact.

My education on the movement stems not only from the exposure to difficult migrant experiences and stories but also from my observations of their debates, their ideological expressions, their analysis of current policy and politics, and their hopes for their future and that of their family members. I have been able to closely follow the political process that has unfolded in the past eight years. Perhaps the most direct personal experience was supporting the campaign to stop the deportation of UIC student Rigo Padilla in late 2009. Colleague Nilda Flores-Gonzalez and I joined several youths and the Illinois Coalition for Immigrant and Refugee Rights (ICIRR) in weekly planning meetings, fax petition campaigns, and events, and even testified in city hall. The stay of his deportation, announced a day before he was scheduled to be deported, was, in hindsight, a meaningful collective victory, as it motivated the undocumented youths who had been involved to continue the work and found the IYJL, which only three months later staged the first "Coming Out of the Shadows" event in the country, announcing that they were undocumented and unafraid.

On a personal level, the campaign solidified my transition from having an academic interest in the movement to being an engaged, activist academic. I never started this project with a guise of purported neutrality or objectivity, two concepts that have been questioned extensively in the ethnographic literature and which I do not believe exist. Yet I did believe it was necessary to keep a certain distance from my subjects in order to better understand their behavior and its implications. However, in time I also realized that this supposed distance contradicted other important goals in research, such as the pursuit of an extended interpretive ethnography, which assumes extensive interaction and exchange and relies on intersubjectivity, and the basic principle of reciprocity—in exchange for their time and attention to my research, activists asked me to carry out a variety of activities to support their goals, and I have also had the opportunity to mentor and support several undocumented youths at UIC and beyond. In the process, while I have tried to maintain a balance, I am aware that I have been perceived as closer to or more distant from certain groups and that, inevitably, those relationships have shaped how other sectors of the movement may see me. I do not think this reciprocity, participation, and intervention, or the relationships I have forged, impede or thwart my analysis, which is a critical questioning of what family represents and how it is informing and informed by movement goals, identities, strategies, and tactics. Eight years of fieldwork is quite extensive. It has allowed me to develop a rapport with very sophisticated interlocutors who have come to understand and trust that I am not interested in comparing organizations or strategies or evaluating them as better or worse, but in "reading," interpreting, and writing about their narratives and actions as significant and meaningful political processes. I remain convinced that this analysis would have been impossible to do from a distance, since it requires being a close interlocutor, always engaging respectfully with organizers, and sharing my own perspectives as well. Another key aspect of my field research has been an ongoing conversation established with many of the people I have studied throughout the last few years. Some of the activists I discuss below have joined me in reading groups, been my students, attended talks on this book, and shared crucial insights that have informed my revisions of the manuscript. My methodology has striven not simply to observe them as objects of analysis but also to remain engaged in a constant dialogue that extends to a broad and diverse sector of movement participants, Latino communities, and academia.

A reflection of my field experience raises two important circumstances. First, the vicissitudes of an associate professor position juggling administrative and teaching duties while being a single mother to two young boys meant that my research and writing period have been more extensive than average. I realized a while back that this extended study of an ongoing movement that has faced many challenges and achieved very few gains has allowed me to engage in an extended ethnography in which I have been able to identify small changes in ideology and strategy, something that ultimately has become a strength in a book that focuses on the subtle changes in a politics of family. A much shorter ethnography would not have allowed me to identify certain shifts and changes, however small, compare them to previous modes of politics, and place them in a larger context. Second, living in the field means that I never go away and that many of the connections as well as close relationships I have developed in the process remain active to this day. In my view, this has only given me a greater sense of urgency and responsibility to complete the manuscript in the most careful and honest way possible.

I would like to acknowledge that some sections of chapters 2 and 3 were previously published as "Representing La Familia: Family Separation and Immigrant Activism" in *Marcha: Latino Chicago and the Immigrant Rights Movement*, coedited by Nilda Flores-Gonzalez and me (University of Illinois Press, 2010), and a section of chapter 3, cowritten with Nilda Flores-Gonzalez, was previously published as "Regarding Family: New Actors in the Chicago Protests," in *Rallying for Immigrant Rights: The Fight for Inclusion in 21st Century America*, coedited by Kim Voss and Irene Bloemraad (University of California Press, 2011).

This book is dedicated to all the activists and organizers who opened their doors to me and continue to believe in the possibility of creating change. I would like to thank the organizers and activists who were extraordinarily generous with their time, explaining their visions: Jacobita Alonso, Kathy Archibald (RIP), Elvira Arellano, Toribio Barrera, Chris Bergin, Diego Bonesatti, Irma Cabrera (RIP), Rosi Carrasco, Walter "Slim" Coleman, Flor Crisóstomo, Fr. Brendan Curran, Jenny Dale, Jhonathan Gómez, Rachel Heuman, José Lopez, Roberto Lopez, Emma Lozano, Ashley Moy-Wooten, Angélica Rivera, Nathan Ryan, Katty Salgado, Yesenia Sanchez, Micaela Saucedo (RIP), Alma Silva, Fred Tsao, and Martin Unzueta. Youth organizers who have taught and continue to teach me every day include Cindy Agustín, Cynthia Brito, Fanny López-Martinez, Lulú Martinez, Sean McCllelan, Jorge Mena, Alaa Mukkahal, Rigo Padilla, David Ramirez, Anita Rico, Jonathan Rodrigues, Arianna Salgado, Isaac Silver, Xanat Sobrevilla, Yaxal Sobrevilla, Ireri Unzueta, Tania Unzueta, Janeth Vazquez, and Reyna Wences.

I would also like to thank civil society leaders in the following organizations: Chicago Community and Workers Rights, IYJL, ICIRR, Latino Policy Forum, Latinos Progresando, LOYAL, National Alliance of Latin American and Caribbean Communities (NALACC), Nuestra Voz, Undocumented Illinois, and West Suburban Action Project (PASO).

I cannot imagine a better institution from which I could be doing this work. Students, faculty, and administrators at UIC have supported this project in myriad ways. The Institute for the Humanities and the Great Cities Institute awarded me fellowships that allowed me to focus on research and writing. The Latin American and Latino Studies Program, the Political Science Department, and the College of Liberal Arts and Sciences have also provided meaningful contributions in research assistantships and other forms of support.

I have had several interlocutors and colleagues in and outside of UIC who have helped me develop and think about this project from its inception. They include Leisy Abrego, Frances Aparicio, Xóchitl Bada, Linda Bosniak, Jennie Brier, Miranda Cady-Hallet, Mark Canuel, Ralph Cintron, Stephen Davis, John D'Emilio, Molly Doane, Stephen Engelmann, Nilda Flores-Gonzalez, Jonathan Fox, Ruth Gomberg-Muñoz, Elena Gutierrez, Sue Levine, Juan Martinez, Shannan Mattiace, Ellen McClure, Maura Moro-Torn, Michael Rodriguez-Muñiz, Nena Torres, Stephen Warner, and Pat Zavella. Thanks to all of you for the many direct and indirect ways in which you helped make this possible. I am also forever indebted to my research assistants, undergraduates Winne Monu and Jose Espiritu. My graduate assistants Vanessa Guridy and Roberto Rincon provided crucial assistance in fieldwork, offered insightful comments, and helped with extensive copyedits.

My parents and siblings—Carlota, Victor, Carla, Victor, and Jerry—have been a pillar of strength and support, always believing I could complete this. It was perhaps poignant to be writing this book as there were life-changes occurring in my own family. I am so grateful to my sons, Antonio and Pablo, for weathering those changes with such strength, as well as for the wide range of things they have done on a daily basis so I could complete this book, from accompanying me to marches, rallies, acts of civil disobedience, and overnight vigils, to engaging in quiet time so that I could work on a chapter. Most of all, I thank them for making sense of my research on their own terms and never doubting for a second the importance of this work. Finally, my partner, Jack, who came into my life five years into this project, has been a source of love, joy, and support through most of the writing stage. I am deeply indebted to all of you.

I dedicate this book to all the undocumented activists who struggle every day for justice and dignity, and especially to Elvira, Fanny, Flor, and Rosi.

ABBREVIATIONS

AEDPA	Anti-Terrorism and Effective Death Penalty Act, 1996
CIR	comprehensive immigration reform
CSF	Centro Sin Fronteras
DACA	Deferred Action for Childhood Arrivals
DHS	Department of Homeland Security
DREAM Act	Development, Relief, and Education for Alien Minors Act
FU	Familias Unidas (United Families)
GLBT	gay, lesbian, bisexual, transgender
ICE	U.S. Immigration and Customs Enforcement
ICIRR	Illinois Coalition for Immigrant and Refugee Rights
IIRIRA	Illegal Immigration Reform and Immigrant Responsibility Act, 1996
INA	Immigration and Naturalization Act, 1965
IRCA	Immigration Reform and Control Act, 1986
IYJL	Immigration Youth Justice League
LFLU	La Familia Latina Unida (The United Latin Family)
LOYAL	Latino Action Youth League
LPR	legal permanent resident
NACARA	Nicaraguan Adjustment and Central American Relief Act
NAFTA	North American Free Trade Agreement
NALACC	National Alliance of Latin American and Caribbean Communities
NCLR	National Council of La Raza
NHCLC	National Hispanic Christian Leadership Conference
NIYA	National Immigrant Youth Alliance
OCAD	Organized Communities against Deportations
PRD	Partido de la Revolución Democratica (Party of the Democratic Revolution)
PRWORA	Personal Responsibility and Work Opportunity Reconciliation Act, 1996
RIFA	Reform Immigration for America
UWD	United We Dream

FAMILY ACTIVISM

INTRODUCTION
Immigrant Rights Activism
and the Family Paradox

   In the past decade, due to legal and political changes that have dramatically curtailed the legalization options for people who are in the United
States without legal status, millions of undocumented immigrants and their
families have experienced the threat or reality of deportation and family separation. Faced with the increasing inability to make any individual claim to remain
in the United States, undocumented immigrants, their relatives, and supporters
have organized around the notion of family as a political subject whose rights are
being violated upon deportation. Insofar as many of these families are mixed-
status families, meaning they have at least one undocumented member and one
who has legal status, immigrant rights advocates have claimed that a citizen's right
to a family (many of them children) is being violated, as are the collective rights
of families (regardless of the citizenship of its members) to remain together.
While the former claim is centered on the right of the citizen member to have
a family, the latter is based on personhood—that is, on the claim that all people,
regardless of citizenship status, have a right to care and be cared for by immediate family members. While neither of these rights has been recognized in U.S.
courts of law (except in extraordinary cases of extreme hardship to a citizen), in
recent years the claiming of the right to remain a family has become a powerful
basis for arguing against deportation and for legalization of the undocumented.
   This book explores the significance of family as a political construct in the
contemporary immigrant rights movement. Drawing from Mae Ngai's description of the undocumented as "impossible subjects" who are constructed as
being outside of the polity, it focuses specifically on the "impossible activism"
of undocumented immigrants, whose political rights are not recognized as
legitimate (Ngai 2004). As the legally excluded and their supporters challenge

this "impossible" context, they have relied on the politicization of a basic social institution such as family and the implementation of family-based relational strategies to question the justice of contemporary immigration law. Family has become politically significant in at least two ways. First, family has been created as a political subject as activists rely on relational strategies, meaning that they draw on the familial connections among individuals as a primary axis of identification and ideology. Second, family has become a central site of collective identity as representations and discourses of the family have assumed increased significance in debates between pro-immigrant rights groups and their opponents and state officials, as well as within immigrant and Latino communities.

Exploring this first dimension involves tracing how family has been constructed as a political subject in the past decade, focusing on the discourse of family and family rights stemming from grassroots campaigns, immigrant rights organizations, politicians, churches, and interfaith coalitions. Based on ethnographic research and interpretive analysis of seven years of advocacy campaigns and trips, marches, protests, vigils, hunger strikes, acts of civil disobedience, and a wide variety of actions, I explore the different ways in which family becomes politicized, and what different representations of the family teach us about immigrant subjectivities, the agency of mixed-status families and immigrant youth, and the activism of and for the undocumented. Further, I analyze the ways in which immigrant movement strategies that I label tangling, intersecting, and crossing are evident in these different family politics.

Second, I highlight the distinct ways in which narratives and performances of family serve as a site of collective identity, acting as both a source of unity and distinction (and at times division) within the immigrant rights movement. The immigrant rights movement does not share one collective identity stemming from a singular process of identification among movement participants—there are many differentiations among movement adherents. It would be a mistake to assume, for example, that all the immigrant rights marchers in 2006 and 2007 were undocumented. A great majority were citizens, both naturalized and native born (Pallares and Flores-Gonzalez 2010). Organizers themselves are divided among immigrants with legal status (including non-Latino leaders), undocumented immigrants, second- and third-generation Latinos, and non-Latino natives who became active in the movement through their labor, civil rights, or religious identifications and affiliations. While some participants were part of a mixed-status family and are therefore directly affected by the possibility of deportation in their family, many were not. Hence, allegiance to or solidarity with the undocumented is not something to be assumed, but to be explained. Additionally, even looking solely at immigrants, there are key differences that make the forging of a collective identity difficult to do: not only are they divided by status—documented and undocumented—but among the undocumented distinctions are made between those who have overstayed their visas and those who crossed the border. (The former, made up of more Europeans and Asians but also some Latin Americans, sometimes minimize the extent to which they broke the law since they entered the country legally but overstayed their visas.) All these elements together mean we cannot speak of one collective identity but of multiple communities coming together in different moments or campaigns, not unlike the civil rights movement, sharing a general goal, but multivocal, with important ideological and strategic differences that are either minimized or negotiated as they strategize and move forward.[1] These fragmented identities are tied together with shared frames that are sustained on discourses of civil, religious, and human rights. The concept of family and family unity plays a key role in this collective bonding.

Both in terms of subjectivity and collective identity, it is relevant to note that family is also a site of racialization and racial resistance. Studies of postracial discourse have argued that locating racism in the post–civil rights era requires looking beyond more obvious discriminatory expressions and actions and focusing on issues, debates, and policies that disproportionally affect populations of color, including debates on culture, nation, religion, education, and immigration (Balibar and Wallerstein 1991; Bonilla-Silva 2012; Gomberg-Muñoz 2012). This is especially relevant when one analyzes discourse about the deserving and undeserving poor, the deviant and nondeviant, and the worthy and unworthy immigrant. While plenty of restrictionist or anti-immigrant rhetoric seems obviously racist, there are also less blatant forms of racialization that are embedded in discussions and policies dealing with immigrant families, deportations, and family separation. I argue that these racial meanings are significant to explain not only the devaluation of immigrant families in the broader polity but also the new consensus for legalization among Latinos.

To understand the politicization of family in the immigrant movement, this book engages in a dialogue with three main areas of scholarship: the theorization of noncitizenship or alienage, the political dimensions of family, and undocumented political subjectivity.

THEORIZING NONCITIZENSHIP AND THE QUESTION OF "WORTHINESS"

What is the basis upon which people who lack legal status can claim to belong to the polity? Do people who are undocumented in fact have any rights-based claims, or does lack of access to citizenship make them excludable? In *The Citizen and the Alien* (2008) Linda Bosniak claims that it is not a contradiction to talk about the citizenship of the undocumented. This is the case, she claims, because citizenship in liberal democracies is hard on the outside but soft on the inside, due to the expectation of a certain level of egalitarianism supported in liberal regimes. Thus, while undocumented immigrants may be denied formal citizenship, they do have access to certain social and labor protections on the basis of their territorial presence and personhood, as conveyed in the equal protection clause of the Fourteenth Amendment, which is not exclusive to citizens. Hence, Bosniak argues, the division in the immigration debate is between those who, like Bosniak, think that the spheres of citizenship should be separate—that is, formal illegality should not be used as a basis for denial of basic rights on other fronts—and those who claim that these spheres are conjoined and should not be separate, therefore justifying denial of a broader range of rights based on a lack of formal citizenship status. While Bosniak argues for the former, she admits that there is an ambiguity between these two positions and that it is not possible to keep them totally separate. Ultimately, Bosniak argues that lack of status should not be used as a basis for denial of personhood rights.

In response to Bosniak, Muneer Ahmad (2011) claims that Bosniak's argument for the separating out of personhood rights is not feasible because the two spheres have been inevitably conjoined. While he agrees with Bosniak's claim that they are indeed separate, he also argues that personhood rights and citizenship rights in the United States are tethered, so that the personhood regime does not exist independently from citizenship, which has the higher priority. Hence, Ahmad concludes, the lack of citizenship status threatens the enjoyment of substantive rights even in the cases where rights are based on personhood.

So if citizenship trumps personhood, then how does an undocumented person claim the right to citizenship? Both a legal scholar and a practicing lawyer, Ahmad argues that lawyers' narratives to defend the rights of immigrants involve citizenship scripts, which he calls the routinized performances of cultural, economic, and civic understandings of the citizen, that are needed, even in instances in which a person's status is irrelevant to his or her right to legal protection. So what exactly are these routinized performances Ahmad refers to, and why are they so necessary? In court settings it is not unusual, he explains, for individual immigrants to adopt narratives of worthiness. "In the context of immigrants' rights, the worthy immigrant is, in many respects, an idealized citizen, living a life of robust economic productivity, civic engagement, and familial responsibility" (Ahmad 2011, 5). Ahmad quotes Margot Mendelson's description of how these narratives work in the courtroom: "When granting relief from deportation, judges heap praise upon immigrants for working seven days a week and marrying their high school sweethearts. Court decisions wax poetic about immigrants who attend church every Sunday, coach local little league teams, and raise their children speaking English. These values and lifestyles (many of them family-centric) are understood to be quintessentially American, and it is by proving one's American credentials that one may be exempted from imminent deportation" (Mendelson 2010, 1015). Ahmad concludes: "A rights-asserting immigrant is a model citizen in every way but for status citizenship. Indeed, not only are the clients made out to conform to citizenship scripts, they over-conform, performing a kind of supercitizenship that is neither expected nor typical of the status citizen, and yet is demanded of them precisely because they are definitionally noncitizen." The problem Ahmad sees is that worthiness narratives "may expand the contours of the rights-bearing community, but do so at the risk of reinforcing the subordinating regime that produces the substantive inequality in the first place" (2011, 6), and may reinscribe patriarchal or heteronormative structures. Instead of questioning the basis for citizenship, they are reinforcing citizenship.

Drawing from Bosniak and Ahmad, one can reach two important conclusions about the belonging of noncitizens. First, while personhood is not earned but citizenship is, the right to personhood of noncitizens is not always recognized, and second, undocumented immigrants still must strive to be like citizens in order to be recognized as persons, what Ahmad calls the worthiness quest. This quest is based on the premise that the noncitizen who is deemed worthy is entitled not just to rights but to the free exercise of rights, because of the behavioral similarity he or she bears to idealized status citizens. Thus, even when asserting seemingly personhood-based rights, what Mendelson calls the powerful myth of citizenship is sustained. In other words, for undocumented immigrants, their personhood is not enough, in and of itself, to claim citizenship. Therefore, they must increasingly rely on another basis to claim citizenship: a form of merit or worthiness based on the performance of an ideal citizenship in a context of uneven and limited recognition of personhood.

While Ahmad's work primarily rests on court cases to stop deportations, a similar rationale of worthiness permeates the immigrant movement and informs strategies. In a social movement context, however, this worthiness logic is supported not only through immigration laws and practices but also through the racialization of Latinos as foreigners. Performances of worthy citizens are not only ways of gaining potential legal recognition but also are counters to existing representations of immigrants as outsiders and even threats to the nation. Scholars of Latino studies have explored these linkages by focusing on the ways in which Latinos more generally, and Latino immigrants specifically, are racialized and excluded. What makes these analyses more complicated is the fact that this slippage between the categories of Latinos and immigrants is not accidental, but actually reflects the ways in which people are othered and excluded. While Latinos have different statuses (native-born and naturalized citizens, legal permanent residents, work visa holders) and histories in this country (ranging from recent immigrants to centuries of family history in the United States), images and depictions of immigrants often refer to all Latinos as foreign "others"

(Oboler 1995). The recent Twitter responses to eleven-year-old Mexican American mariachi singer Sebastien de la Cruz singing the national anthem during the NBA finals and to Marc Anthony singing "America the Beautiful" in a baseball All-Star game—both native-born citizens and both rejected as "foreigners" and "illegals" who should not be singing patriotic songs—are only the most recent examples. This is why the immigration issue is not only relevant to immigrants but also is a springboard or platform from which to speak about all Latinos, as well as other minorities who are viewed as foreign "others" regardless of their citizenship status. Hence, immigration discourse and policy are used to justify exclusion of non-immigrants: they do double work.

The exclusion of Latino immigrants from the nation is sustained ideologically through the use of repeated images and representations that help to create and reinforce exclusion. Leo Chavez (2008) and Otto Santa Ana (2002) have analyzed the specific discourses and metaphors used to locate immigrants of Latin American origin as outside of the nation. Santa Ana (2002) has argued that the primary metaphor used to depict immigration is that of dangerous waters, depicted as a flow or a sea of brown faces, which must be contained or shut off in order to protect the "house" that is the nation.[2] Uncountable and dehumanized in these images, undocumented immigrants are rejected as part of the nation. Additionally, Santa Ana argues that another common metaphor for undocumented immigrants is that of animals, a metaphor that also depicts immigrants as lacking citizenship potential.

Chavez (2008) argues that while all Latinos are affected by images of the "Latino threat," these images are primarily based on depictions of immigrants of Latin American origin. Immigrants are viewed as undermining American culture and not assimilating. When using resources and social services, they are viewed as challenging or undermining the privileges of citizens and of citizenship. Chavez's research confirms one of Amhad's main points: that citizenship is often understood as the bestower, the be all and end all, of rights, and therefore the personhood of noncitizens is not recognized. When formal citizenship becomes the bestower of rights, then any access of noncitizens to the rights and privileges of citizens is viewed as inherently unfair because it transgresses a boundary and undermines national sovereignty. Understood not only as the excluded who help to define the included (Honig 2001; Bosniak 2008) but also as a threat to the privileges and resources of those who are included, undocumented immigrants are often rendered deviant and less than human. This is why their personhood, while it exists, without citizenship status, has to be proven and claimed.

How, then, can undocumented immigrants be included as citizens if they are also defined as outsiders who are a threat? How is it possible for them to move from threatening others to being members of the polity? This book claims that in the increasingly challenging quest for worthiness, the political construction of family plays a key role. As immigrant individuals' rights to claim citizenship or to appeal deportation have been curtailed in the past two decades, an appeal to the family and to the role and worth of the individual in a family context has become an increasingly important way of proving one's worth as a potential citizen, both in the courtroom and in the social movement sphere. The reliance on "family" as way of addressing the problem of noncitizenship is the subject of this book.

THE POLITICS OF FAMILY

While family and discourses on the family have played important roles in the political sphere across time and place, there is no systematic, comparative analysis of the role and significance of the family as a political construct (and not a social institution). However, there are case studies and analyses of the political meaning of family or familial relationships (such as motherhood) in specific nation-state politics as well as in social movements.

In the U.S. context, Robert Self (2012) compares the meaning of family in the discourse of Democrats in the 1960s. In the 1960s, the survival of family was a basic rationale for supporting antipoverty programs, whereas by the 1980s a conservative movement promoting family values had used the political meaning of family to justify a very different policy direction, one that attacked social programs. Self argues that a traditional notion of family (emphasizing and privileging the male breadwinner) was utilized to justify both sets of policies, one that favored more state support and intervention in addressing poverty and one that attacked the programs.

Several other scholars have focused mainly on the contemporary discourse of family values, emphasizing its ideological origins and showing how conservative claims that families were more "traditional" and heteronormative in the past are a myth (Gillis 1997; Coontz 1993), as well as analyzed the ways in which contemporary families are far more complex, diverse, and structurally conditioned than what is assumed in family values discourse (Gerson 2011; Coontz 1998; Sarkisian and Gerstel 2012; Stacy 1997). Janet Jakobsen (2000) reminds us that while the contemporary debate on family values has focused on the heteronormative inclination and homophobic nature of this discourse, family values discourse does much more than justify antigay policy. She argues that family values discourse, since its inception, has excluded racial minorities, and not only sexual ones. She claims that talk about family values is not simply homophobic or heterosexist discourse, but refers to various social hierarchies condensed within the symbol of "family values," including class and race. Jakobsen reminds us that "family values" provided the legitimating discourse for both the Defense of Marriage Act (DOMA) and the welfare reform bill in the summer of 1996, allowing for regulation through budget cutting of all those queer bodies that did not fit into a mold of white middle-class privilege (2000, 19). While she does not mention it, this is the same welfare reform bill that severely cut the welfare rights of legal permanent residents.

Both Self and Jakobsen highlight the political significance of family and reveal the interconnections between "family" and racial categories and hierarchies. While the Lyndon B. Johnson administration expressed a more inclusive vision that bridged race by highlighting the similarities among families of different races and economic status, the contemporary version reflects values of nuclear families that are viewed as self-reliant, devaluing those who are dependent on the state. In contemporary discourse, the representations of those who do not fit the mold are racialized (examples being the African American welfare mother from Chicago or the Mexican pregnant woman crossing the border to give birth as undeserving and state-abusing mothers). These associations are so powerful, in fact, that undocumented immigrants are often viewed as dependent on welfare even though they do not qualify for it. Hence, in Jakobsen's view, queer bodies are not only those considered outside the heteronormative norm but also those considered outside a middle-class white norm. Jakobsen concludes that "family values" provides the punitive discourses about women, poverty, race, and sexuality that short-circuit counterclaims for economic and racial as well as sexual justice.

Jakobsen's argument helps to explain the apparent contradiction between a supposedly neutral "family values" discourse and a lived reality in which families of color are not as valued as white middle-class families. The family activism I study in this book highlights this contradiction and attempts to reproduce a "family values" discourse that does not discriminate on the basis of legal status or race, close to the 1960s ideal of family described by Self. However, the latent presence of race and citizenship, the very constitution of family values discourse, renders this separating out of a more democratic discourse a difficult challenge for both civil rights and religious leaders emphasizing the family.

In terms of social movement activism, there has been significant work on social and political mothering in the United States, Latin America, and many other parts of the globe (Agosin 1990; Grayzel 1999; Guzman Bouvard 2002; Jetter et al. 1997; O'Reilly 2007; Swedlow 1993; Van der Klein et al. 2012). This mothering politics has been used for more progressive directions (suffrage, rights of poor immigrants) and more conservative tendencies (sanitation, curbing prostitution, eugenics, and so forth). However, it is important to note that conventional notions of motherhood have been used in support of radical politics, as evidenced in the U.S. Strike for Peace movement, when women struggled against nuclear arms and intervention in Vietnam by invoking their traditional feminine and motherhood roles (Swedlow 1993). Perhaps one of the most notable cases of reliance on traditional motherhood is that of the Mothers of the

Plaza de Mayo, created in 1970s Argentina, who relied on notions of traditional motherhood roles to demand information about their disappeared children during the repression or "dirty war" of the military dictatorship. Scholarship on this case maintains that their claims did reinforce traditional motherhood and that this was a strength because it helped them avoid being viewed as a threat by the state in their early activism and pointed to the contradictions between a military state that claimed to defend the Argentinean nation and families against the threats of Marxism and the reality of state torture and executions (Agosin 1990; Bosco 2006; Guzman Bouvard 2002). In this instance, the very same assumptions of the state about what was the proper place of women served as a mechanism of subversion. However, scholars who have followed the trajectory of the mothers in the decades after the transition to democratic rule have argued that far from reinforcing traditional notions of motherhood and family, the Mothers have been very supportive of youth movements and other progressive and GLBT organizations and have come to understand their mothering as a form of social mothering, supporting and nurturing postdictatorship activism in the country (Bosco 2006; Guzman Bouvard 2002).

Additionally, more recently there has been some work on the role of political motherhood in the antifemicide movement in Ciudad Juarez, questioning the emancipatory potential of political motherhood. While Melissa Wright (2001) claims that motherhood politics in the movement renders it more conservative and less contestatory, Fernando Bosco (2007) disagrees and explains that as mothers become activists, they also develop a more radical notion of motherhood and align themselves with antiglobalization movements. Bosco's argument is that actors emphasizing their motherhood are not, by definition, conservative or progressive, and that it would be premature to consider the struggle of mothers against femicide in Juarez a conservative one.

I have encountered similar questioning of my emphasis on family while presenting my research at conferences. I am asked whether I think this politics of family in the immigrant movement is problematic since it reinforces traditional norms and can therefore not be progressive—the conversation ranges from more general reminders of intersectionality, or, more specifically, power differences within households as a cautionary tale against romanticizing the family, to more pointed critiques similar to Ahmad's claim that performing conventional hypercitizenship reinforces the status quo and does not challenge the state's immigration regime. While I do acknowledge the critique of how such performances can conform to conventional norms (and I share this critique in different sections of the book), we should not assume that a politics that relies on a reproduction of conventional norms always means or implies a lack of emancipatory potential. One should not discard it and instead at the very least analyze the work that family does. There are a number of reasons why this is the case. First, as we can see in the example of the Mothers of the Plaza de Mayo, the reliance on conventional images and norms can underscore the contradictions between state rhetoric and state practices, in essence shaming the state into having to explain why it has not protected the values/communities/norms it purports to protect or stand for. While this reinforces certain norms, it may also push the state to revisit its own position and implement certain policy changes, such as in the case of U.S. Immigration and Customs Enforcement (ICE) altering its guidelines for detentions of breastfeeding mothers.[3] Additionally, conventional discourses may resonate more broadly and appeal to potential allies because they do not feel threatened, but rather identify with these issues. In the case of the Mothers of the Plaza de Mayo, their plight appealed to a global human rights community—in the case of the migrant family claims in the United States, as chapter 3 shows, family claims have proved pivotal in the forging of alliances with religious communities and leaders. Second, it is problematic to conflate conventional discourses with conventional actions or effects. Activists may rely on conventional discourses to engage in very novel and nonconventional actions—the example of Elvira Arellano, discussed in chapter 2, is a case in point. She relied on her claim as a mother who did not want to be separated from her son and on her citizen son's right to grow up with a parent. In doing so she resisted her own deportation by speaking out for her case (a public coming out and seeking of agency that was very novel at the time for any undocumented person) and seeking sanctuary in a local church, inviting the state to come get her there if it wanted to. Her discourse and action were subjects of local, national, and global debate, and it was as common to hear some state that her goals were very conventional and others state that she was quite radical. I would sustain she was both, and that it is premature to assume that conventional discourses are always accompanied by conventional strategies or lead to conventional effects.

Finally, as the last part of this book shows, it is important to keep in mind the polyvalence of family in a social movement setting. I explain how some sectors of the movement have relied on less conventional understandings of the family to create stronger bonds among native-born citizens and immigrants of different statuses and sexualities as well as between mixed-status families and entirely undocumented families. In other words, I argue that in later phases of the movement, newer actors (in this case, organized undocumented youth) have, in opposing deportation, challenged conventional understandings of family and suggested alternative ones. In sum, to dismiss the role, significance, and effects of family in the movement with the critique that the defense of family relies on conventional and therefore nonliberating strategies not only throws the baby out with the bathwater, it also ultimately means a "not seeing" of the movement or of the work of "family" as a producer of meaning within it.

Lest the reader view in this perspective a romanticization of the family, let me clarify that I am not interested in any essentialized vision of the family. I focus on the family as a political construction (with associated frames, ideologies, strategies, and tactics), and not as some fixed and idealized social institution. Nor am I necessarily adopting the perspective that Latinos are more culturally prone than other ethnic or racial groups to value families as an explanation for the political activism I seek to explain. In a review of research on Latino families, I examined several scholarly works on the topic of Latino familism, most of which are psychological studies, none of which focuses on political activism (Okagaki and Frensch 1998; Oyserman, Coon, and Kemmelmeier 2002). Matthew Desmond and Ruth Lopez-Turley (2009) define familism as a social pattern whereby individual interests, decisions, and actions are conditioned by a network of relatives who take priority over the individual. Basic dimensions of this familism, which is understood primarily as a cultural variable, include high levels of perceived family support and a strong perception of family as referents, both of which decline with more acculturation but remain higher than those of non-Hispanic whites. Other scholars have argued that Hispanic adults and adolescents value interdependence and family support and obligations more than whites do (Fuligni, Tseng, and Lam 1999; Harrison et al. 1990; Sabogal et al. 1987); report higher degrees of familial cohesion and intimacy than whites do (Niemann, Romero, and Arbona 2000; Sabogal et al. 1987); assist family members more than whites do (Sarkisian, Gerena, and Gerstel 2006); and live in larger and denser kinship networks than whites do (Sarkisian, Gerena, and Gerstel 2006; Valenzuela and Dornbusch 1994).

Some scholarship, however, questions familism as a useful explanation for many different attitudes and behaviors among Latinos. For example, Caroline Hartnett and Emilio Parrado (2012) found very weak support for the idea that familism undergirds ethnic differentials in fertility for native Hispanics. They suggest instead that socioeconomic characteristics and migration experiences, rather than the cultural orientation of familism, explain fertility differentials. Other scholarship has questioned the differences in rates of familism among different groups, suggesting that Hispanics do not appear to have higher levels of familism than other groups (Schwartz 2007).

While family networks are indeed more important in disempowered and low-income communities who rely on them for self-help, I am not convinced that familism is easily generalizable across status, place of birth, generation, or national origin, or that one can always find consistent relationships between familism and individual behavior without accounting for socioeconomic factors. In other words, familism may be more of a mediating variable, and something else—time of migration or socioeconomic status or education level—may explain a propensity to familism. Therefore, I am not persuaded that Latinos as a totality (not controlling for income, generation, and so forth) take family more seriously than other groups, or that familism in and of itself explains the role of family or the politicization of family in the immigrant movement.

Hence, I argue that the politics of family in the movement cannot be explained by or derived from a fixed concept of Latino familism as a cultural phenomenon. I argue that this reliance on family is not something solely cultural but a response to political and social developments that have separated families in rather arbitrary and violent ways via deportation as well as increased enforcement that keeps families separated. A major premise underscoring this argument is a conceptualization of family as a social and even political construct and not only as an institution. This conceptualization allows us to see the immigrant movement's focus on the family not as some inevitable, culturally informed, or determined expression of "Latino familism," but as a powerful and political construct of meaning that is shaped by deportation policies and politics and in turn informs immigrant movement ideologies, organizing, and strategizing.

UNDOCUMENTED SUBJECTIVITY: CREATING SPACE THROUGH ACTION

If activists have been relying on a politics of family to claim their "worthiness" in their antideportation struggles, the final question in the puzzle is how do they do so, and more specifically, how do undocumented activists do so? While scholars of citizenship have begun to point to the need to critically examine the exclusionary aspects of citizenship that shape the experience of undocumented residents as the "present absents" in the U.S. polity, it is the task of social movement scholars to turn their focus on the specific agency of the undocumented—that is, on the relationship between the exclusion from citizenship and the forms of political representation, strategies, and identities that undocumented people can potentially deploy.

Much of American social movement theory attempts to identify patterns and/or create a template that would allow us to make generalizations about a social movement's causes, strategies, and effectiveness. The assumption is that, irrespective of the actors, there are certain basic features shared by all social movements and that we can engage in a comparative analysis that helps us understand how these actors deploy strategies and resources differently (Kriesi et al. 1995; McAdam et al. 1996; Meyer 2009; Meyer and Whittier 1994; Tarrow 1994). Rarely, however, does this scholarship engage in a critical discussion of how the subject position of a social movement actor may affect the possibilities of the deployment of these strategies, identities, and resources.

New social movement theory did pioneer a focus on collective identity in shaping a movement's causes, actions, and effects. Alain Touraine (1988) pointed to the relevance of understanding why individuals and groups may imagine or reimagine themselves in new ways and how this may lead to new forms of organizing. Jean Cohen (1985) and Joshua Gamson (1995) explored the relationship between identity and strategy, discussing the ways in which collective identity and strategy may be in a dynamic interrelationship mutually shaping and constituting each other. This provides a more useful way of thinking about how movements work. It seems, however, that there is a mediating factor that receives very little attention: the relationship between identity and strategy might be shaped by the restrictions or limitations on political subjectivity—that is, both identification alternatives and strategies one may develop in response to a third pivotal factor, which is political subjectivity. In other words, how does one's political subjectivity or location constrain or enable opportunities for resistance? Specifically, in this case, how do the restraints of noncitizenship, for example, affect what activists can make possible?

Some significant work has been done on how the boundaries that distinguish the documented from the undocumented enable and reinforce the latter's subordination and exclusion, ranging from the political construction of the border that creates illegality, as explained by Mae Ngai (2005) and others; the condition of deportability and inclusion through exclusion analyzed by Nick de Genova (2010); the simultaneous inclusion as persons but exclusion as aliens analyzed by Bosniak (2008); and the need to "earn" personhood when you are not a citizen discussed by Ahmad (2011).

Most scholars agree that the paradox of the undocumented is that while they are physically present in the millions, they are excluded completely from the body politic, its imaginary, and the sense of belonging to the "nation" that informs and is informed by formal citizenship. Bosniak (2008) asserts that even liberals who argue for separate spheres and are open to the idea of equal social and economic rights for noncitizens draw the line at political rights. They tend to uphold an unexplained assumption that voting rights and political representation should be off-limits to noncitizens. While not historically accurate, this assumption is shared by most of the citizenship theorists Bosniak discusses and by many in the general population. Noncitizens are viewed as outsiders primarily on the legal and political fronts, and their political agency and participation are not only not recognized but also denied as a possibility. They are, as Peter Nyers (2010) has explained, impossible activists.

How, then, may this exclusion as political actors be informing undocumented immigrants' subjectivities, especially in the context of movement activism? As actors who are creating a new space in which they can constitute themselves as subjects, the undocumented are engaged in what Hannah Arendt (1958) and Jacques Ranciere (1995) have called a world-building activity. Mustafa Dikeç (2013) analyzes the activism of the Sans Papiers in France, and relies on this notion of a world-building activity, claiming that the undocumented transgressively occupy roles that they are not associated with in order to be considered equals. When those who were thought unable to do something show that they can, Dikec explains, they are producing political subjectivity (and not merely disclosing a previously conformed one). He states: "Political subjects are not created *ex nihilo*, and politics, rather than taking place in specific realms, is in fact a space-making action that blurs—rather than abides by—divisions" (Dikec 2013, 88). Equally, Cristina Beltran discusses the 2006 immigrant marches as a space of appearance: "When subjects enter the public realm they are not simply enacting their already existing commitment" (2009, 616). Instead, she argues that subjectivity is produced and transformed through these civic encounters. She adds that for this type of subjectivity to be effective, it would most likely need to continue in future actions to enact what seemed politically improbable prior to its performance.

Similarly, in his analysis of the activism of Algerians facing deportation in Canada, Nyers (2010) relies on Bonnie Honig's discussion of the foreigner as a "democratic taker," which is "the practice of taking rights and privileges rather than waiting for them to be granted" (Honig 2001, 79, 99, 101, quoted in Nyers 2010, 424). Like Dikec, Nyers also relies on Ranciere to argue that when abject subjects (those who have no part in the social order) act as equal speaking beings and articulate a grievance, they enact an interruption that Ranciere defines as a radical moment. Also relying on the work of Engin Isin (2002), Nyers continues by explaining that such moments "enable the excluded or the abject to 'constitute themselves as political agents under new terms, taking different positions in the social space than those in which they were previously positioned'" (Isin 2002, 275–276, quoted in Nyers 2010, 424).

An additional key insight stems from Susan Coutin (2000a), who has analyzed how Central Americans have historically tried to conform to the stereotype of the model immigrant but also challenge the basis of their exclusion (the notion of "no human is illegal" comes from this period). Coutin claims that excluded immigrants both conform and transgress, comply with and challenge, the dividing lines as well as the criteria of worthiness. This suggests the importance, perhaps even the necessity, of a moving positionality, or a politics of motion, to which I will return.

In work not directly related with social or political activism but with the everyday survival of the undocumented, scholars have emphasized the "in-betweenness" of migrant consciousness. Leo Chavez (1997) has relied on the notion of liminality to describe the settlement of undocumented immigrants in Southern California, living in a marginal position, neither belonging nor being fully excluded. Linda Basch, Cristina Blanc-Szanton, and Nina Glick Schiller (1992) proposed a transnational framework in order to understand the myriad ways in which migrants inhabit two different social spaces that they carry with them at all times. In their aptly titled article "I'm Here but I'm There," Pierrette Hondagneau-Sotelo and Ernestine Avila (1997) have written about transnational motherhood to analyze strategies used by women in caretaking positions in the United States with children in their country of origin to mother from afar. Pat Zavella (2011) warns that this form of existence, of being in-between, is a difficult one, as people feel like they are neither from here nor there, with lives shaped and informed by both countries, but never fully belonging in any one place. There is a double vision where thoughts and actions about lives, perceptions, and relationships are grounded in both countries. In her ethnography of indigenous migrants from Oaxaca, Mexico, who periodically migrate to Oregon and California, Lynn Stephen (2007) opts for the term "transborder" as opposed to "transnational" because she considers the national as only one subset of the borders that migrants traverse. "Transborder," Stephen argues, better captures the indigenous migrants' crossing of ethnic, racial, class, gender, and regional boundaries, as well as different labor, communication, and transportation systems across and within both countries. The multiple "homes" or sites that they inhabit may be defined as a shared social field, but they are also discontinuous spaces (Stephen 2007, 8–9). Migrants, Stephen explains, are connected to networks that are in turn linked to other networks, creating multisited "meshworks" that inform a complex web of relationships that are local, regional, national, transnational, and global. She argues that all the people living within these meshworks share this transmigrant subjectivity, even if they rarely or ever migrate (Stephen 2007, 19–23).

Stephen's notion of "transborder" is reminiscent of other works in Latino and Chicano studies that have suggested that this "in-betweenness" is not only about a crossing of territorial spaces or even the social imaginaries of two nations but also about crossing multiple intersecting lines while growing up and living in the United States and negotiating the many divisions or borders experienced between Mexico and the United States as well as among Mexicans, Mexican Americans, and other Latinos in the United States. Hence, it applies to both immigrants and nonimmigrant Chicanos and Latinos as well, and in addition to nation refers to class, gender, sexuality, and race as borders. For example, Pat Zavella (2011) analyzes these differentiations among Mexican immigrants and non-immigrants as key factors that shape how people experience their familial, social, and political relationships in the United States.

These perspectives are informed by the work of Gloria Anzaldúa (1987), who discusses borders both as a physical space and as a social, political, spiritual, and emotional one. Inhabiting the borderlands, she explains, refers to always being in different worlds and negotiating between them. Anzaldúa visualized the border between Mexico and the United States as an open wound that bleeds repeatedly.

But the physical border is also a metaphor for other crossings in multiple social, sexual, and geopolitical contexts between cultures but also within one's own culture. Anzaldúa claims that surviving and even thriving through this open wound requires healing; yet this healing does not involve choosing one or the other side or being permanently split among them. It involves tolerating and learning from the ambiguity, producing knowledge as both insider and outsider, straddling the different worlds and transcending the duality in one's own terms in order to create a third space that can lead to numerous possible outcomes. Anzaldúa explains this new mestiza consciousness: "Though it is a source of intense pain, its energy comes from continual creative motion that keeps breaking down the unitary aspect of each new paradigm. . . . Because the future depends on the breaking down of paradigms, on the straddling of two or more cultures" (1987, 102). This notion of a continual creative motion that breaks down paradigms is similar to the notion of a politics of motion described in the discussion of immigrant subjectivity above.

Works that have focused specifically on legal status and its social and political effects have also relied on the notion of liminality. These include Susan Coutin's (2003) discussion of legal nonexistence in which people are physically present and socially active but lack legal recognition, participating in some spaces and not in others, and Cecilia Menjívar's (2006) discussion of the permanent temporariness of Central Americans whose status, due to legal and historical circumstances, can change from deportable to nondeportable more than once. Menjívar argues that immigrant assimilation theories do not consider status and do not accord sufficient attention to the state's role in shaping the subjectivities of immigrants who lack status or are shifting between statuses and therefore living suspended lives, existing in a state of what she calls liminal legality. She claims that while anthropologist Victor Turner referred to liminality as a temporary or transitional stage between two fixed states, in the case of undocumented or sometimes undocumented immigrants, this state is not temporary but extended and can last most of a person's life. Finally, Roberto Gonzales and Leo Chavez (2012) also address the question of how undocumented status affects political, civic, and social selves by relying on the notion of abjectivity, first used by Sarah Willen (2007) in an effort to bring together status and subjectivity. To be abject, according to the authors, is to be cast away, expelled, or excluded, to inhabit a liminal space, simultaneously being part of and not being part of the nation.

Combining existing literature on transborders, undocumented activism, and the effect of status on subjectivity, I argue that the activism of undocumented immigrants forces us to think about a politics of simultaneous liminality and motion, in which those who inhabit the hard outside but soft inside discussed by Bosniak share a subjectivity that permanently occupies the borders and an agency that involves a crossing of the lines of status as a political construct, of inclusion and exclusion, of citizenship and alienage. If in a legal court context they are always arguing for inclusion and in order to do so mostly reinforcing standards of worthiness, in a social movement context they inhabit and activate the borderlands, engaging in a politics that is both conforming and challenging, accepting and reinforcing state norms and categories of belonging, but also questioning and interrupting them, hence always engaged in a politics of motion.

Following Coutin's insights about activists both conforming and challenging, I am interested in the questions of how we can theorize this politics of motion. I would argue that not only Salvadorians but also all those who are deemed excluded or excludable, irregular, unauthorized, undocumented, or illegal are engaged in a politics of constant motion. Hence, when they deploy relational strategies (strategies in which they emphasize their relationship to a family/families), they engage in three specific tactics or types of tactics: tangling, crossing, and intersecting. While I argue that these politics characterize different areas of realms of organizing, I focus on the politics of family (and its concomitant relational strategy) as a window or frame through which this politics of motion can be rendered visible. While tangling and intersecting are initiated and pursued by organizers of all statuses, the politics of crossing is usually initiated and led by undocumented organizers and activists. I argue that these tactics need to be understood as tactical forms with varying content (they are not limited to undocumented activists and can be used by activists of many different ideological tendencies for very different purposes). However, I argue, as well, that among the three tactics, crossing has the most emancipatory potential, since it is most likely to challenge and even disrupt previous arrangements or imaginaries, and facilitate or enable the creation of new political spaces.

By "tangling," I refer to the tying together of the lives and futures of the documented and the undocumented by underscoring the role played by the undocumented in the lives and caretaking of residents and citizens, and the ways in which deporting the undocumented leads to a dramatic decline in the affective, economic, and social conditions of the documented. While ties among residents in a city or neighborhood are also examples of this, in my research I emphasize the extent to which an emphasis on family ties in mixed-status families means that the vulnerability of millions of undocumented people leads to the vulnerability and declining life conditions of millions more.

By "intersecting," I refer to acts that emphasize different aspects of immigrant lives and identities, in the process questioning the dividing lines between deserving and underserving immigrants or legal status as the most determining or constitutive aspect of a person. Personal narratives and "Coming Out of the Shadow" speeches help to illustrate the different layers and relationships that characterize speakers' lives, underscoring the ways in which status alone does not define them, as well as highlighting the similarities between those who are undocumented and those who are not. While some of these may not challenge the dividing line between documented and undocumented itself, they can certainly problematize it. Importantly, intersecting also allows for the creation of collective identity with others who are not undocumented, most clearly along ethnic, racial, faith, and sexuality lines.

Crossing is a tactic that goes beyond tangling and intersecting by acting out of place, openly challenging the categories of who is part of a group (and who is not) and which behaviors are allowed and not allowed of immigrants. Crossing is a tactic that can only be performed by undocumented immigrants themselves or their immediate family members. While tangling and intersecting are tactics deployed by most sectors of the movement, crossing is a tactic more likely to be used by more critical or radical sectors of the movement (day labor, youth, and some grassroots organizations and networks) and usually attempts to challenge existing notions of worthiness and create new ones. An example of this would be that of undocumented youth who defended themselves in a Washington, D.C., court after being arrested for engaging in civil disobedience during a DREAM Act protest in August 2010. While they had access to legal counsel, they chose to defend themselves in an effort to perform citizenship and to occupy a place from which they have been habitually excluded, occupying roles with which they are not associated. However, in very conservative contexts, even intensive lobbying is considered subversive and may be considered a form of crossing. While tangling and intersecting are often claims to similarity to citizens in order to gain recognition as possible citizens, crossing involves enacting or performing citizenship, not asking for it.

Why is it important to be engaging in the improbable, to be tangling, intersecting, and crossing in new ways? To never sit still? If we return to Bosniak's metaphor of the hard edges and the soft core and balance it against Ahmad's claims that recognition of personhood relies on the ability to be "worthy" of citizenship, we find common ground—they both recognize that personhood and citizenship coexist, even if Ahmed acknowledges that it is very hard to separate them. Undocumented subjectivity involves not only activists' recognition that both exist but also activists' performance of both citizenship and personhood and of the complicated relationship between the two in the context of a state that hardened the lines between them. In other words, as the immigration system has become less porous and flexible, the soft spaces have counted less and the hard lines have counted more; the enforcement of sovereignty has gained priority over the personhood of noncitizens. The politics of "worthiness" seeks to preserve these soft spaces or remind the state of their existence.

However, the politics of worthiness is not enough. Immigrant politics in a social movement setting entails going beyond the politics of worthiness or preservation to a politics of claiming and creating new spaces. I agree with

Dikec that immigrant subjectivity is not only about preserving or space-saving, but about space-making as well. Space-making entails shifting, moving over, altering existing divisions and categorizations, and proposing new and more inclusive ones. If the privileging of citizenship masks personhood, immigrant tactics involve bringing personhood to the surface in different ways in order to claim citizenship. In tangling, intersecting, and crossing, immigrant activists are both relying on existing forms of worthiness and creating new ones, engaging in the art of the politically improbable but not impossible. I am not speaking of revolutionary shifts but of small instances of space creation that can be seen in the "family politics" of the immigrant movement as it evolved between 2006 and 2014.

This study is based on ethnographic research of the immigrant rights movement conducted over an eight-year period (2006–2013). In spring 2006 I started researching La Familia Latina Unida (LFLU), a group of thirty-five families arguing against the deportation of their own family members in a context of a highly mobilized political period, right after the March 10 and May 1 Chicago marches. Moved by the dire situation of many of these families facing deportation and intrigued by the activism of the families' undocumented members, I decided to focus on family activism and the creation of the family as a political subject that underscored the relationships among mixed-status families. This seemed to me a stark contrast from dominant discourses that individuate undocumented immigrants and criminalize them. This was my focus in a chapter in my coedited book, Marcha: Latino Chicago and the Immigrant Rights Movement (2010), and is developed more specifically in chapter 2 in this book. However, as I studied the broader movement composed of different organizations relying on different strategies, I realized that studying the creation of the family as a political subject alone did not capture the different aspects of what family represented or the work that family was doing in the movement. I realized that family was becoming a site of collective identity across people of different origins, races, classes, and religious identification, as well as a reflector of ideological tendencies, as different groups emphasized different rationales and justifications for family unity and represented the family in different ways, some focusing primarily on mixed-status families, others minimizing or erasing the distinction between mixed-status and entirely undocumented families. However, I also realized that many different organizations (not only those made up of mixed-status families or explicitly created as organizations of families like LFLU) were speaking of the family and for families. As new youth organizations such as the Immigrant Youth Justice League (IYJL) and Nuestra Voz started to "come out" and negotiate their own positions in relationship to the family claims, I realized that family politics was not merely a key social movement frame, but could provide a window into immigrant activists' political subjectivity.

By 2010, I had expanded my project from how a certain organization or group of "family" organizations engage in antideportation and prolegalization poli tics to study what the family represents in the movement, including its different ideological expressions, the relational strategies connected to it, the tactics utilized by activists, and the role played by different organizations in the creation of ideas, strategies, and tactics. I focused on four main cases: the sanctuary experience of Elvira Arellano (2006–2007), the Chicago-based LFLU campaign (2005–2008), the national Familias Unidas (FU) campaign (2008–2009), and the advocacy of IYJL (2010–2012). I utilize these cases to show how the use of family as a point of reference for activism remains a constant, but the way in which family is framed differs and evolves according to the group involved, the strategies used, and the historical and political context. My research methods include eight years of participant observation of meetings, retreats, press conferences, rallies, religious ceremonies, marches, protests, and acts of civil disobedience. While most of these observations have occurred in Chicago, I have also traveled to Washington, D.C., several times, as well as to Tijuana, San Diego, and Mexico City to observe events or conduct interviews. Additionally, my research assistant, Vanessa Guridy, traveled to Texas and Florida following the FU campaign. I have also conducted approximately 120 hours of interviews with activists and organizers from LFLU, Centro Sin Fronteras (CSF), IYJL, Nuestra Voz, and Illinois Coalition for Immigrant and Refugee Rights (ICIRR), as well as a wide variety of politicians, grassroots community and religious leaders, and immigration attorneys. In the cases of Elvira Arellano, Flor Crisóstomo, and members of IYJL, I have also spent years visiting and interacting with these activists on a regular basis. Additionally, I have relied on several informants whom I have been in regular conversations with about different developments in the movement both in Chicago and at a national level. Finally, I have read and analyzed relevant organization literature; newspaper texts; press releases; online literature, posts, and debates; policy briefs; government documents; public opinion surveys; bills; laws; congressional hearings; and court cases.

The book follows a chronological order. Chapter 1, "From Reunification to Separation," overviews the historical, legal, and political changes that have led to the record rates of deportations and related family separations. I review the immigration laws implemented in the mid-1990s and analyze how they dramatically altered the existing legal framework, paying particular attention to how policy changes and their implementation have affected families' ability to stay together. I consider the different legal options available to undocumented immigrants in these situations and explain why they are very limited and very rarely lead to exceptions based on family claims. Finally, I review the social and economic effects that these deportations have had on families that have been affected.

Chapter 2, "A Tale of Sanctuary: Agency, Representativity, and Motherhood," discusses the case of Elvira Arellano, the president of LFLU, who sought sanctuary in a Methodist church in order not to be separated from her citizen son. This chapter explores what happens when an undocumented mother relies on her relationship with her son to claim political agency and struggle against her own deportation. I analyze the potential and limits of this strategy through a discussion of the mainstream media's questioning of her agency as well as the ambiguity of other immigrant movement supporters around the case. The final section compares Arellano to Flor Crisóstomo, another mother who sought sanctuary in the church after Arellano's deportation, to show the limits of the mixed-family strategy in its exclusion of parents who do not have citizen children.

Chapter 3, "Regarding Family: From Local to National Activism," analyzes the evolution of the family as a political subject and social movement frame from the creation of LFLU in 2005 through the end of the FU campaign in 2009. I look at both a Chicago-based grassroots campaign as well as a national campaign in order to explain the rationale and ideological constructs that have informed this frame; the ways in which each campaign performed or enacted the family, highlighting salient similarities and differences; and the empowering potential as well as social and political limitations of the family frame in each of the two cases. By starting with the local grassroots campaign and then analyzing a national campaign visualized by the same CSF leadership, I seek to understand how the family frame evolved and how it was able to take hold beyond members of mixed-status families and inform broader political imaginaries, playing a key role in the building of support from religious and other political allies as well as other Latinos not directly affected by deportation.

Chapter 4, "Our Youth, Our Families: DREAM Act Politics and Neoliberal Nationalism," analyzes the case of Chicago's IYJL to argue that undocumented youth advocating for the DREAM Act initially relied on a different form of worthiness than that used by the families discussed in chapter 3. They relied on a frame that presented them as talented, innocent, and American individuals who should be evaluated separately from the parents who brought them. This juxtaposition of youth and family as dichotomous is also reproduced by critics of the DREAM-only strategy within the movement in 2010. After the failed DREAM Act vote of December 2010, the youth responded by questioning this neoliberal mode of representation and self-representation and by relying increasingly on the embracing of a relational strategy, highlighting their connection to family to pursue an alternative agenda and strategy and engage in a more autonomous struggle.

The conclusion, "Moving Beyond the Boundaries," first provides an update with a review of the politics of the 2013 Comprehensive Immigration Reform Act. Next, it draws some general conclusions about why and how the family, in the context of the struggle for undocumented immigrant rights, is an object of continuous political construction and change. I specifically focus on the significance of the changing representations of family. I also reflect on the theoretical implications of this research, emphasizing its impact on how we theorize citizenship, undocumented immigrant subjectivity, and family. I reiterate my arguments that the family—and the relational strategies pursued—has played a central role in immigrant activism in a context of limited recognition of personhood. I conclude that movement activism and the family frame have informed each other—that the political meaning of family can be both exclusionary and inclusionary, emancipatory and exploitative/subordinating, and empowering and disempowering at the same time. What it definitely has been, and remains, is significant.

1 · FROM REUNIFICATION TO SEPARATION

The preservation of family unity has become a common referent for immigrants and their descendants as well as for a broader community of support. Spearheaded by community, political, and religious leaders, this defense of family is mainly informed by the shared lived experiences of immigrants facing the prospect of deportation in a historical and legal context that had privileged family reunification and unity for almost four decades. As immigration policy changes seek a diminishment of the family reunification rationale to one that emphasizes "highly skilled" professionals, today's immigrants are experiencing an unprecedented reality: the contradiction between a history and official discourse that has prioritized family unity and reunification and a reality that threatens the survival of undocumented and mixed-status immigrant families already living in the United States. This chapter reviews the legal and political changes that have led to the current record rates of deportations and related family separations and the decline of family unity as a state goal. Additionally, I analyze the economic and social effects of immigration policy changes in the past fifty years, which have led to a dramatic increase in detention and deportations and increased the vulnerability of the undocumented and their family members.

Immigration policy analysis matters not only because the laws expand or curtail the possibilities of legalization but also because policy directly affects trends. Migration patterns and migration "crises" are caused both by demographic and economic trends and by immigration policy, which shapes who can or cannot migrate and how they can or cannot migrate. One clear example is Douglas Massey, Jorge Durand, and Nolan Malone's (2003) persuasive argument that intensification of border enforcement in the past two decades has impeded circulatory migration (a previously common pattern) and forced migrants to bring their families to settle without status rather than risk going back and forth to visit them. In this way a policy designed to diminish undocumented migration actually increased it.

Even a policy that aims to be inclusive can be exclusionary if it is designed in a way that prevents millions from accessing the pursued good. As I review below, with one exception, the capacity of the family reunification visa system has remained the same for decades, creating a backlog that has led to more undocumented migration. Hence, U.S. policy (on both the admissions and enforcement ends) has facilitated the existence of eleven million migrants who are undocumented, made "illegal" and therefore deportable. As Mae Ngai, Cecilia Menjivar, Nicholas De Genova, and others have argued, illegality is created by a system that creates the boundaries of legality and illegality, and "illegals" are a production of the state.

IMMIGRATION LAW, FAMILY IN(EX)CLUSIONS, AND MIGRATION PATTERNS

Before the 1950s there was no consistent policy of family inclusion for migrants, and there were several instances of family exclusion targeting non-European migrants, such as the Chinese Exclusion Act, which would not allow the Chinese to bring spouses, or the bracero program, specifically targeted toward men who, in a time of labor shortages during World War II, were recruited to come alone and work and return to Mexico. The lack of concern for the family rights of Mexican immigrants was made even more evident in the massive repatriations in the 1930s, when citizen adults and children were sent back to Mexico along with their noncitizen relatives. In fact, according to Edward Telles and Vilma Ortiz (2007), 60 percent of the "repatriated" in this period were citizens. It was not until the 1950s that family reunification was explicitly included as a category that made someone eligible for admission. The McCarran-Walter Act of 1952 was the first to introduce a system of preferences for the selection of immigrants applying for admission that was based on both skill sets and family reunification. However, because it still continued the national origins quota system that gave preference to immigrants from those populations already here, this policy favored mainly Western European applicants.[1]

The 1965 Immigration and Naturalization Act (INA), by contrast, which was informed by the civil rights movement, did away with the national origin preference while maintaining the skills category and expanding the family emphasis (adding parents of U.S. citizens over age twenty-one to the list of immigrants not subject to numerical limitations, and altering the size of preference categories so that family reunification was emphasized). According to Charles Keely, this expansion was due to the negotiation of two philosophies of immigration, one that emphasized humanitarian values and one that was concerned with maintaining American culture (1971, 8). Humanitarians favored repealing the national origins quota and expanding the family numbers, as there had been a backlog since the passage of the McCarran-Walter Act. Those concerned with the "preservation of American society" wanted to continue the national origins quota system and were open to family reunion with the condition that the American economy and labor were protected. The 1965 law reflected compromises by both factions (the death of the national origins preference and emphasis on family reunion were concessions to the humanitarians, while efforts to protect American jobs via labor certification and to curtail Western Hemisphere migration favored the preservationists). Eliminating the national origins preference allowed for the significant expansion of non-European migration. However, it was a controlled expansion, as there was a numerical restriction of 170,000 individuals for the Eastern Hemisphere, and a 120,000 ceiling on Western Hemisphere migration.

Hence, since the 1950s there has been an immigration norm that prioritizes family reunification in cases of family members abroad, and family unity in cases of families who reside in the United States. This includes not only prioritizing family members for visas (regardless of race) but also facilitating legalization for those who married in the United States. Citizenship was bestowed to partners and parents of minors (and siblings) of citizens and residents, although the latter have a longer wait for reunification. Very close relatives of citizens were not subjected to the numerical limitations of the quota system. In no legislation have children (under the age of twenty-one) ever been able to bestow citizenship upon their parents.

This creation of a family reunification system that prioritizes the nuclear family (in the immediate family relatives category) and locates siblings and adult children in a secondary category (in the family preference system, which has a limit) reinforced what Monique Hawthorne (2007) considers a very limited North American model of family that does not consider different cultural constructions of family, and does not even reflect the different models that exist in the United States. According to Pat Zavella, including only spouses and children under the age of twenty-one as part of the family unit is a provision that "codifies a heterosexual nuclear family and excludes other types of family structures that are prevalent in the United States and Latin America—such as single parents, the elderly, multigenerational, extended, those headed by minors, or same-sex families, as well as children born 'out of wedlock' or who have informal foster relationships with parents (in loco parentis) such as children cared [for] by their grandmothers when parents migrate" (2012, 1). This restricted model has not been altered since 1965, with the very recent and important exception of the recognition of same-sex marriages in visa petitions starting July 2013 and of same-sex partnerships in prosecutorial discretion (in cases of individuals facing deportation) since October 2012.[2] While an analysis of how these very recent policies may affect immigrant family policy and politics is outside the scope of this chapter, the positing of a nonheteronormative model of immigrant families by youth activists, discussed in chapter 4, certainly indicates a better fit with the youth activists' model of family than with the traditional one.

However, while all these nuclear families were considered equal in theory by the 1965 INA, they were not equal in reality due to the differences in the volume of migration across the country. Mae Ngai (2013) discusses how Senator Phillip Hart's proposal prior to the 1965 act that would have allotted 48 percent of all visas to countries that were the largest senders in the previous fifteen years was not accepted by the Kennedy administration, which was pursuing a civil rights–era ethos of equality and insisting instead on the visa system that allotted an equal number of visas to all countries. This meant that citizens of the countries that send the largest number of immigrants, such as Mexico and the Philippines, have much longer waits for visas. Since all countries have an equal limit of visas, regardless of sending patterns, citizens' relatives and even very young children have had to wait years or decades before being able to enter the United States.

Despite these limitations, which led to different lived legal experiences among immigrants of different national origin, this policy not only shaped law but also immigrant communities' understanding of the law and their expectations that family was the primary rationale for migration and legalization. One cannot overestimate the discursive power of these family reunification policies. The prioritizing of admission based on family reunification has informed immigrant communities' notions of what is fair, just, and achievable, and these notions are shared by most immigrants, regardless of their legal status.

While one could argue that these reunification policies apply only to legal migration and do not include those immigrants who did not enter legally, these distinctions are problematic to make retroactive for at least a couple of reasons. It is not until the 1980s debate on the Immigration Reform and Control Act (IRCA) that the issue of "illegality" surfaced as a central concern, which remains prevalent through today, and that the distinction between "legal" and "illegal" became a central focus. Second, because of IRCA, many people who were undocumented were able to legalize—subsequent reunification of families has therefore included the reunification of family members of individuals who were once undocumented but gained legal status and were able to petition for family members. The fluidity between the undocumented and the legal migrant, between the citizen and the noncitizen, suggests that this norm of family unity is widespread and porous, predates the stark illegal/legal divide, and continues to be shared by most immigrants. As the visa backlogs became longer, many immigrants who were related to citizens opted to migrate without authorization and felt morally justified doing so. Insofar as the U.S. immigration system has prioritized and recognized a need for family (the basis for this is discussed later in this chapter), the standards and norms have relevance for the undocumented immigrants' sense of what is fair.

By the mid-1980s, the United States had already experienced a family reunification system that was limited in its breadth and would become more so in subsequent decades. The economic crisis of the late 1970s and early 1980s, conjoined with the migration influx of Central Americans (in addition to the substantial migration of Cubans coming from the Port of Mariel), led to the intensification of public concern about immigration and to the development of a national agenda and legislative process that concluded with the passing of IRCA in 1986. IRCA is the federal government's first attempt to manage and control "illegality" by combining an amnesty program that legalized about two million people who could prove they had arrived in the United States before 1982, but also created employer sanctions to punish those who hired undocumented immigrants. Like the 1965 act, it was a trade-off between immigrant rights supporters, who sought a human solution for the undocumented, and restrictionists, who conditioned the amnesty on establishing measures that would impede and/or disincentivize more undocumented migration. No significant changes to the numbers of the visa quota system were made in this or any subsequent bill, nor was there any provision that would expand the restricted family model created by the INA.

In fact, newly legalizing family members was quite restricted, as IRCA did not allow for the legalization of spouses and minors of applicants who had arrived after 1982 to legalize as derivatives as long as the newly legalized had temporary status. (It took four years from the granting of temporary status to becoming a legal permanent resident [LPR], which then qualified an immigrant to petition for family.) Hence, IRCA is the first policy to create split families among those living in the United States, consisting of those who qualified and those who did not, leading to deportations of many of those who did not qualify. This development led to pressure from immigrant rights supporters for the 1994 modification of section 245 I of the 1990 act, in which an adjustment of status provision allowed for undocumented family members of residents and citizens who had been residing in the United States to petition to legalize without having to leave the country and wait.

Because these new family legalizations were added to the caps in the visa list (and the quota was not formally expanded to accommodate the post-IRCA demand), amnesty made backlog longer, significantly slowing the process for future applicants and further lengthening already lengthy waits. The Immigration Act of 1990 made a one-time adjustment in order to accommodate IRCA beneficiaries' petitions, raising the maximum number of visas per year from 500,000 to 700,000. This was the first and last time the cap was adjusted. However, given the number of years it takes for an immigrant to become a resident and then a citizen and petition for family, the greatest number of IRCA-related petitions have come after 1990, with no subsequent updates to the caps.[3] While neither perfect nor permanent solutions, both the creation of 245 I and the expansion of the caps did reinforce the family reunification norm and signaled that family unity of mixed-status families already residing in the country was also a priority.

While IRCA led to the temporary expansion of visas to accommodate the relatives of those who qualified, it also created a backlog that extended even further the wait of future applicants. This backlog problem pushed family migrants residing in the United States to opt to migrate illegally. Policy makers of different stripes made this connection explicit in the Independent Task Force on Immigration and America's Future, which reported in 2006: "The system's multiple shortcomings have led to a loss of integrity in legal immigration processes. These shortcomings contribute to unauthorized migration when families choose illegal immigration rather than waiting unreasonable periods for legal entry."[4] Statistics support this task force observation, since the problem has only become exacerbated after 245 I was eliminated in 2001. A significant percentage of the estimated eleven million unauthorized immigrants in the United States are spouses and minor children of LPRs who have been approved for family-based visas but are caught in the years-long preference category logjam. But if they come and then try to legalize, they are barred for ten years and then "become part of a growing underground of undocumented people who are subject to exploitation and abuse."[5]

The bar referred to in this passage is the one in the 1996 Illegal Immigration Reform and Immigrant Responsibility Act (IIRIRA), which stipulated that a person who was unlawfully present in the United States for one year, upon leaving the country, would be barred from returning for ten years. While this was passed in 1996, it was only felt to its full extension when section 245 I's second extension expired. This meant that an undocumented family member of a citizen who wanted to apply for legalization could no longer do so from the United States and would have to leave the country and apply at a consulate. However, leaving the United States to do this immediately triggered the bar. The ability of citizens to petition their family members living in the United States and legalize their status was thwarted.

If the situation of undocumented family members already living here was impossible, the prospects of family members living abroad and seeking to reunite here was not exactly easy or quick. Because the quota has never been based on realistic matching with demands of the economy, or been adjusted to expand for the largest sending countries, the problem just perpetuates itself and becomes more severe. The 2007 bill as well as the 2013 Senate legislation did nothing to expand the number of visas; instead, both sought to reduce family-based migration and increase skill-based visas. Specifically, the 2013 bill would have eliminated the sibling family preference category, making it impossible to sponsor siblings. To address the demands of agriculture and service industries, both bills proposed a form of temporary guest worker program that would not grant visas to the families of workers.

Another legacy of IRCA was the criminalization of deportation by equating a deportation order with a felony conviction, and barring those with felony convictions from ever legalizing. Thus IRCA barred the previously deported from being able to apply for legalization, eliminating the possible use of waiver (212 I) that had allowed the possibility of pardoning any felony with the exception of drug-related ones.[6] This permanently prevented families that had a member deported previously from being reunited.

The decade between IRCA and IIRIRA was characterized by the rise of strong anti-immigrant sentiment expressed in an intense restrictionism that sought increased external and internal enforcement and exclusion of immigrants (documented and not) from state services and resources. The immigrant family came to renewed attention in the debate and mobilization over Proposition 187 in California, which aimed to deny education, social services, and most health services to undocumented immigrants and required local police, health, and social service officials to report undocumented immigrants to the federal government. Mexican women, in particular, were represented as hyperfertile, their reproductive expenses costing taxpayers highly.

The view of immigrant and specifically Mexican immigrant women as a reproductive threat is not necessarily new. In a study of mainstream journalism's perceptions of Mexican and Mexican American women's fertility between 1965 and 1999, Leo Chavez (2004) found that journalists associated these women with high fertility and population growth, and therefore more likely to use medical and other services for their children. He claims that anti-immigrant sentiment during the 1980s and 1990s focused on the reproductive aspects of Mexican immigrant and Mexican-origin women. Both Chavez and Jennifer Hirsch (2003) show a more complicated story of fertility than the alarmist stereotypes of mainstream media. Relying on California-based data, Chavez (2004) showed that Mexican-origin women have had a drop in fertility, but that the steep decline in the fertility of white women and the fact that the fertility of immigrants remains higher than that of native white women have led to alarmist but unfounded claims of hyperfertility. Hirsch (2003) argues that while fertility rates of Mexican women did increase in the 1980s and 1990s, fertility in Mexico has declined significantly in the past three decades, and that fertility tends to decline with migration. Some of these statistics may point to the life-cycle and relative youth of migrants more than to hyperfertility.

Irrespective of its accuracy, the claim of hyperfertility has had a deep impact on health and immigration policies. Elena Gutierrez (2008) has aptly argued that in the 1970s, the forced sterilization of Mexican and Mexican American women (of different legal statuses) was a form of eugenics in response to the perceived threat of Mexican women's reproduction. In the 1990s, this attack on Mexican women's fertility assumed a different path, focusing not on eugenics but on a discourse of "economic costs" (which erased or minimized economic contributions of immigrants). Hence, in the 1990s the reproductive threat left the realm of hospital and street and became part of the public discourse on immigration policy—becoming a central rationale or basis for excluding immigrants from rights and public services.

While Proposition 187's victory did not lead to its implementation due to immediate challenges in the court system, it did inform national politicians and debates, as anti-immigrant organizers moved from the state to the national scene, seeking legislative support for a bill that would advance the restrictionist agenda. IIRIRA, the Personal Responsibility and Work Opportunity Reconciliation Act (PRWORA), and the Anti-Terrorism and Effective Death Penalty Act (AEDPA) all passed in 1996, and all contained provisions that restricted the rights of immigrants. IIRIRA limited legalization options and expanded enforcement; PRWORA excluded immigrants from state resources and services; and AEDPA expanded the powers of local police to arrest immigrants. The strict and punitive implementation of these enforcement measures especially became far more widespread after the post–September 11, 2001, creation of the Department of Homeland Security (DHS) in 2002, which took over immigration affairs from the Department of Justice and added a security rationale to its immigration external enforcement through the U.S. Customs and Border Enforcement Protection and internal enforcement through U.S. Immigration and Customs Enforcement (ICE). Enforcement intensification continued and became exacerbated after 9/11, when national security became a new framework of justification for further immigration enforcement and border control. This was due in great part to the substantial increase in the budget for arresting, detaining, and deporting noncitizens once immigration came under DHS (Golash-Boza 2012, 40).

IIRIRA and AEDPA led to important changes, including restricting of family petitions and a bureaucratic path to legalization; facilitating the increase in enforcement; and restricting or minimizing legal recourses for those facing deportation.[7] Each of these three measures bears relevance for immigrant family unity and requires further examination.

First, the new law restricted family petitions by creating a requirement that an individual petitioning a relative had to be 125 percent above the poverty line. Because this made it very hard to sponsor relatives, some families who would have petitioned formally had no option but to bring their relatives through alternative means. Additionally, the bureaucratic relief to facilitate legalization mentioned above, 245 I, was cut—prior to October 1994, most undocumented residents were required to leave the United States and acquire a visa abroad from the Department of State, as they are again now. As I stated earlier, when Congress created the adjustment of status part to Section 245 I, this allowed undocumented residents to adjust their status without leaving the country. IIRAIRA stipulated that this part of Section 245 I could only be extended until 1997. However, President George W. Bush approved a temporary extension in January 2000 to include anyone who was present in the United States before December 2000.

A second set of measures combined new laws and new enforcement programs that expanded "illegality," and the number of deportations skyrocketed. First, the new laws grandfathered no one, and thus targeted all noncitizens with a previous infraction (felony, misdemeanor), which could be applied retroactively, even after time was served. When the criminal act was implemented, there was no grandfathering that would exclude people who had committed previous infractions. This is why one of the first ways in which IIRIRA was felt was the unprecedented deportations of people, including many LPRs who were deported, sometimes upon applying for citizenship, for having a criminal record or immigration infractions that were now considered felonies. In other words, IIRIRA criminalized immigration. Reentry, or returning after a deportation, was a felony, as were a number of other immigration-related acts, which made it possible for people who committed these acts to be called "criminal offenders," likened to violent criminals or serious offenders, and made, by definition, ineligible for any form of relief and most likely ineligible for any form of legalization in the future. The very creation of a criminal alien category and the targeting of those with a record who were not fleeing the state initiated the deportation increase even before other forms of enforcement were intensified. Moreover, the further criminalization of immigration violations made it increasingly easy to place many of the undocumented on the list of "criminals" who had committed a misdemeanor or a felony, and should therefore be deported.

IIRIRA also created three-year bars from returning for people who have been deported once and ten-year bars from returning for people who have been deported twice. Additionally, as mentioned earlier, the law also prohibited anyone who has left the country after having been here a minimum of six months without permission from reentering the country for three years—regardless of whether they have qualified for an immigrant visa through family or employer sponsorship. Those here for twelve months or more were prohibited from reentering the country for ten years. This places immigrants in a Catch-22: many immigrants who are in the United States without permission, but who have qualified and are on the verge of gaining immigration status, are required to leave the country to pick up their immigrant visas in their home countries. After the elimination of the section of 245 I, discussed earlier, they were not able to leave to adjust their papers without triggering the bars. This is perhaps the system's most pernicious contradiction or trap since the bars make legalization of most people who are undocumented here impossible. These immigrants face the choice of a very long separation from their family or remaining in the United States with no status and forgoing the immigrant visa for which they have qualified.

Currently a waiver for the bar to reentry is available only to an individual who can show that a U.S. citizen or LPR spouse, child, or parent would suffer "extreme hardship" if the individual were to be forced to remain outside of the United States for a long period of time. Even if an individual qualifies for the waiver, the application process itself may result in a long period of separation. Currently, this waiver is obtained at a consular post abroad, and it may take up to a year for a decision to be made. In April 2012, the Obama administration proposed a new waiver process that would allow applicants for these waivers to remain in the United States while their application is adjudicated. This would cut down on the amount of time families are separated while waiting for the waiver to be processed. However, the onerous "extreme hardship" standard must still be met to qualify for the waiver. Because the implementation did not start until March 2012, it will be some time before we know how easy or difficult it is to get such a waiver and what percentage of applicants are accepted. Despite the obvious problems that these bars present for people who are members of mixed-status families in the United States, neither version of a comprehensive reform bill, either in 2007 or 2013, has proposed the elimination of these bars. Together, the elimination of 245 I and the continuation of the bars since 1990 reveal the lack of a political will to resolve the legal status of mixed-status families outside of a massive legalization bill, which remains elusive.[8]

In addition to these changes, there was an increased focus on enforcement, some measures stemming from IIRIRA and AEDPA and others stemming from subsequent piecemeal enforcement bills. In terms of external enforcement, there was the creation of expedited removal, which allowed border agents to deport people they caught crossing or on the U.S. side, a power they did not have prior to IIRIRA. Expedited removal meant an immigrant could be deported without having her or his case considered by a judge. Additionally, there was a significant expansion of border security via patrol reinforcement, new equipment, and wall construction (Hold the Line, 1993; Operation Gatekeeper, 1994; and Operation Desert Safeguard, 2004). Two consequences of this external enforcement intensification have been the rising expense of crossing (leading drug cartels to become involved in the industry) and the rising number of deaths of migrants in the desert as enforcement in California and Texas led migrants to opt for Arizona. In terms of internal enforcement, work-site raids increased dramatically between 2004 and 2007, and the proliferation of agreements between DHS and local police departments (thanks to the 287 G provision in IIRIRA) allowed local enforcement officers to detain people for immigration-related purposes, leading to more arrests and deportations. With these new arrangements, even routine traffic violations could lead to detention and deportation. More recently, DHS's Secure Communities program has relied on integrated databases and partnerships with local and state jailers to identify, detain, and deport more immigrants, many of whom do not have any criminal record.

Given these new conditions that eliminated most options for legalization and dramatically increased deportations, what recourse did families facing deportation and separation have? Very few, given IIRIRA's specific criteria about who is deportable under what conditions, which meant the minimization of judicial discretion. The new rules, which criminalized many immigration offenses, did not easily allow judges to balance a person's contributions and ties when considering a deportation case. In fact, in some cases, such as reentry (when a person had a previous deportation), a person was deprived of the right to go before an immigration judge. While "suspension of deportation," the last recourse available to immigrants pre-IIRIRA, allowed a judge to consider how deportation would cause extreme and unusual hardship to the individual migrant making the appeal, IIRIRA canceled suspension of deportation and replaced it with cancellation of removal, which was more stringent. Now, the potential deportee no longer had to prove that deportation would lead to extreme and unusual hardship for herself or himself, but for others.

There is a maximum of 4,000 approvals for cancellation of removal for non-LPRs per year, and the standard for granting approval is quite rigorous. Immigrants first must apply to the attorney general's office, which frequently reviews them without a full judicial hearing. After a cancellation of removal is denied at the level of the attorney general, it can move on to very busy circuit courts with very limited prospects. IIRIRA policy severely restricts the ability of immigrants to seek a remedy through the judicial courts when they receive an order of removal. Sometimes referred to as the "jurisdiction stripping rule" by the circuit courts (see *Morales-Morales v. Ashcroft*), 8 USCS 1252 (a)(2)(B) states that no court should have jurisdiction to review previous judgments on granting relief, or any other decisions of the attorney general or the secretary of DHS. In other words, the courts cannot "reverse" or alter the outcome of the attorney general's decision. Law 8 USCS 1252 (a) (2) (D) still allows the courts to review "constitutional claims or questions of law." This latter point constitutes the basis for most of the suits heard in the circuit courts.[9]

DEPORTATION, DEPORTABILITY, DETENTION, AND THEIR EFFECT ON FAMILIES

While there are an estimated 11 million undocumented immigrants, adding their family members means there are approximately 16.6 million people who are directly affected by deportation or the possibility of deportation. The number of children of undocumented immigrants increased by 1.2 million from 2003 to 2008, totaling 5.5 million children (DHS 2009).[10] Most of the growth is due to more births in the United States; 4 million of the 5.5 million children (or 73 percent of the children of the undocumented) are U.S. citizens. The number of undocumented children, by contrast, has remained level at approximately 1.5 million in that five-year period (DHS 2009, 7). Eighty-two percent of children of undocumented immigrants are in mixed-status families, while 18 percent, or 792,000, are not (DHS 2009, 8).[11]

According to ICE's own figures (released after a Freedom of Information Act [FOIA] request by the online news outlet Colorlines and published on December 17, 2012), between July 1, 2010, and September 30, 2012, nearly 23 percent of all deportations—or 204,810 deportations—were issued for parents with citizen children, averaging about 90,000 deportations of parents per year (Wessler 2012). According to Colorlines journalist Seth F. Wessler, "the new figures show that rates of parental deportation have remained largely level since Congress ordered ICE to begin collecting the data, quashing hopes from some advocates that the agency's 2011 prosecutorial discretion guidelines would lead to a decline in these removals" (Wessler 2012). Because there is no data prior to 2010 about the percentage of people deported who were parents, it is impossible to know what the average was for the last decade and if levels have gone up or down. However, this two-year snapshot gives a sense of the severity of the issue; with 90,000 parents deported a year, we can assume that significantly more than 90,000 citizen children are affected. However, despite this data limitation, one Human Rights Watch report estimates that since 1997, at least 1.56 million family members—including husbands, wives, sons, and daughters—have been separated from loved ones by deportation, and that many of those affected are citizens and lawful residents.[12]

These parent deportees would include not only undocumented immigrants but legal residents as well, even though we do not know the exact breakdown (DHS data does not distinguish between LPRs and the undocumented when reporting removals, nor does it distinguish among nonviolent felonies such as drug convictions and illegal entry or other immigration-related felonies). This happens because, as stated earlier, IIRIRA made permanent residents subject to deportation after having served criminal sentences, even in the case of nonviolent offenses with a short sentence.[13] In terms of criminal offenses, it is important to note that the 1996 law added seventeen offenses to the category of aggravated felony. Before IIRIRA, offenses were only aggravated if the term of imprisonment was five years or more, but with IIRIRA, offenses became aggravated if the term of the offense was one year. Additionally, the federal law respected state sentences, so an LPR might be deported for an offense that had a one-year sentence in one state, while another one with the same offense in a state with different laws might not. According to Human Rights Watch (2007, 42), in fiscal year 2005 only 20 percent of deportations for criminal offenses were charged with violent offenses, whereas 64.6 percent were for nonviolent cases, including theft offenses, and 14.7 percent were "other."

In sum, the effects of the policies of 1996 and subsequent policies have led to unprecedented rates of deportation. In the ten-year period between 1998 and 2007, for example, the number of deportations more than doubled, from 179,000 to 359,000 (see figure 1.1).[14]

While there was a dramatic increase in deportations in this ten-year period, the high numbers maintained in recent years have remained stable. Between 2008 and 2012, deportation rates maintained the high rate obtained in 2008, fluctuating between 350,000 and 400,000 individuals,[15] despite the steep decline in actual rates of migration in recent years (Passell and Cohn 2010). This has meant that in order to maintain its 400,000 annual deportation quota, DHS has relied on increased internal enforcement by ICE, which is more likely to target immigrants who have been here for many years and have formed families (rather than recent border crossers).

Together, this intensification of border enforcement, the minimization of judicial discretion, the limit of administrative limits to relief from deportation, and the lack of any legislative action that creates a path to legalization (the only exception being the deferred action for youth discussed in chapter 4) mean that the mass deportation and family separation issue, and its detrimental economic, social, and psychological effects, has not only continued in the past decade but has become more severe in the last five years.[16]

What exactly have been the effects of deportation on families? In addition to the child and adult trauma, insecurity, and anxiety that stems from the

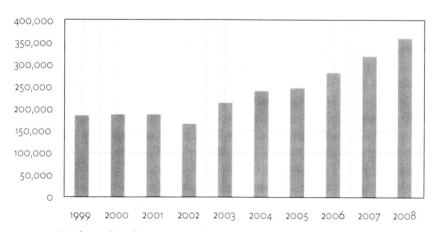

FIGURE 1. Total Number of Deportations by Year
Created by Roberto Rincon.

experience, research has shown that it damages family structure and personal relationships and leads to a substantial decline in the household economy. Joanna Dreby (2012) found that there were three main directions that families could take after deportation, each with detrimental outcomes. One is the case of a spouse remaining in the United States with children (mostly women since the majority of deportees are men); another would be the moving of most or the entire nuclear family to Mexico or another country of origin; and a third would be the placement of children in foster care. The first option most often leads to the creation of single-mother households, whose income goes from low to poverty level after a spouse's deportation, and who do not qualify for unemployment or welfare relief. Additionally, their spouses are usually returning to countries where it is hard to find a job that allows them to support themselves, much less their families. In many cases, women end up sending money to the deported spouse. This arrangement also tends to restructure the family, as older children are forced to assume child-care responsibilities when the mother works, and deported spouses sometimes become estranged from their spouse and/or children. In fact, David Brotherton and Luis Barrios (2011) have found that while male migrants who leave voluntarily tend to maintain their relationship with their children, deportation tends to sever bonds with children, as deportees experience high levels of rejection and demoralization in their country of origin. The long-term outcomes of this option vary. In some cases the deported spouse returns illegally. In other cases, and if viable and affordable, the children and spouse regularly visit the deportee in order to maintain family ties. In other cases, all or most of the family travel to Mexico. However, such arrangements may take a long time, since paying for passports and tickets is a large financial burden (Dreby 2012). Less research has been done in the case of deported mothers, although most cases I have encountered have led to women taking small children with them and leaving teenage or older children with a spouse or relatives to avoid disrupting their lives and schooling. For women who leave children behind, their child's legal status determines their ability to receive visits from their children.

In the case of the family's departure to Mexico, in addition to the economic difficulties entailed in finding work, it can have disruptive effects on children born and educated in the United States. For example, research on the children who have returned to Mexico (a number that the Pew Hispanic Center calculated at 300,000) has found that the children feel like exiles, have difficulties with the language and a very different education system in school, and are deprived of certain health benefits they had in the United States, something especially important in the case of children with learning disabilities. Additionally, their educational achievements and aspirations often suffer (Boehm 2011; Chaury et al. 2010; Dreby 2012; Yoshikawa 2011; Zuniga and Hammond 2006).

Finally, the foster care option has been recently noted in the Colorlines report "Shattered Families," as research has uncovered the tragic ways in which the detention and deportation of parents have led to charges and findings of parental neglect and the subsequent entering of children into the foster system. Once deported, parents have very little recourse to argue their case and regain custody of their children. In many cases where parents have expressed their desire to have their children cared for by relatives, the state has denied this request, finding undocumented relatives poor prospects for foster parenthood on the basis of their status. The report estimates that there were at least 5,100 children living in foster care whose parents had been detained and/or deported. All three of these possible directions mentioned by Dreby—leaving children in the United States, moving them to the country of origin, or placing them in foster care—lead to severe distress, dramatic family changes, a decline in family income, and a loss of opportunities for children.

As explained in the first section of this chapter, the policy of family reunification and family unity, despite its limitations, was sustained for thirty-six years, between 1965 and 2001 (when section 245 I ended). It remains the main logic for the admission of people who are not in the United States, but has been severely curtailed for those families seeking to remain united here. In 2003, family reunification was the largest category of entry (categories include family, work, refugee and asylum, and diversity-based migration) and accounted for two-thirds of permanent migration to the United States every year.[17] However, despite this persistent rationale, because of the changes explained above, families of mixed status in the United States have found their ability to regularize their status impeded, and families that are entirely undocumented have waited for years for a legalization bill that would regularize their status and allow them to come out of the shadows in an age of intensified deportation. Moreover, prior to IIRIRA, judicial discretion allowed judges far more flexibility in balancing an immigrant's infractions and the individual's standing as a family member with responsibilities and rights. While the right to family has been recognized in several international human rights treaties, including the Universal Declaration of Human Rights and the Convention of the Rights of the Child,[18] this recognition has not permeated the legislative process or significantly mitigated enforcement. These contradictions, made painfully evident in the enforcement policies that have truncated over 90,000 families per year, have become the basis for the politicization of family for undocumented immigrants and their families, legal immigrants, and the wider Latino communities in which they reside. For them, seeking justice and recognition of their personhood has become deeply intertwined with the defense of family unity. This process, its meaning and its effects, is the topic of the remainder of this book.

2 · A TALE OF SANCTUARY
Agency, Representativity, and Motherhood

I fight not for myself but for my U.S. citizen son, so that he will know that he is
a child of God and not a piece of garbage that can be used and thrown away.
—Elvira Arellano, press conference upon
entering sanctuary, August 15, 2006

This chapter focuses on Elvira Arellano, a Mexican undocumented
immigrant mother and founder and president of La Familia Latina Unida
(LFLU) who, facing deportation, sought sanctuary in Adalberto Unido Methodist Church in Chicago in August 2006. Arellano's action gained national and
international recognition, shedding light on the increasing deportations and
creating a platform for the voice and agency of an undocumented mother. An
analysis of Arellano's case provides insight into the relationships among political
motherhood, agency, and representativity. I explore what her appeal to motherhood meant for her as an undocumented immigrant, for the immigrant rights
struggle, and for a broader public. Finally, I also explore the potential and limits
of the Arellano case by comparing it to the case of another mother, Flor Crisóstomo, who sought sanctuary in the same church. The comparison provides a
useful window into our understanding of undocumented immigrant agency and
representativity, which points to the limits of the family frame with a specific
emphasis on motherhood.

Motherhood has been relied on by different groups and social movements
as a source of political legitimacy and agency, as exemplified by the Mothers of
the Plaza de Mayo in Argentina as well as other groups of mothers organized
around issues of violence and human rights, such as Conavigua in Guatemala
and Comadres in El Salvador.[1] What these groups share is their reliance on traditional notions of motherhood as a source of political legitimacy. Interestingly,
through their claim that they have been denied their traditional reproductive

role, mothers organize and assume a political agency that is not customary. While their agendas evolve and may eventually assume gender claims that question conventional gender norms, their starting point is usually their role conceived in a traditional way.

Likewise, Arellano's main claims were based on her role as a mother. She emphasized her right to stay with her citizen child in the country where he was born, and his right to be mothered without having to leave the United States. Born in Maravatio, a small town in the state of Michoacán, Arellano first crossed into the United States in 1997 but was deported (at that time, she states, she did not know she was being deported, but simply returned to the Mexican side of the border). Later that year she returned to the United States and moved to the state of Oregon, where she worked and had a relationship that did not last long, but resulted in a pregnancy. In 1999 she had a son, Saul, and in 2000 she moved to Chicago, where she worked primarily in cleaning positions and was finally hired to clean airplanes at O'Hare Airport. On December 10, 2002, she was arrested in the early hours of the morning in her home in front of then three-year-old Saul. Her arrest was part of Operation Chicago Skies, an investigation that was one of several federal stings planned after September 11, 2001. According to the *Chicago Reporter*, most of those rounded up were not terrorists but undocumented immigrants, forty-five low-level airport workers, mostly baggage handlers, janitors, truck drivers, and food-service employees (*Chicago Reporter*, 2003). Arellano was charged with fraudulently obtaining airport security clearance with an invalid Social Security card, which is considered a federal offense. She was released on bail. After three appearances before a federal judge, she pleaded guilty to document fraud in March 2003 and was given three years probation. She never went before an immigration judge; her deportation proceedings were the outcome of a civil process run by the Department of Homeland Security (DHS) (something only possible after the 1996 law).

After being released on bail, Arellano became actively involved in mobilizing around her case, working first with the Illinois Coalition for Immigrant and Refugee Rights (ICIRR) and later with the Centro Sin Fronteras (CSF), where she joined efforts with the organization's president, Emma Lozano, and other members to create the LFLU campaign (see chapter 3). Together, Arellano and her supporters made her case public in an effort to raise awareness about the detention of undocumented immigrants and their separation from their citizen children. She was granted three stays of deportation between 2003 and 2005, with the support of Senator Dick Durbin, based on the claim that Saul had ADHD and other health issues that could not be adequately addressed in Maravatio. Arellano's case was also included in the private bill that LFLU families filed but which was never addressed by Congress. In 2005, Durbin did not file for an extension of her case, claiming that Saul's condition had improved and that he wanted to focus on immigration reform for the collective good, rather than on single cases. Arellano was left with no recourse but to face imminent deportation in August 2006.

As president of LFLU, Arellano had presented the family cases in numerous advocacy efforts in local and national government; trips to Washington, D.C.; public talks; marches; protests; a twenty-day hunger strike in May 2006 in Pilsen, Illinois, for the rights of IFCO workers; and more broadly for legalization, family reunification, and a moratorium on all raids and deportations.[2] Finally, facing her own deportation, Arellano engaged in an unprecedented act that gained national and worldwide attention. She sought sanctuary in Adalberto United Methodist Church. In doing this, she was invoking not only an ancient tradition of churches harboring those seeking a safe haven but also the more recent U.S. political experience of sanctuary provided by churches to Central American refugees fleeing persecution in the 1980s, in which the Chicago Religious Task Force on Central America played an important role as national coordinator.[3]

Upon entering the church, Arellano held a press conference where she appealed to a higher law and her motherhood to justify her decision: "I am prepared to face the consequences of my actions, even if it means serving ten or twenty years in prison. I have made this promise to God, and God will determine what will happen to me. I am not a terrorist. I am not a criminal. I am a mom."[4]

As I discuss further below, Arellano herself became a national symbol, adopted and supported by some pro-immigrant organizations and movements throughout the country while vilified by restrictionist groups (those that seek deportation of most or all the undocumented and severe curtailment of any future immigration).

Once Arellano entered the church, many events were held to maintain attention to her plight and that of other families facing separation. Arellano held several press conferences explaining her position as well as introducing local and national political and religious leaders who supported her. Arellano's seven-year-old son, Saul, pursued and lost a federal lawsuit in which he claimed that in deporting Arellano, the federal government was denying his rights as a citizen.[5] Prosecutors were able to successfully dismiss the case, stating that deporting Arellano did not violate any of Saul's constitutional rights and that granting her a stay would provide a benefit that Congress never intended.

Saul and other children of LFLU members traveled to Washington, D.C., where they marched and delivered a letter to President George W. Bush. Saul also traveled throughout the United States and Mexico, calling attention to the cause. Saul and other children of LFLU members testified before groups ranging from the Cook County Board of Commissioners to the United Nations, and joined other children in the country to file "4 Million Kids," a class lawsuit presented to the Supreme Court in an effort to protect the rights of citizen children (the case was never reviewed by the Supreme Court). Additionally, CSF worked closely with Congressman José Serrano to promote the Citizen Child Protection Act, which would return more discretion to judges in cases of possible parent separation from a citizen child. This bill was never discussed and was reintroduced in Congress in January 2011 as H.R. 250, where it did not leave the committee.[6] In January 2007, representatives from eighteen cities, over fifty churches, and twelve different religious traditions met to create the new sanctuary movement, which was officially launched in April of that year. While not all churches would harbor people facing deportation, they would offer support in different ways. People who were being harbored would move from church to church to share responsibility. The idea was to focus on a few cases to draw national attention to the cause. Within the first year more than twenty other people entered sanctuary in different churches across the United States. In more recent years, new sanctuary movement organizations throughout the country have continued the work, mostly focusing on assisting and ministering to people facing deportation as well as engaging in political advocacy. Sanctuary, or the actual harboring of the undocumented as a strategy, however, did not grow significantly.

In summer 2007, immigration activists experienced great disappointment when the Senate failed to reach cloture on the Comprehensive Immigration Reform Act (S. 1348, 100th Congress). While this bill had been opposed by labor and by many activists who believed that it excessively increased enforcement and was not generous enough in legalization, it had also been opposed by restrictionists who opposed any form of legalization. It was ultimately the restrictionists who mobilized effectively to stop the bill (for more, see Pallares and Flores-Gonzalez 2010). The unlikelihood that any new effort at reform would succeed before the 2008 elections produced a widespread sense of disappointment among immigrant communities that had built up expectations for reform since the 2006 marches. Arellano, in consultation with her pastor and CSF activists, opted for a change in strategy. In August 2007, she held a press conference to mark her one year in sanctuary and announced that new, undisclosed actions would be revealed soon. Shortly after, she left Adalberto Unido Methodist Church by car, driving with Saul and other CSF leaders to California. While she left clandestinely, she sent out a press release in which she communicated that in order to reinvigorate the immigrant community, she would visit sanctuary cities throughout the nation, holding a press conference at each site, ending in Washington, D.C., in September, where she would hold an action outside of Congress. She stated that she was prepared to be publicly arrested, if it meant renewed attention to the cause.

Arellano was not able to complete her tour as she was arrested in Los Angeles, the first city that she visited, on Sunday, August 19, 2007. She was detained right after leaving the church of Our Lady Queen of Angels, in La Placita, a historically Latino area of the city. The Immigration and Custom Enforcement (ICE) office deported her within hours of her arrest, probably hoping to avoid any further spotlight on her case.

REPRESENTING THE UNDOCUMENTED:
THE QUESTION OF AGENCY

How was Arellano's sanctuary experienced and understood by others? In contrast to the 1980s, when Central Americans in sanctuary usually masked their faces while others spoke about their cases, Arellano did not disguise herself while in sanctuary and spoke openly to the press, in Spanish, about her case. This provoked a very strong reaction from columnists in the mainstream local press. The controversy surrounding Arellano's decision to seek sanctuary rather than to be deported included the comments of columnist Mary Mitchell of the *Chicago Sun Times* and Eric Zorn of the *Chicago Tribune*. In their different ways, both suggested that she was out of place in her activism and that it was not her place to resist deportation.

In her column entitled "Elvira Arellano Is No Rosa Parks," Mitchell (2006) opposed Arellano's right to use the example of Rosa Parks as a model for her activism. While clearly informed by the complicated and ambivalent relationship of African Americans to the immigration issue, Mitchell's column stated that Arellano, unlike Rosa Parks, did not have the right to resist because what she did was out of bounds legally, morally, and historically. As an undocumented immigrant, Arellano had broken the law, whereas Rosa Parks technically, at least, had not.[7] Mitchell's column implied that Arellano, as a recent immigrant, had no right to draw any relationship or comparison between the historical oppression of African Americans and migrants' inferior place in the labor market. Erasing the labor history of Mexicans and Mexican Americans in the United States, Mitchell's argument about Arellano's illegality in opposition to Park's "legality" also erased the illegality of the acts of many abolitionists in the nineteenth century and civil rights activists committed to ending segregation and disenfranchisement in the 1960s. In a narrative that places her outside of the law, there is no figurative or real space for Arellano to claim any rights from the state.

Eric Zorn (2006) from the *Chicago Tribune* argued that Arellano was not the ideal poster child for this cause because she broke the law by reentering after a prior deportation and by using false documents. He wrote:

> Our leaders can't summon the political will to secure our borders and enforce our laws. But Arellano's not helping things. She's not a particularly good cause celebre, as these things go. She has twice entered the country illegally, has been

convicted of carrying a false Social Security card, speaks very poor English for someone who has been in this country nine years, and she plays her so-called "anchor baby," a 7-year old son who is a U.S. citizen because he was born here, as her trump card.

"Anchor baby" is a term usually used by restrictionists to describe children who, they claim, are being used by their parents as a means to access citizenship. While the assumption that children can legally sponsor their parents is inaccurate in the current legal system, it is often referred to by restrictionist activists to illustrate the ways in which they believe that undocumented immigrants are cheating or rather gaming the system (Chavez 2008).[8] While he later apologized for the anchor baby comment (in response to many letters of outrage), acknowledging that it was not a neutral term he should use as a journalist, Zorn never expanded further on the question of Arellano's worthiness as a cause célèbre.[9] Given that Arellano's case is not atypical from that of tens of thousands of undocumented immigrants, Zorn's commentary begs the question: who is the ideal poster child? Zorn has no answer for that, and his silence on this issue is telling. There is no ideal poster child, because there is no place for the undocumented person's political voice.[10]

I would argue, in contrast to Zorn, that Arellano's case is not atypical. What is atypical of Arellano is the fact that she did not accept her deportation fate and actively resisted it. In fact, Zorn develops his position against Arellano further by explaining that her defiance "drips with a sense of entitlement that many Americans find off-putting." It is therefore this act of resistance, or defiance as Zorn calls it, in and of itself, that ultimately makes her an inadequate cause célèbre and justifies the displacement of her voice as one that legitimately speaks for herself or others like her.

A final relevant column is "Immigrant Mother Hurts Her Cause with Standoff," which appeared in the *Chicago Sun Times* on December 21, a few days after Martin Barrios, a member of LFLU and father of two children, was deported. His coming out in a newspaper had resulted in the loss of his job as well as his detention and deportation. Additionally, Barrios had received inadequate counsel on his case: his lawyer had made serious mistakes in the past that had made him unable to appeal his case. Despite these factors, Barrios was officially given a notice of deportation in 2005. His current lawyers had attempted to delay it but were unsuccessful. During the months of waiting to learn if his deportation could be stalled, Barrios did not seek sanctuary, like Arellano, but continued his regular family life at home. When the agents arrived a few days before Christmas, they found Barrios in his pajamas and arrested him in front of his family. The *Sun Times* column portrays a sympathetic picture of Barrios and his plight, contrasting it to a negative portrayal of Arellano in what appears to be a good immigrant/bad immigrant juxtaposition: "Martin Barrios stuck his neck out on this issue and is paying the price for his activism. You have to respect him for that. But the longer Arellano is allowed to flout the law, the more intolerant people will become about immigration reform."

Now here, again, one has to read between the lines and ask what is left unsaid. What exactly is the difference between Barrios and Arellano, since they were both LFLU activists and both were undocumented? Is it that Barrios complied with being carried away by immigration agents? That he seems like a conventional family man, in contrast to single mother Elvira Arellano? That he waited for the inevitable in the privacy of his home? While Barrio's illegal entry receives nary a mention, Arellano's is emphasized. Moreover, she is single-handedly blamed for increasing opposition to immigrant legalization. The column suggests that while the likes of Barrios will make us more tolerant, the likes of Arellano test our benevolence.

Taken together, these three columns beg the question of whether the issue at hand is only, or primarily, about illegal entry or about what increasingly gets viewed as an out-of-place political agency. If she was not being challenged on the basis of her motherhood (in the case of Zorn), her right to have rights becomes the target. If one takes this column's message seriously, then the only meritorious undocumented immigrant, the only one who will be tolerated, is the one who either avoids being caught or, if caught, accepts his or her fate and goes away quietly, unseen. The "price to pay" for assuming political agency is to be deported.

This denial of the agency of the undocumented is not limited to Arellano. During the May 1, 2006, march of 600,000 people, the *Chicago Tribune* interviewed several people on the street concerning their opinion on the marches. One man stated that he was sympathetic to the plight of undocumented immigrants but they should not have shown themselves. While the man interviewed reproduces the mistaken assumption that all marchers were undocumented, it confirms a prevalent view that the undocumented can be tolerated or tacitly accepted if they physically remain in hiding.[11] It is as if the performance of the vulnerability of being deportable requires silence. Likewise, in their different ways, the columnists suggest that Elvira Arellano should have remained in hiding by not advocating for herself, or not resisting her deportation. It is, in fact, in this context, quite ironic that to make her case politically visible, Arellano had to isolate and sequester herself physically, rendering public the impossibility of her situation.

The mainstream media's reaction to Arellano vividly shows the difficulty faced by undocumented immigrants who attempt to speak for their own case. In the case of Arellano, the lack of a citizen husband and the young age of her child did not allow for the option of citizen or legal family members eloquently speaking for the undocumented, as has been common in many representations of family in the movement. This only underscored and highlighted her individual visibility and made her more likely to be an individuated target, the opposite of what she had sought to do by emphasizing a relational strategy that underscored the entanglement of her and her child's futures.

REPRESENTATIVITY

The question of representativity took on additional meaning for immigrant communities and Mexicans in Mexico both during and after Arellano's sanctuary experience. If the discussion of columnists' responses earlier in this chapter speaks to the problem of individual agency, the critique of Elvira Arellano from within the movement after her deportation underscores the issues and contradictions raised by questions concerning personal morality and child activism. In both instances, from within and without the movement, her representativity is questioned. While the columnists seem to suggest that Arellano could not speak even for herself, several members of the immigrant activist community questioned whether she could represent others, a topic that became an object of heated discussion when she was deported. The question of whether Arellano truly represented the immigrant population revolved around issues of authenticity linked to notions of morality.

Representativity refers to the extent to which someone stands or acts for another, usually for a collective or constituency. As Jose Antonio Lucero has argued in his work on indigenous movements in Ecuador and Bolivia, representativity in social movements is produced politically and culturally through local and transnational interactions, and operates from above and below. Lucero explains that elections are only one of several arenas for the politics of representation (others are popular support and recognition of state and international actors), but also more subjective determinations such as resources, status, and style. In the case of the indigenous, this is shaped by notions of authenticity (reflected in culture, language, religion). Also looking at indigenous people, Kay Warren and Jean Jackson have maintained that representativity focuses on the practices and discourses that situate some subjects as more culturally authentic and more politically consequential than others (Lucero 2008; Warren and Jackson 2003).

Immigrant representativity presents its own particular issues. The question of whether non-immigrants should speak for immigrants has become an issue of contention and of competing claims for authenticity. In many instances spokespersons for immigrants are civil rights activists, grassroots organizers, or social-service providers who have gained their status through their work for immigrant communities. Sometimes they are immigrants, but more frequently they are children or grandchildren of immigrants, second- or third-generation Latinos.

While they are not always elected, they do have a base or constituency and have obtained recognition after years of working for and among immigrants. That model has been questioned by organizations such as the National Alliance of Latin American and Caribbean Communities (NALACC), which contends that only immigrants should be at the head of the advocacy organizations that claim to represent immigrants.

In the case of Arellano, her plight as an undocumented mother facing certain deportation generated name recognition and empathy from many members of the immigrant community. Clearly, Arellano perceived herself as being a representative of the people, not only because her story was similar to that of millions but also because of divine guidance. In one press interview she stated, "I represent millions of people. I've been chosen by God to be this symbol."[12] In the Chicago area, there was an extensive awareness of the Arellano case among immigrants who were politically mobilized. In several states there were marches to support her, both after she entered sanctuary and after she was deported. For example, Javier Rodriguez, organizer of a march in Los Angeles one month after Arellano entered sanctuary, stated that Arellano represented "the face of thousands of women" and her son represented "the face of millions of American children" whose parents face deportation.[13] However, while her supporters in Chicago and elsewhere staged mobilizations throughout the country chanting "todos somos Elvira" (we are all Elvira), for immigrant rights supporters who were not vocal pro-Arellano advocates, the case raised a series of questions, most notably: does Elvira Arellano represent us? There was undoubtedly a recognition of her agency and its importance, as she was the first undocumented immigrant to publicly challenge her own deportation and highlight the family separation issue. But there were also concerns about whether her particular case and story, while powerful, helped or hurt the cause, as well as whether the excessive focus on one individual hides or erases the plurality of voices. Some activists asked if there were other strategies or alternatives of representation that would be more viable and politically effective.

Unlike the competing claims over indigenous authenticity, which are based on culture, language, and dress, the claims concerning the authenticity of a spokesperson for undocumented immigrants are primarily based on issues of morality that inform the concept of "worthiness" discussed in chapter 1. For example, as chapter 3 explains, the LFLU families created an online photo album that stressed the "worthiness" of each family, emphasizing their strong work ethic, excellent parenting, religiosity, and "traditional" values. In the case of Arellano, moral questions that were raised by people within the movement included whether she was a good mother, a deserving immigrant, and in fact an upstanding protocitizen. These questions of moral authenticity are not news, as they have been used in courts. Recently, however, they have become more prominent in immigrant movement activism, as evident not only in the critiques of Arellano but in many efforts to show and create model immigrants as well.

The rationales given among movement activists for doubting the effectiveness of Arellano's claim, and, most important, for questioning her representativity, can be divided into the following two sets of critiques: one was a question of her "worthiness," given that she had a prior deportation and that she had been convicted by a criminal court for the use of false documents. This does not mean that activists believe that a prior deportation should be a basis for criminalization, but that they have developed an acute sensitivity to the ways in which immigrants are criminalized and seek to present cases that are farthest away from any possible criminalization. Not unlike Zorn, immigrant rights activists wondered if a better spokesperson could have been found, a youth, an Iraq veteran, someone who would be considered more worthy, who would be a "better representative" of immigrants.

For example, interviewed by Mary Schmich on August 22, 2007, Univision radio DJ Javier Salas stated:

> This is not about bashing Elvira . . . my heart goes to her. I wish her the best in Mexico. But there are 12 million other lives and stories to make the case for humane immigration reform. Hers is not the best. Better would be the soldier dying in Iraq. The undocumented sick who can't find decent care. The undocumented college students who came here as kids and can't get financial aid.

The soldier dying in Iraq presents a very disturbing image—worthiness comes from the ability to sacrifice life, a worthy representativity that is earned by death or near death. Arellano's motherhood in and of itself did not seem sufficient to mitigate or erase her proximity to criminality.

In another instance, when a *Sun Times* liberal columnist asked if there was a better example, one immigrant rights organization proposed "Oscar," a young man who had pulled himself up by his bootstraps, who had paid his way through college, and whose parents had brought him to the United States when he was small, as a better example of a deserving undocumented person, worthier because he is not complicit in illegal entry.

In both instances the counterexamples were young men who had been brought by their parents when they were children, hence tapping into the DREAM Act advocacy discourse that emphasized the innocence of youth. Furthermore, both suggestions gendered the ideal candidate male and did away with what can be at best characterized as an ambivalent position toward single motherhood. Intersectionality matters when discussing "representatives" because the tangling of the mother and child does not seem to do enough to uphold the worthiness of the mother. Somebody who is a soldier or a college student would be capable of highlighting intersections that would mitigate their status; mother-hood alone does not seem sufficient.

The second main criticism concerned Arellano's mothering, especially with regards to her son's activism. As described in the next chapter, one of the strate-gies pursued by LFLU was a transition from family marches and family lobby days in Washington, D.C., to one that highlighted the children acting alone. Saul, who turned eight during their year in sanctuary, traveled at different times to Washington, D.C., California, Texas, and Mexico to advocate for his right to not be separated from his mother. After Arellano was deported, Saul remained in the United States for a month and traveled through several states as well as D.C., where he participated in a mobilization that led to a couple of arrests. While Saul's role was often a target of criticism when his mother was in sanctuary, it was more so once Arellano was in Mexico and he remained in the United States engaging in political actions. Many people found it hard to believe that an eight-year-old would be willing to participate in these activities voluntarily.

While the question of children's political agency is controversial because chil-dren are not believed to fully comprehend their actions or consent to them the way adults do, rather than pick sides in this debate, I would like to point to a rel-evant issue here, which is who is assigned responsibility for the conditions that lead children to engage in this activism. Are parents entirely responsible for the conditions that lead children to become child soldiers in Sudan, or activists in 1970s South Africa, for example? Or could one argue that the set of conditions that render people of all ages and all members of families vulnerable also lead children to engage in adult activities of different types: work, soldiering, protest? While one could argue that children in families with undocumented immigrant members are more vulnerable to state deportation policies, onlookers frequently assign the moral responsibility for these children's situation exclusively on the parents and not on the law or the state. For example, when ICE deported Arel-lano in front of her son, critics blamed Arellano, not the state, for placing her son in the situation of being a witness to her deportation.

This critique also highlights some of the strategic limitations of the family frame. The same appeal to family that Arellano had relied on to make her case was used to question Saul's actions and scrutinize her choices, which were con-strained due to her single motherhood.[14] While the Mothers of the Plaza de Mayo had been questioned by elites and upper-class citizens as having raised children with a propensity to leftist politics (something that in some circles was viewed as bad or irresponsible mothering), the aspect of their mothering that remained visible and most politically effective was the grief and anger associ-ated with their loss. Arellano's mothering of a young, live child, by contrast, was placed under a microscope, observed, and evaluated. In the case of the Mothers of the Plaza de Mayo, we see the opposition between grieving parent and state as the responsibility over the child's death is laid squarely on the state. In the case of Arellano, there are clearly two visions, a more mainstream one that views the parent as fully responsible for the child and makes the state invisible, and the view of Arellano and her supporters who point to the state's responsibility in protecting the rights of its citizen children. For the former vision, the individual parent is assumed to be capable of shielding the child from all conditions and threats, no matter how large. Hence, Arellano's claims based on her motherhood also opened her up to a questioning of her "aptitude" by not sufficiently protecting her child from the effects of deportation policy.

Throughout her sanctuary and after her deportation, the worthiness question remained among immigrant rights communities. Was she a worthy representative, or was her purported criminality a major issue? Wasn't her purported use of her son an obvious indication that she was not a good mother and therefore not deserving? In order to address the question of her representativity, it became necessary to question her authenticity, which seemed to be linked to questions of morality: was she a good mother, was she a deserving immigrant, was she in fact an upstanding "substantive" (if not formal) citizen?

This intense concern with Arellano's worthiness as a representative reflects an internalization of mainstream views of immigrants and, more specifically, immigrants of color. Latino and other immigrants of color are overly concerned with the gaze of the mainstream white non-immigrant community because their claims for legalization and an end to deportation require a shift in popular sentiment, which, in many an activist's view, could happen if mainstream citizens identify with immigrants and their stories. In sum, it is not novel to claim that for disempowered peoples, representativity seems to matter more than it does for those who are privileged. We do not witness this kind of angst over whether any white person's actions (criminal or not) or views do or do not represent his or her population category. Whites are understood as representing a particular position or viewpoint, whereas people of color are burdened with representing their race, and foreign nationals as representing all people of their national origin. Additionally, for undocumented immigrants, this reality is made even more complicated by the fact that they are impossible activists—that is, they are denied political agency, and their ability to represent at all (even if only themselves) is denied by their very status. Claiming political rights and political agency becomes in and of itself an act of insubordination. While the immigrant community was mostly concerned with Arellano's morality as a gauge of her worthiness, this was not the main issue for outsiders. Ultimately, this attempt to represent herself in a very vocal way is her biggest sin to the mainstream gaze, and most delegitimized her right to represent others. Hence, ultimately the media's as well as anti-immigrants' interpretation of her resistance as an act of insubordination upsets Arellano's opponents within the movement, who have tried to be viewed as good, morally upright citizens. In this context, it is perhaps her political agency, as a strong, working-class single mother, and not her previous deportation or use of false documents, that is the ultimate "immoral act," rendering her unworthy and occluding the recognition of her personhood.

In addition to immigrant rights activists in the United States, Mexican politicians and community organizers also weighed in on the case, as her deportation led to very mixed responses. On the one hand, she was briefly acclaimed upon her return for her activism for immigrant rights. However, there were also very critical comments that questioned her actions, considering them a defiance of U.S. law and a threat to U.S. sovereignty, and providing a negative image of Mexican immigrants. Some were particularly upset by her request to then president Ernesto Zedillo that she be named honorary ambassador of immigrants and be granted a diplomatic visa to the United States. This was seen as an insult to the Mexican government that could endanger U.S.-Mexico relations. Arellano soon began working with the Partido de la Revolucion Democratica (PRD; Party of the Democratic Revolution), and these politicized positions furthered as affiliates of the National Action Party (PAN) and the Institutional Revolutionary Party (PRI) questioned her right to speak for all immigrants. In one telling event, at a migrant parliament inaugurated in November 2007, a Panista congresswoman stated that she sympathized with Arellano as a mother but could not support her because she violated both Mexican and U.S. sovereignty.[15]

Since her return, Arellano has remained politically active. She first worked with the state of Michoacán to assist immigrants from Michoacán, and then left that job to run for representative of Baja California for the Mexican Congress in the election of July 2009 (she did not win). In Tijuana, she has supported the shelter for deported women, Casa Elvira (funded by Hermandad Mexicana Transnacional), and has advocated continuously for the rights of migrants. She has also worked closely with Enrique Morones, of Border Angels, in that group's annual marches of migrants and other direct actions. Since her loss in the 2009 election, she has continued to advocate for migrant rights and has traveled to several countries to spread her message. Currently she is working on migrant rights issues with a special focus on the human rights of Central American migrants crossing through Mexico and the rights of Mexican deportees and their families. Most recently, in March 2014 she returned to the United States with fourteen-year-old Saul and her infant son Emiliano and dozens of other members of separated families, as part of the "Bring them Home" campaign designed to shed light on the role of deportations in the displacement of individuals and families, and claim the right to return.

The controversy over Elvira Arellano reflects an ambivalence about the rights of Mexican immigrants in Mexico, where notions of proper and improper behavior for migrants also prevail. Migrant activists who gain

Arellano's case had wide resonance throughout the United States. Many immigrant activists supported her and admired her ability to highlight the family separation issue, which had not gained meaningful press attention until she sought sanctuary. There had been a few cases of family separations covered by the mainstream press, especially around the 2006 megamarches, but no undocumented parent or person had engaged in such a dramatic political act and obtained such consistent, sustained media attention on her or his case. Arellano's case acted as a form of threshold; the dozens of family cases that were covered in subsequent years were facilitated by this mainstream media opening to the issue. In subsequent years, cases from LFLU and other organizations throughout Chicago and the nation were highlighted by politicians and the media, and some people were able to gain stays from deportation due to a combination of politicians' interventions and organization campaigns. As discussed in chapter 3 in much greater detail, after the Arellano case the family separation issue became widely disseminated and relied on as a key platform for immigrant rights organizations, religious leaders, and allies throughout the country.

As I have discussed, however, Arellano's reliance on the family frame was a double-edged sword, as it opened up the space for both empathy and criticism based on prevalent notions of moral and responsible motherhood, but did not automatically lead her agency or representativity to be recognized. Moreover, her mothering was always criticized not only by the restrictionists but also by immigration activists. Undoubtedly, some of that vulnerability was facilitated by the reality of her single motherhood, which, interestingly, contrasted with the image of the traditional family promoted by LFLU. However, while Arellano used the family frame she also challenged conventional notions of family. A single mother who was estranged from her son's father, she represented a gendered hybridity, both the caretaker and breadwinner for Saul. She turned down multiple marriage proposals from men drawn to her cause, a conventional, if at this point suspect, solution to her plight. Her work as an organizer was fraught with difficulties, as working with fathers of families at times instigated the suspicions and jealousy of their spouses. She was never supported by any man, working since she was a teenager, then working to support herself and her son in Chicago and Aurora, Illinois, and finally, supported by the congregation of Adalberto United Methodist Church and activists from CSF. Her act of seeking sanctuary in the church and remaining there was also understood by some as an act of gender crossing. For example, one older Mexican woman hugged Arellano and slipped her some money after a religious ceremony in the church in October 2006. The author overheard her say, "Estamos contigo, mijita. Sigue adelante. Tú si tienes los pantalones bien puestos" (We are with you, my dear. Keep going forward. You are wearing the pants).[16] This is a point of marked difference between immigrant communities and outside perceptions. While the author never heard one criticism of Arellano's single motherhood in six years of interviewing activists in the immigrant community (some of them quite critical of Arellano), it was clearly a point of contention among restrictionists' comments and blogs. For example, a blog by Mothers against Illegal Aliens written after the organization attempted to visit Adalberto Unido Methodist Church (they were not allowed in) questioned why there was possibly no father's name on the birth certificate and tied Arellano's estrangement from the father to possible government support for her son (all speculative but common criticisms).[17]

Another problem with the motherhood claim as represented by the media was its depoliticizing potential. For example, Arellano was often described solely as a mother who refused to leave her son, as opposed to an activist and president of an organization who was claiming to represent the cause of millions. This became more apparent after her deportation when media reports as well as popular blogs and conversations emphasized her act as a mistake that led to her deportation, eliminating any legal chance for her to stay. All of these observations disregarded her role as an activist who had for more than a year claimed that she knew her own case was hopeless but was doing this for the cause rather than for herself.

However, as problematic or ambiguous as the case was, it did set out a path for the immigrant rights movement, a singling out of the family separation issue via a motherhood angle that made the issue visible and opened the door for future cases. Arellano's case relied primarily on her status as the mother of a citizen child, and while that was both a source of empathy and attacks, it remained an undeniable fact. What happens, however, in the case of migrant mothers who do not have citizen children?

A TALE OF TWO MOTHERS

While the focus on family separation was becoming a powerful new social movement frame that opened up opportunities for some but also closed it for others, a significant proportion of the undocumented population either do not have children or have children who are not citizens and in some instances not even in the United States. As we shall see with the case of Flor Crisóstomo, Arellano's case was a hard act to follow. Five months after Arellano left Adalberto Unido Methodist Church, Flor Crisóstomo, a former IFCO worker, fellow CSF member, and activist, sought sanctuary after receiving her letter requesting that she voluntarily deport. While she spent twenty-one months in the church where Arellano had been staying, her sanctuary experience was different on a number of fronts.

After two attempts at crossing the Arizona desert, Flor Crisóstomo arrived in Chicago in 2001 looking for work after the superhighway built from Monterrey to Acapulco displaced her mother's restaurant business in the state of Guerrero.

A single mother of three children, Crisóstomo migrated to sustain her children, leaving them with her mother. In Chicago, where she had two brothers, Crisóstomo eventually found work at IFCO, a pellet factory, where she was one of the workers arrested during the nationwide IFCO raid of 1,100 people in April 2006. CSF became involved in the case, and its attorney represented several of the IFCO workers, including Crisóstomo. Soon after her arrest, Crisóstomo joined Arellano and a couple of other activists in a twenty-day hunger strike in Pilsen for the rights of all the IFCO workers arrested. The group ended the hunger strike on the day that an immigration judge decided to defer the IFCO case for several months, buying the workers more time to resist their deportation. When Arellano sought sanctuary in August of that year, Crisóstomo and her then partner moved in with her to provide support. Crisóstomo continued to work with CSF from its office, located on the second floor of the building that housed Adalberto Unido Methodist Church. Here she participated in and helped to plan several political actions and demonstrations. She also played a key role in supporting the growing struggle for immigrant rights in the suburb of Waukegan, Illinois, during the summer and fall of 2007. After Arellano was deported, Crisóstomo continued to stress family activism, emphasizing her own role as a mother of children in Mexico:

> I am here today, like my sister Elvira Arellano, who is in front of the American Embassy in Mexico City, because we are mothers and we demand respect, commitment, actions, and solutions for us and our families on both sides and by both governments.... As a mother I came to work because I have to work to provide for my kids what this system has shamelessly taken away from us.[18]

As she matured and gained experience as an activist, Crisóstomo also started identifying with her indigenous roots. Her father was a Zapoteca indigenous man from Oaxaca, where Crisóstomo had lived as a child close to her paternal aunts. When her parents separated, Crisóstomo and her siblings left for Guerrero with their mother. While Crisóstomo does not speak Zapoteco and had not returned to Oaxaca, she began to develop ties with indigenous activists in Chicago, Mexico, and California. In April 2007, the author accompanied her to New York to speak at a special session on migration of urban and indigenous peoples at the United Nations in coalition with Red Chicana Indígena, a California organization that conjoins the displacement of Chicanos in the Southwest and indigenous peoples in the Americas. Crisóstomo's experience in this encounter was a transformative one. Surrounded by indigenous peoples from everywhere in the world, she claimed her place as an indigenous woman displaced twice, first from her home in Mexico and then from her home in Chicago, emphasizing the roles of racism and neoliberalism in the denial of economic opportunities for her in

Mexico, leading to her migration to the United States. Upon her return to Chicago, she rejected Christianity and began practicing indigenous rituals as well as dressing in indigenous garb. She also joined a local group of Mexicas, part of a broader cultural movement of people who seek to claim Mexica traditions and beliefs by learning and using the Nahuatl language, dancing Aztec dances, and practicing Aztec rituals.

After the Bureau of Citizenship and Immigration Services denied her right to an appeal, Crisóstomo was given a January 28, 2008, voluntary deportation date. On that same date, after extensive consultation with CSF president Emma Lozano, Reverend Walter "Slim" Coleman, and other organizers, activists, and supporters, she entered Adalberto Unido Methodist Church to seek sanctuary. She vowed to continue this struggle through her sanctuary for all her pueblo, which she defined broadly as all undocumented people. Keenly aware that, unlike Arellano, she did not have a citizen child, Crisóstomo emphasized her breadwinner role, arguing that she was a single mother who had been forced to separate from her children in Mexico in order to feed them. When reporters asked her why she did not self-deport and return to her children, she stated that she had no choice, that her return would be a hunger sentence for them. On several occasions she explained her need to remain as a second but no less important rationale: "On the one hand the family, faith and community ties are too strong for people to self-deport, and on the other hand, the devastation caused by NAFTA [North American Free Trade Agreement] and other exploitative policies of 'free' commerce make it impossible for the undocumented to return to their countries of origin since they cannot support their families."[19]

Her angle was to link her struggle to NAFTA, highlighting its role in displacing people who had earned their livelihoods in small businesses and agricultural work. This was the continuation of a public education campaign on NAFTA that she had initiated with CSF months before she went into sanctuary. Lacking the constant attention of the mainstream press that Arellano had garnered, Crisóstomo sought to develop her own media niche. She created a blog, "Floresiste," and recruited several young people to help her raise funds for it. She used the blog and strategic events such as press conferences, hunger strikes, and cultural programs to raise awareness. With no alternative income to support her children, she made and sold jewelry and tamales. She also continued her work with CSF, conducting phone and Internet promotion events and campaigns.

As the months passed, Crisóstomo's indigeneity became a more central part of her identity. She participated extensively in dances and other pre-Columbian rituals performed by a Mexica (Aztec) group that she founded, which met frequently at the church. She made jewelry out of natural materials and used native themes. She imported textiles made by her aunt and other Zapoteca women for sale. And she began to actively advocate for the rights of indigenous people and indigenous migrants in particular. Crisóstomo's apartment on the second floor of the church building gradually became a meeting center for local artists, Mexicas, and young activists who were not necessarily directly linked to CSF or other immigrant organizations, but were drawn to Crisóstomo's message, which intertwined opposition to trade liberalization and concerns about cultural and economic displacement, indigeneity, racism, and transnational motherhood. Her message was attractive to youth and second-generation Latinos because of the variety of themes and the fact that they did not rely primarily or exclusively on the family frame. While most of these youth cared about family separation issues, this alone was not sufficient to attract them to the movement. Additionally, most of them were hesitant to join more traditional immigrant rights organizations as they sought less formal spaces for political and cultural discussions in which they could articulate their views openly and freely. When she was arrested, Crisóstomo employed a methodology that involved collective decision making and collaborative exchange and learning among youth.

In the final months of her sanctuary, Crisóstomo began to question if the strategy had outrun its course. Despite being in sanctuary more than a year and conducting two separate hunger strikes, she had received very little media attention and feared that she was not playing an effective role in the immigration debate or a central role in CSF's mixed-status family-centered agenda. In 2009, CSF had devoted most of its energy to building alliances with Evangelicals and other religious groups in the Familias Unidas (FU) campaign (discussed in the next chapter), taking the family frame to its fullest national extent. In this context, Crisóstomo's story, which increasingly focused on her indigeneity, did not appear to be a good fit. In October 2009, Crisóstomo left sanctuary to move to an undisclosed location. In a press release she explained that she had left because in her case the sanctuary strategy had lost its effectiveness. Since her departure, Crisóstomo has remained in the United States, albeit with a low public profile, though still engaged with indigenous migrant and labor issues.

While there was some media attention on Crisóstomo's case when she first sought sanctuary, it soon fizzled and was not comparable to the sustained attention Arellano had received. Why was Crisóstomo's plight so invisible compared to Arellano's? One possible explanation is that Arellano had been the first to seek sanctuary, and that by the time Crisóstomo sought sanctuary, there was a level of media weariness. Moreover, her case also seemed less compelling, given the lack of an embodied citizen child at her skirts. The presence of a citizen child in U.S. territory had allowed for the highlighting of Arellano's motherhood in a way that Crisóstomo's transnational motherhood had not.

While the visibility of the undocumented mother and the citizen child is often a source of interracial tension and opposition to immigration, most noticeably in the Proposition 187 movement, it remains something to contend with, not easily set aside or dismissed, despite the efforts of those who seek to challenge the Fourteenth Amendment and eliminate birthright citizenship. Crisóstomo's motherhood plight, by contrast, represents a transnational motherhood that, in the case of Mexican immigrants, has been invisible for decades. Historically a far more common form of separation, it involves the externalization of reproduction, as children are left in another country, cared for by grandparents or other relatives. As Pierrette Hondagnou-Sotelo and Ernestine Avila (1997) have explained in their analysis of Latin American domestic workers in the United States, the real cost of raising children is externalized, enabling U.S. employers to hire their parents as cheap and flexible labor. Employers do not have to deal with the costs and inconveniences of child care, and can count on these workers during extraordinary hours. Mothers suffer the duress of separation, but learn new ways of mothering. These transnational forms of motherhood involve practices in which they continuously communicate with their children and caregivers, a model that Hondagneu-Sotelo and Avila describe as "I'm here but I'm there." However, as studies have shown, the costs of transnational motherhood are not small, as relations between children and their parents are forever transformed, and expectations on both sides when they finally meet again or live together are often not met.

As a factory worker, Crisóstomo worked all day and would not have been able to afford child care and to support her children in the United States. She was, however, able to live on a minimum amount in a small apartment she shared with her then partner while sending a large part of her salary to her family in Mexico. Like Crisóstomo, many mothers (and fathers) have engaged in these kinds of arrangements for very lengthy periods with the purpose of supporting their families. Crisóstomo's case, in many ways, was therefore not news because it was not extraordinary; the plight of her children and her need to stay in the United States in order to financially support them were minimized because the absence of the migrant parent has been such a long-standing and common story—in many ways, what is expected of immigrant workers, a "necessary" sacrifice. One common assumption is that her situation is as it should be, a migration that is perceived as a choice, and that she made a free choice to leave her children. While Crisóstomo stressed the NAFTA angle to explain her lack of real choice, it was a very difficult frame because the global political economy that is most evident to migrants is also most easily set aside or rendered invisible by those outside the migrant community. Hence, erasure of the global political economy also makes invisible the family separations that enable migration, the externalization of reproductive costs, and the transnational parenthood of migrants like Crisóstomo.

But as different as they may seem in their identities, subjectivities, and situations, Crisóstomo and Arellano are also similar. Both have seen their reproductive roles as mothers threatened or severed as a consequence of their migration. Both appeared to have made a "choice" even if in very restricted conditions. (For Crisóstomo, the choice was to stay in Mexico and see her children hungry or leave her children before migrating, and for Arellano, to agree to be deported and leave her child here or to return to Mexico and essentially deport her citizen child from the United States.) In distinction from Arellano, Crisóstomo's choice to stay in the United States, however, was not seen as selfless, sacrificial, or necessary by many critics (and seen as unnatural by some, who asked if she was a good mother, wouldn't she want to return?). Because leaving children before migrating is something that has often been invisible and assumed to be an external issue (while being very much part of what makes immigrant labor so much cheaper and flexible), her right to continue to do that, to remain separate from her children in order to be the breadwinner and earn a wage that could sustain her family, was not necessarily recognized, as views on motherhood (unlike fatherhood) are often characterized by an overvaluing of the affective dimensions of mothering over its economic or material dimensions. Her breadwinner argument was not considered sufficiently valuable, and her plight was not considered comparable to Arellano's.

By contrast, Arellano's strategy of risking it all to remain with her child underscored the affective dimension, with no emphasis on the fact that she was also the wage earner. Her emphasis on the affective dimension is precisely what led to media puzzlement when Crisóstomo sought sanctuary in order not to return to Mexico to be with her children. It made her motherhood seem less affective and more "unnatural" compared to Arellano's "understandable" desire to remain physically close to her child.

Because of this difference based on gender roles and expectations, Crisóstomo could not readily rely on the family frame to make her case. She had to move from the family frame to one that underscores the global political economy's effect on life-chances and migration decisions. In her quest for a rationale that could explain her actions and make them meaningful to a broader public, Crisóstomo relied on a notion of displacement, first one that emphasized neoliberalism and specifically NAFTA's impact on the Mexican population in general, followed by one that placed a specific emphasis on the displacement of indigenous peoples and her own displacement as an indigenous migrant. She did the latter by tying together a millenarian struggle of indigenous people displaced from their land in Latin America with their contemporary exclusionary status in the Americas. She claimed that undocumented indigenous migrants in the United States were doubly displaced as they migrated due to poor opportunities in Mexico that are not only linked to a lack of economic opportunity but also to racial discrimination toward indigenous people. Economic displacement, she explained, was not a choice, but a process that forced her, as a single mother, to leave her children in order to provide for them.

By explaining her migration as forced rather than voluntary, and offering a racial logic in addition to the economic one, Crisóstomo provided a unique and alternative angle, but one that did not easily tie into the family frame pursued by CSF and others in the immigrant movement who were increasingly relying on the notion of family as a plural subject as articulated by relatives who are documented or citizens, and focusing on the rights of the citizen children of undocumented parents. The invisibility of her transnational motherhood appeared to render her less relevant for the broader Latino family frame that had become central for the movement, leading her and others to question the effectiveness of her sanctuary.

FRAMING THE FAMILY

Elvira Arellano's case provides a window into some of the conditions facing undocumented immigrants seeking their own political agency as they face deportation. Arellano's rights to articulate a political position and champion her own cause were regularly questioned. While she spoke frequently in the name of herself and her son, claiming a plural agency and utilizing a relational strategy by emphasizing her motherhood, she was also individuated/individualized, singled out, and accused of utilizing her son. Moreover, the very frame that allowed her to make her motherhood central allowed critics to question her mothering as well as her moral authenticity. In sum, motherhood as a political strategy did not provide her immunity. Motherhood, and the responsibilities that Arellano attached to it, became a powerful basis for her relational strategy and tangling tactics, but was not, in and of itself, sufficient to supersede or overcome the problems of agency and representativity—and was also a source of challenge itself.

The recognition of agency and representativity is a problem historically shared by many subordinated populations. While on the surface agency and representativity seem quite different (agency being more questioned by the mainstream media, representativity by the immigrant community), the intersection of agency and representativity is aptly illustrated in the Arellano case. The questioning of her agency informed perceptions of her representativity, and questions about her representativity informed debates about her agency. While immigrant worthiness, as I have explained, is often evaluated according to conventional standards of morality (often expressed as law-abiding, hard-working, religious, and heteronormative), it is ultimately the questioning of her right to a voice, of her act of resistance, of her political agency, that most informs notions of her worthiness. Her resistance is deemed out of place and understood as an act of insubordination. And it is ultimately the media as well as anti-immigrants' interpretation of her resistance as an act of insubordination that upsets Arellano's opponents within the movement, since for them, Arellano's actions lead them all to be viewed as radicals when they have tried to be good, morally upright citizens. It is her unwillingness to play "by the political rules," her political agency, and not her previous deportation or use of false documents, that is the ultimate immoral act.

How can we reconcile the rendering of Arellano as a radical with her seemingly quite conventional political appeal of her right to mother? Why and how is her activism perceived as both conventional and radical at the same time? The discussion of movement tactics introduced in chapter 1 proves useful here. In highlighting her motherhood, Arellano was apparently simply tangling, that is, challenging the individuation of undocumented immigrants by showing, in multiple ways, how her life and that of her son's were deeply intertwined and could not be separated. She was engaging in a relational strategy that problematizes liberal individualism through the idea of a plural subject, citizen child and undocumented mother. However, as her agency and representativity were questioned and challenged, it became more evident that she was also "crossing," that is, charting new territory, occupying a new space where none existed before, engaging in actions from which undocumented subjects have historically been excluded. It is this crossing that seems so radical, so disruptive and audacious, while the claim to motherhood on the basis of moral responsibility and religious claims appears so conventional. Arellano is both conforming and challenging, occupying her rightful place as a mother but stepping outside of "her place," transgressing as an undocumented subject. Her status, and the concomitant denial of her political agency, rendered her conventional appeal an unconventional form of activism.

The legacy of Arellano's case is significant. As contradictory and complicated as her case was, it resonated in important ways among immigrant and non-immigrant publics as it dealt with a topic so universal and intimate—family—that most people felt obliged to stake a position in one way or another. Years after her sanctuary stay and deportation, the family frame has solidified its place in the immigrant rights movement, becoming possibly the main rhetorical anchor utilized by groups ranging from grassroots activists to religious leaders, policy wonks to national politicians.

However, Crisóstomo's very different sanctuary experience and reception reveal the exclusions implicit in appeals like Arellano's. Crisóstomo's agency and representativity were, by contrast, not so much questioned but ignored or viewed as insignificant because her case did not seem meritorious. It seemed like the farther her distance from the increasingly dominant family frame, the more challenging it became for her to situate herself in the immigrant rights debate.

While her increasing focus on indigeneity and double displacement is an emerging frame, for now it occupies a minority position in the immigrant movement. Hence, the family frame is both empowering and limiting, an advantageous double-edged sword for Arellano, but an almost insurmountable hurdle to overcome for migrant mothers like Crisóstomo who do not have a citizen child.

The following chapter steps outside of these two individual cases and explores the collective potential of organizing around family in the three years following Arellano's deportation.

3 · REGARDING FAMILY

From Local to National Activism

In a Cook County Board of Commissioners meeting held in September 2006, then Cook County commissioner Robert Maldonado requested that Chicago be symbolically declared a place of asylum for undocumented immigrants. Several activists and representatives of immigrant organizations, community organizations, and churches spoke. Ninety percent of the speakers were in favor of the declaration. Raquel Jiménez,[1] a member of La Familia Latina Unida (LFLU) and an undocumented immigrant who was almost deported while pregnant two years earlier, approached the podium. In fluent if slightly accented English, she introduced herself, stated that she was undocumented and that she had three children, and then informed the board that her son would speak. Her son, a twelve-year-old boy wearing a suit and tie, spoke briefly and eloquently in nonaccented English about why it was important for him to have his mother remain in the country. Raquel Jiménez remained in the background and did not speak again. After his short speech, several members of the press immediately followed the boy to interview him. The strategy had clearly paid off. That evening both Spanish-language news stations showed primarily footage of the boy as the spokesperson for the issue, in addition to footage of the two opponents who spoke. No other spokesperson was presented, and Raquel Jiménez was entirely absent in the media coverage.

While the media appeal of the very poised boy was clear, I could not forget Raquel Jiménez's brief appearance and disappearance. A young, sharply dressed, and articulate woman who had a compelling personal story to tell (she had been shackled and separated from her family while four months pregnant) had remained silent while her son, the young citizen, spoke. While I understood the appeal of the citizen child in an effort to garner media and public support, I was ambivalent about a self-presentation that focused on the child to the exclusion of the mother. On the one hand, I wondered if something was lost when Jiménez did not speak. I also wondered what were the particular political effects or consequences of having a stand-in represent Jiménez and others like her. However, I also realized that while she barely spoke, she did appear, and established her legal status, her role as mother, and her relationship to her son. It would have been possible for her son to appear alone from the beginning. However, this would defeat the point. Her son was not merely a stand-in but a continuation of her, intrinsically connected to her, a member of her family. Together, with her citizen husband and children (one who was testifying that very week in the United Nations in Geneva), they constituted a family as political subject. And family as a political subject is at the center of strategic political identity formation deployed by members of the LFLU campaign as well as other antideportation activist groups throughout the country.

Centro Sin Fronteras (CSF), the home organization of the LFLU campaign, was the first Chicago organization to launch a campaign organized by families where one or more members had been deported or were facing an eventual order of deportation. While CSF had existed since 1987, the campaign initiated by thirty-five families is a newer effort, created in 2005 as an antideportation campaign and presided over by Elvira Arellano. By 2008, the efforts initiated by CSF had led to a broader emphasis on the family in the immigrant movement as well as a national campaign—Familias Unidas (FU), or "United Families"— coordinated by CSF director Emma Lozano, Congressman Luis Gutierrez, and the Congressional Hispanic Caucus, and organized by hundreds of community organizers and religious leaders throughout the country.

This chapter analyzes the evolution of the family as a political subject and social movement frame from the creation of LFLU in 2005 through the end of the national FU campaign in 2009. I look at both a Chicago-based grassroots campaign as well as a national campaign in order to explain the rationale and ideological constructs that have informed this frame; the ways in which each campaign performed or enacted the family, highlighting salient similarities and differences; and the empowering potential as well as social and political limitations of the family frame in each of the two cases. By starting with the local grassroots campaign and then analyzing a national campaign visualized and planned by the same CSF leadership, I seek to understand how the family frame evolved and how it was able to take hold beyond members of mixed-status families and inform broader political imaginaries, playing a key role in the building of broader support from religious and other political allies. Throughout the chapter, I consider both the internal and external resonance of the family frame. In other words, I analyze the resonance of specific ideological content that provides meaning to this family frame for movement actors and immigrant and Latino communities, as well as discuss the ways in which the family is represented to external audiences and potential allies.

LFLU—BACKGROUND

LFLU is an organization focused on stopping deportations and fighting for the reunification of families that have been separated through deportation. The campaign is housed in CSF, based in Pilsen, Illinois, a primarily Mexican neighborhood in the Near West Side of Chicago, and its founding president was undocumented immigrant Elvira Arellano, who was initially detained in 2002 and who, after five years of activism, was forcefully deported in August 2007 (see chapter 2). Between 2005 and 2008, LFLU focused on lobbying for a private bill that would benefit thirty-five families that had been separated or were facing imminent separation due to deportation of one of the family members. All of the members were part of mixed-status families—that is, families that have at least one member who is undocumented and at least one member who is a resident or citizen. In most of the thirty-five cases, people left the United States to visit a very sick or dying relative and were detained and deported upon their return, and were banned from attempting to enter for ten years, a ban triggered when an undocumented person leaves the country and is caught when attempting to return. All of them, however, found a way to return to reunite with their children and spouses in the United States. Some were detained twice (in which case they were banned from attempting to return for twenty years) but returned nonetheless. Before their trips, some of these individuals were in the process of being formally requested by their spouses.

LFLU members raised awareness of their situation and collected funds for their campaigns by outing themselves as undocumented, making the details of their cases known to community members, religious congregations, and local, state, and national politicians. They lobbied the Chicago City Council and the Cook County Board of Commissioners in actions such as the one described above, successfully obtaining the approval of resolutions that denounced deportations and family separation, and asked for a moratorium on deportations and for immigration reform.

Faced with no further legal recourses at their disposal, the thirty-five families opted to pursue a political strategy of lobbying for a private bill sponsored by Representative Luis Gutierrez and Senator Dick Durbin. They also took several bus trips to Washington, D.C., where they met with congressional representatives to discuss their private bill, but also to advocate more broadly for legislation that would assist all families like them. They traveled as families, and children and parents together lobbied politicians. While the bill was first introduced in Congress in 2005, there were new attempts to reintroduce it in 2006, 2007, and 2008, with no success.

Another strategy was participating in marches and rallies designed to stop deportations that separate families. As the national movement for immigration reform intensified in the marches of 2006, members of LFLU were active mobilizers who were constantly underscoring the importance of stopping the raids and deportations. After the marches in March and May, they helped organize a march in July that focused on stopping deportations and raids.

The paralysis of the private bill and the urgency of a politicized national environment led LFLU activists to pursue more radical strategies. Their focus on the detained and deported led them to adopt the cause of the IFCO workers arrested in April 2006, many of whom had resident or citizen family members. Since 2005, IFCO, a company that produced wooden pallets, was being investigated by U.S. Immigration and Customs Enforcement (ICE) for hiring undocumented workers. On April 20, 2006, ICE apprehended 1,187 IFCO employees in twenty-six states in what is considered to be the first massive raid held after the March 10 march. In Chicago, sixty IFCO workers were detained. Several immigration activists in and outside of LFLU viewed this raid as both a governmental response to the March 10 march and a warning as they prepared for the May 1 march. In May 2006, Elvira Arellano joined Flor Crisóstomo, one of the detained IFCO workers, in a hunger strike in Pilsen that lasted forty days and was designed to pressure for a fair hearing of the IFCO workers in court. Once the judge who heard the cases granted them several months to prepare their case, Arellano and others ended the hunger strike. Finally, in August 2006, faced with an order to report to the local immigration office for deportation, Arellano sought sanctuary in Adalberto Unido Methodist Church. While Arellano's sanctuary experience is covered in the previous chapter, it is important to point out that although she was president of LFLU, the media's focus on her individual story meant that, with a couple of exceptions, very little attention was given to other LFLU cases.

LFLU AND THE MIXED-STATUS FAMILY AS A POLITICAL SUBJECT

When organizations such as LFLU advocate, lobby, march, and protest for the rights of families, they are creating a plural and relational subject that highlights the social relations between undocumented and citizen relatives, which tangles or ties together their destinies and livelihoods, complicating the distinction between outsiders and insiders. This relational subject is simultaneously about and not about the undocumented immigrant. In this context, somebody's place, or position in relationship to the state, or his or her right to belong, is advocated on behalf of the rights of citizens, and their ability to be deported is presented as a threat that transcends the deportable person and directly impacts those who are viewed as legitimately belonging. This critique of the separation of the parent and child as detrimental to the well-being of the citizen child is one of the most powerful dimensions of the defense of the family subject. While it has not proved successful in most court cases or in achieving broad immigration reform, it is an important basis of support coming from Latino families not directly affected as well as from religious communities, and has informed current state categories of prosecutorial discretion that would prioritize reconsidering the deportation of people with citizen children.

As described in the introduction, the idealized family is one that fulfills dominant ideas about traditional heteronormative nuclear families, and LFLU members definitely embraced this image. An online scrapbook of the families, with photographs and descriptions of the families, usually depicted them in formal Sunday clothes and included descriptions of their seemingly perfect lives before they were disrupted by the threat of deportation. Family members are usually described as pillars in their communities, church-attenders, with hard-working parents and academically outstanding children. The smiling faces seem full of portent of more happy days and promising futures. Their case narratives typically emphasize how their detention and deportation proceedings were usually triggered because of the familial commitment of one of the parents who returned to his or her country of origin to visit a dying parent. Familial love and responsibility, the very things that are most emphasized in these stories, are also portrayed as the cause of their potential deportation. Their only fault, it seems, is to have been too loving and responsible. It is hard to interpret the interruption of this future as anything but devastating. The purpose of these representations is to simultaneously convey the "worth" of these families according to dominant standards of family values and the impact of deportation's potential destruction on family members and on the broader community.

However, the representation of family is not only a process of mere "messaging" or instrumental framing but also a way of conveying the beliefs, values, and ideas that inform their own ideologies. It is not only that antideportation groups have gambled on the appeal of the family as the most viable or "marketable" option, it is also the case that they are firm believers in its importance. Family—its unity, continuity, and reproduction—is a primary axis of political identity, even as it is constructed differently by different actors. Hence, commonsense understandings of who and what constitute the family, and the political process of creating an alternative political subject that goes beyond the individual subject, are constantly informing and reinforcing each other. Below I discuss some of the main themes revealed in interviews with ten families of LFLU between June 2006 and January 2007.

THE FAMILY MEMBER/PARENT AS A
RESPONSIBLE CONTRIBUTOR

For many of the interviewees, civic responsibility is measured first and foremost by one's loyalty and commitment to family. The parents interviewed understood parenting as a social responsibility and believed that their ability to carry it out ensured a better and more secure society and more responsible future citizens. The families often referred to their commitment to the idea of family, which they frequently use to distinguish themselves from others and to explain why they had to break the law (by leaving to visit ailing or dying relatives). Several of them understand caretaking as a form of social citizenship that benefits not only one's children but society as a whole. I often encountered arguments explaining how, in caring for her children in low-income urban neighborhoods, an undocumented mother is ensuring that they will not be involved in gangs or become criminals; or how, in being a hard worker and also a constant presence in his children's lives, an undocumented father keeps his children motivated and off the streets. In aiming to deport them, the state interrupts the parents' task of making children socially responsible citizens. Deportations, therefore, in LFLU members' views, not only disrupt their families but also undermine the social order.

This discourse is not that dissimilar from dominant family values discourse that regularly draws a relationship between the decline of family and social disorder (see Gillis 1997). This view is intimately connected to a more individual self-presentation of these undocumented parents as morally ideal individuals (law-abiding, tax-paying, nongovernment-dependent individuals). It represents a more collective extension of this individualized image, introducing the notion of an ideal protocitizen as a family- and community-building, church-attending model parent and example for her or his children. Benjamin, a citizen father of three citizen children and husband of a woman facing deportation in September 2006, talked about his wife's case:

> She has never worked. She has always stayed home and taken care of the kids. No one can say anything bad about these kids. They are very good. I work so that my salary is enough so that she can stay home and take care of her children, instead of them being with somebody bad or becoming involved in gangs. But this is something the government does not recognize. . . . The work she does is probably not well recognized but it is something very noble and she is a good person. We are proud of her. So what happens? We want our kids to be better citizens, having their mother in the house, to take them to school, pick them up from school. . . . This is a contradiction of the very system of government that we have in this country. We immigrants have very big values, we were raised with moral values over there with mothers and fathers and everything. And you get

notoriety become stand-ins not only for all Mexican immigrants but for all Mexicans, becoming national markers. Hence, their actions are evaluated in relationship to how they present Mexico on an international front and how they may inform Mexico-U.S. relations. Many did not view Arellano as a model migrant, even though her plight was recognized as something shared by many migrants. The sympathy for her situation is widely shared; unlike the U.S. restrictionists, Mexicans did not usually question her right to be in the United States or the tragic nature of her situation. But her suffering was not enough. They were divided about her strategy, according to their ideological positions, as Arellano positioned herself on the left of the Mexican political spectrum, aligned with the PRD and various leftist organizations. For those on the center and right, Arellano's sanctuary act was neither legitimate nor necessary; some even considered it shameful. For those who did support her, she represents a more radical perspective, one that challenges Americans to face the real consequences of their dependence on labor migration, holds them responsible for the fate of her citizen child, and underscores the connections between productive and reproductive immigrant work.

Among the general public, among immigrant communities, and in Mexico, Arellano's representativity was up for question. While the restrictionist groups and mainstream press's critiques focused on her right to agency, immigrant organizers and Mexicans in Mexico focused on questions of authenticity, not on whether she could represent herself but on whether she could claim to represent others. Clearly, Arellano's motherhood strategy was not impervious to attempts to individualize and criminalize her, or to question her right to have rights. The next section focuses more on the specific strengths and limits of the motherhood strategy for women like Elvira Arellano, but also for other migrant women in different circumstances.

THE POLITICS OF MOTHERHOOD

Like the Mothers of the Plaza de Mayo, Arellano relied on traditional representations of motherhood to make her appeal. In fact, she increasingly relied on a sacred model of the single mother, the Virgin Mary, deemphasizing her sexuality while emphasizing her religiosity. As the months in sanctuary passed, Arellano wore more veils, posed near the Virgin of Guadalupe, and included references to God in her justification of her actions and predictions about the future outcome of her case. One predominantly displayed photo in the chapel featured Arellano hugging Saul with a background image of the Virgin. She increasingly projected an otherworldly aura, of someone whose mission lay in the hands of God. Hence, Arellano relied on the iconic image of the suffering mother protecting her child as a source of legitimacy for her political actions.

here and suddenly I am going to destroy your family because your wife or husband is breaking a law? That doesn't work or make sense. It's ridiculous.

As Benjamin suggests, civic responsibility also entails a personal morality that privileges loyalty to family above all other principles, laws, and concerns. It is this primary responsibility that many parents use to explain their activism under such difficult and tenuous conditions. LFLU parents often define their struggle first as being about and for their children. Several interviewees maintained that if they were alone, they would have given up long ago and somehow gotten by in Mexico. For the children and youth of LFLU, their main responsibility lies in doing well in school, obeying their parents, staying out of trouble, and both protecting and advocating for their deportable parent(s). Many of the LFLU children have been increasingly active in public forums and events in Chicago, the United States, and abroad. When asked why they are engaging in these activities, several children and youth stated that they could not imagine doing otherwise, and that they would feel useless and powerless if they felt they could not do anything.

For both adults and children, their activism around this issue is understood as the next logical step for them, the ultimate assumption of responsibility that is part and parcel of being a family. They also expand this notion of civic responsibility to include not only their own families but also the broader community of families who cannot or do not speak for themselves. When faced with the question of whether they actually represent the undocumented, they argue that because many of the undocumented cannot speak for themselves, they must speak for many more families than their own.

Beyond their parenting roles, the immigrants interviewed also frequently describe themselves as model citizens in their larger financial and social contributions to their communities without receiving any benefits from the state. In their view, they contribute far more than they receive, and therefore, on balance, they are a positive force for the United States. They emphasize that they are law-abiding, pay their taxes, work to support their families, do not receive welfare, and are not a burden on the state. Joaquin, an undocumented father, stated: "They call us delinquents, terrorists. I ask those people who think we are that: who is paying your Social Security check right now? They can come tell me [que me digan a mi]. I have worked twenty years in this country and I have not received a penny split in half of Social Security. But Social Security benefits go to those people who hate me, who want to see my family separated."

My interviewees frequently underscored their responsibility in helping to support the economy, responding to those who create a labor demand for workers and who therefore need them to clean their houses, park their cars, care for their lawns, work in their factories; those who benefit from their private consumption (businesses, banks); and those who benefit from their public con-tribution, including the elderly who receive Social Security, those who benefit from taxes, and even the state, which receives their contributions while simulta-neously expelling them or threatening to expel them.

FAMILY VALUES AND CHILDREN'S RIGHTS

LFLU members sought to embody and exemplify democracy by voicing their views about their own or their family member's deportation, generat-ing their own political agency, and engaging in advocacy. Feeling that they had been voiceless in the immigration debate and in deportation decisions that affected them directly, they have emphasized two political dimensions of their situation that they believe highlight the limits of U.S. democracy and point to a vision of what would be a more just and democratic social and politi-cal arrangement. The first dimension questions the commitment of advocates of family values, emphasizing the disparity between how different families are valued and treated. The second dimension focuses on the lack of rights of citizen children whose parents are deported.

For these families, the unity and continuity of family is in and of itself a value that must be preserved and pursued above the laws of the state. This discourse is founded not only on cultural and religious understandings immigrants bring from Mexico but also in U.S. ideologies that have historically granted privilege to the notion of family reunification in immigration policy and, more recently, to Christian conservatives, who have deployed a discourse about the importance of preserving and exalting family values in their campaigns against abortion and gay marriage. This discourse has permeated both Republicans and Democrats who regularly draw a relationship between the decline of family and social dis-order. LFLU parents are not questioning the discourse of family values, but the fact that their ability to reproduce them is being threatened by deportation. This exclusion of their families, which for them is a glaring contradiction, frequently becomes the basis for a radical critique of American democracy.

Once family is articulated as the main political subject, the evaluation of whether the United States is an egalitarian society is no longer based on an exclusive comparison of individuals or even racial communities, but of mixed-status families and families where everyone is legalized. Because a majority of the undocumented families are of Latin American descent, and all of the LFLU activists were of primarily Mexican descent, this comparison intertwines status and race, as they articulate the ways in which some families seem more equal than others. LFLU activists argue that a real democracy would value all families equally. Instead, they point out that while state policies support some families, they destroy others. They frequently referred in their speeches and literature to dominant political discourse on family values to point out the inconsistencies between what that discourse supposedly stands for and the separation of their own families. For example, the family book created by LFLU with the photos and stories of all the families facing deportation has a cover page of George W. Bush, citing a speech in which he stated that "family values don't stop at the Rio Grande." Additionally, his statement frequently surfaced as a referent in interviews. In an initial interview with Elvira Arellano when she was on a hunger strike in the summer of 2006, we discussed the case of Marta Jimenez, who was detained when she was four months pregnant. Arellano stated: "They speak of family values but when they shackled Jimenez and chained her pregnant stomach, where were their family values? Are not our families worth as much as theirs?"

Parents consistently raise the question of whether it is democratic to have different levels of protection for mixed-status families than exist for families in which all members are citizens. One of their most effective strategies has been to appropriate the family values discourse in order to highlight the contradiction or hypocrisy of the Right, which claims to be for family values but does not value immigrant families. Their critique reminds us of Janet Jakobsen's (2000) argument, which is that family values discourse, since its inception, has excluded racial minorities and not only sexual ones. Jakobsen argues that Christian-identified, right-wing discourses in favor of sexual regulation, particularly the discourse of "family values," should be read and responded to as not simply about sex, or about homophobic or heterosexist discourse, but about various social hierarchies condensed within the symbol of "family values," including class and race. She reminds us that "family values" provided the legitimating discourse for both the Defense of Marriage Act (DOMA) and the welfare reform bill in the summer of 1996, allowing for regulation through budget cutting of all those "queer bodies that did not fit into a mold of white, middle class privilege."[2] (While she does not mention it, this is the same welfare reform bill that severely cut welfare rights of legal immigrants.)

The second dimension present in the discourse of LFLU activists concerns the rights of citizen children, specifically the loss of their future opportunities as well as the schism that these children experience between the promise of democracy and the reality of exclusion of their parents. They argue that the legal protections afforded citizen children should be extended to their noncitizen parents, instead of the legal vulnerabilities of noncitizens being extended to their children.[3] They also emphasize the rights of children as birthright citizens who are in a country with such privileges and that removing them from these privileges (if they have to follow a deported parent) implies an unequal or denigrated citizenship. The children's educational accomplishments and strong feelings of belonging in the United States are underscored, as is the claim that their departure (due to a parent's deportation) will lead to a decline of their well-being, a possible loss of accomplishment, and a denial of opportunity.

Parents often define their struggle first as being for their children, and state that if they were individuals alone, they would have given up long ago and somehow gotten by in Mexico. Benjamin stated:

> The easiest thing to do would be to say: we are going to Mexico. What are we going to do in Mexico? I have no riches over there. We don't have land or a house, I don't have a job and would have to look for one, but that is not the issue. I would be betraying the rights of my children in this country, and I can betray many people but not my children. And they have the right to be here and to be here as a family. My wife is asking absolutely nothing of anybody. Only that they let her remain here with her family, that is all. And they need to respect my rights. **I am an American citizen and I do have rights. That's what I want and my kids want, to be heard** [bold indicates when he switched from Spanish to English]. . . . **My children, as American citizens, their rights have been violated.**

Activists in LFLU argue that children are placed in the impossible situation of having to choose between their country and their family. Even remaining in the country would also mean a decline in accomplishments, opportunity, and well-being as they would suffer the emotional, physical, and financial effects of being separated from one or more parents. LFLU parents stress the trauma that a previous deportation or the threat of deportation already places on their children. They speak with great emotional difficulty about the effect this has on their children's performance in school, their temperament, their relationship to their parents, and their feelings about justice and democracy in the United States. One LFLU child, eleven-year-old Cristina, spoke of her feelings about reciting one particular section of the Pledge of Allegiance in school: "When I am in school I don't say it [liberty and justice for all] and my teachers get angry. They say they will send me to the office if I don't say it. I don't believe in what it says because there is no justice for my mother and they are saying that there is justice. It's a lie. I don't want to say it on any day. Sometimes I don't say it when my teachers aren't looking."

Children like Cristina experience the possibility of their parents' deportation as an ever-present schism between their allegiance to country and to family, and as a reminder that the ideals their country stands for do not apply to one of the persons they most love in the world. Children who have birthright citizenship are also faced with the question of whether they will be able to stay or have to leave without ever having had a choice in the matter. While this recognition of children's lack of choice was a pivotal factor in *Plyler v. Doe* as well as state policies that allow undocumented students to attend college, those policies address the needs of undocumented children, but not the specific situation of citizen children. This birthright citizenship, which in many respects is just like the citizenship of others but in one fundamental way is not, has led LFLU activists and their children to raise the banner of human rights and children's rights as crucial issues that are deeply intertwined with their own personal struggles, and to pursue legal and political strategies that stress the rights of citizen children in a democratic system.[4] For many immigration movement activists, the issue of family resonates not only as a human rights issue but also because many of them have very painful histories of family separation in their own families. To the extent that other immigrants and descendants of immigrants identify strongly with this liminality, this betwixt and between discussed by Leo Chavez (1997) that characterizes the immigrant experience, these questions about the rights of citizen children will resonate among a broader public.

The idea that "we are fighting for the children" is one that has taken central stage in the activism of LFLU, as evidenced by Saul Arellano's lost court case, the pending court case of several children throughout the country, the increases in children's marches and lobbying and other political activities in which the children are the main participants, and the work of CSF in supporting the "Citizen Child Protection Bill" sponsored by Congressman José Serrano.

This emphasis on children's rights has also led to strategies that involve the activism of children. The parents argue that these experiences have not only victimized their children but also politicized them. In several interviews different parents stated that they initially tried to guard their children from the issues and exclude them from their activism, but that the children insisted on participating because they believed that they had to do something. The actions in which the children have participated and in which they appeared separately from their parents (although they were usually nearby) include a trip to D.C. to accompany Saul Arellano to deliver a letter to President Obama, as well as a few actions in Chicago where they have occupied a politician's office and sang Bruce Springsteen's "Born in the USA," changing the lyrics to say "Born in the USA, don't take my mommy and daddy away." These children are also frequently displayed prominently in their brown "Born in the USA" shirts in local actions and protests with other CSF members.

As mentioned in chapter 2, the activism of children is a controversial issue. The activism of young children has been questioned by other sectors of the movement. There are questions about the extent to which younger children have the emotional and cognitive development to understand what they are doing and why they are doing it, as well as the possible effects and consequences. Even other parallel organizations that focus on preventing family deportations, such as Homies Unidos in Los Angeles and Families for Freedom in New York (both of which, unlike LFLU, work with potential deportees who have criminal records), have been reluctant to have children participate openly in rallies, as has LFLU. Among Chicago immigrant organizations, there have been events featuring children by the West Suburban Action Project (PASO) walking from Melrose Park to Broadview on May 9, 2010 (Mother's Day), and children have been present in vigils and protests (Christmas vigil, 2013 and National Day of Action 2014, for example), but until 2012 only LFLU/CSF had staged several actions with children at the center and/or as speakers. The critique was probably most vivid in the case of Elvira Arellano, both when she was in sanctuary and after she was deported, when her son Saul traveled on several occasions (for example, once to Mexico when she was in sanctuary in Chicago, and to D.C. and other cities in the United States once she had already been deported to Mexico, obviously unaccompanied by his mother but accompanied by CSF leaders, who are also his godparents). While this debate was not really settled, the activism of children has declined since older undocumented youth have assumed a more central role in the movement. This is the case even in CSF, which in the past two years has created a youth campaign that is now more present (although some child activism still happens). In sum, concerns about the strong visibility of citizen children include the fear that instead of generating sympathy, it may backfire, because it might discourage the support of those who question the central presence of children and also provoke the restrictionists who continue to advocate an end to birthright citizenship.

LFLU STRATEGIES: POSSIBILITIES AND LIMITS

As the first group of undocumented immigrants to come out of the shadows in defense of their family unity, LFLU activists played a key role in the initial articulation of the family as a political subject, a strategy that was based on underscoring the tied destinies of immigrants and non-immigrants and on emphasizing the effects of the exclusion and deportation of the undocumented on a broader community of legal residents and citizens. In doing this, they highlighted undocumented immigrants' value not only as individuals but also as family members who engaged in socially responsible roles for the benefit of their children and communities. Another important dimension of this group was its public critique of the dominant family values discourse, underscoring the ways in which even those families whose values most reflected the traditional, heteronormative ideals and behaviors reflected in the family values discourse could be separated in an instant if one member lacked legal status.

However, while it does garner public sympathy and may seem in some instances to be the most effective political route, LFLU's defense of the merit of the mixed-status family and accompanying strategies do have their limits. Rosi Carrasco, an activist and member of an entirely undocumented family, made a clarification in one interview when I characterized the movement as one divided between those individuals focusing on families and those like her, who were focusing on workers: "No, that is not true. It is not that they are struggling for families while we are struggling for workers. We are also struggling for families, but we are struggling for every immigrant family, not only the ones with citizen children. That [only emphasizing families with citizen children] is not fair."

By definition, LFLU and other organizations throughout the nation that have advocated the nondeportability of parents in mixed-status families exclude all families whose members are entirely undocumented. They also exclude any claim for parents whose children may be in Mexico so that they can work here, a fact Flor Crisóstomo learned the hard way (see chapter 2). Hence, this claim does not raise issues of justice beyond the filial connection to a citizen, and it does not question the basis for the exclusion of the undocumented for any other reason than their relationship to their children—it simply states that it is necessary to extend legalization rights to the immediate relatives of citizens. LFLU has also made the conscious decision to exclude people with criminal records in its quest to embody model families. While this clearly is understandable as a strategic move, it is not the only option. For example, organizations such as Families for Freedom in New York and Homies Unidos in Los Angeles do include undocumented family members with criminal records.

LFLU also runs into the same obstacles as other children's rights organizations, as children are not recognized as full citizens in most polities, but as protocitizens, with limited rights and responsibilities.[5] The specific ways in which small children are viewed is reflected in the decisions of immigration judges. An attorney who runs a legal clinic with CSF told me that in his experience, judges were more likely to conclude that deportation of a parent would be a greater hardship on youth than on small children. It appears that the older the children, the stronger the argument that their lives are here in the United States and that the disruption would be more severe if they had to leave with their parents to a country they do not know. Younger children, considered more adaptable, are less likely to be viewed as facing extreme hardship. This is ironically somewhat different from more dominant representations of children that see younger children as more worthy of protection and treasurable and older children as more expendable. However, these differences in how children are viewed according to age vary, and while the welfare of smaller children can be seen as less significant in deportation cases, it can also be used to remove them from undocumented parents and more extended relatives and place them in foster care, and even eventually terminate their parents' rights, as has been the case with over 5,000 children (Wessler 2011).

The case of LFLU is one of many. The politicization of the family in the immigrant movement continued in Chicago and throughout the nation. The cases

Elvira and Saul Arellano during service in the Adalberto Unido Methodist Church, where she was in sanctuary between August 2006 and August 2007. Photograph by Toribio Barrera. Courtesy of Centro Sin Fronteras.

Flor Crisóstomo was in sanctuary at Adalberto Unido Methodist Church between January 2008 and October 2009. Photograph by Jhonathan Gómez.

Members of La Familia Latina Unida visit the state capitol in Springfield, Illinois, on May 10, 2005, to ask then governor Rod Blagogevich to support their cause. May 10 is Mother's Day in Mexico. Photograph by Toribio Barrera. Courtesy of Centro Sin Fronteras.

The Unzueta-Carrasco family, all undocumented activists, at the vigil "Night of 1,000 Conversations," which brought several communities and organizations together at the Broadview Detention Center in 2008 to support the right of immigrant families to stay together. Photograph by Jhonathan Gómez.

On April 27, 2010, twenty-three civil, religious, labor, and immigrant rights leaders were arrested for blocking a bus taking immigrants to be deported to the airport. The group began the action chanting "Illinois is not Arizona," and each of the participants hung a photo of an affected family on his or her neck. All of the arrested were citizens or legal permanent residents. Photograph by Stephen Davis.

Congressman Luis Gutierrez attends a Familias Unidas Event in Homestead, Florida in April 2009. He is joined to the left by congressional representatives and brothers Lincoln Diaz-Balart (left), representative of the 21st District (R), and Mario-Diaz Balart (R), representative of the 25th District . Photograph by Vanessa Guridy.

Rigo Padilla, a University of Illinois student who was facing imminent deportation, speaks at an interfaith vigil for immigrant justice in December 2009. His deportation was stopped only a few days later. Padilla is a cofounder of the Immigrant Youth Justice League and remains active in the struggle. Photograph by Jhonathan Gómez.

On March 10, 2010, eight youths came out of the shadows in the first national Coming Out of the Shadows Day organized by the Immigrant Youth Justice League. This was the first coming-out action held in the nation. From the left are Ireri Unzueta, Hugo Esparza, David Morales, Nicolas Gonzalez, Reyna Wences, Uriel Sanchez, and David Ramirez. Tania Unzueta is at the microphone. Photograph by Isaac Silver.

During the Secure Communities action, the Chicago 6 walked to a freeway ramp entrance with signs claiming that Secure Communities was hurting their families and communities. All six were arrested. From left to right: Fanny Lopez-Martinez, Jorge Mena, Arianna Salgado, Ireri Unzueta, and Karla Navoa. In the back: Miguel Martinez. The youth on the far edges, David Ramirez (left) and Andrea Rosales (right), were caretaking, but not participating. Photograph by Sarah Jane Rhee (www.loveandstrugglephotos.com).

Fanny Lopez and her husband, David Martinez, came out as an undocumented family during the third national Coming Out of the Shadows Day on March 10, 2012. David Martinez stated: "Our love is no different than any other undocumented love." Photograph by Sarah Jane Rhee (www.loveandstrugglephotos.com).

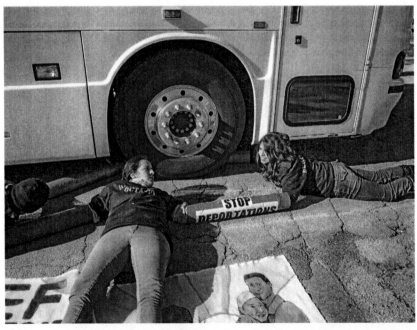

On November 19, 2013, twelve activists blocked a bus transporting immigrants to the airport for deportation. Maria Gonzalez, on the right, and Xanat Sobrevilla, center, and four other immigrant youths attached themselves to the front tires of the bus to stop it from moving. The youths had worked extensively on the antideportation campaign of Octavio, who was in the bus, about to be deported. Photograph by Isaac Silver.

Two weeks after giving the "Dreamer" speech next to Governor Pat Quinn and Mayor Rohm Emanuel during the signing of the Illinois Dream Act, Arianna Salgado participated in an act of civil disobedience in downtown Chicago to protest the Secure Communities program, which facilitated more arrests and deportations. The action was held outside a hearing on the program conducted by a national committee. Photograph by Sarah Jane Rhee (www.loveandstrugglephotos.com).

A few days after crossing the border with the "Bring Them Home" campaign, Elvira Arellano speaks at a rally supporting deparated families shortly after returning to Chicago in March 2014. Photograph by Amalia Pallares.

highlighted in the first half of this chapter are similar to many throughout the country that were felt most egregiously in the cases of raids, in which detention, family separation, and deportation were sudden, unexpected, and devastating to communities. These incidents became more frequent in 2007 and 2008, when activists were increasingly hopeful that a Democratic Congress and a possible Obama administration would lead to legalization. Movement activism turned from megamarches to rallies, local government hearings, and public calls for a moratorium on all deportations. In this time period, the focus on the defense of families and the opposition to family separation begin to surface in a more systematic and collective way.

One of the principal sites for the coalescing of these efforts was Familias Unidas, a national campaign held in fall 2008 and spring 2009. While LFLU members were engaging in a collective struggle, they were primarily focused on advocacy for their own cases, which could be viewed mainly as a defense of their family's rights and therefore a necessary extension of their privatized reproduction. If the state stopped deporting them, they would be allowed to continue their lives as usual, fending for themselves and fulfilling a more neoliberal conception of the role of the family as exclusively private. However, this is not what has happened. The lack of any significant reform has led to a more collective strategy, in which family advocacy is taken outside of the exclusive domain of the mixed-status families to make this issue something that concerns all Latino residents and citizens who are not directly impacted. It has been apparent that the work of affected families is no longer enough, and the survival of immigrant families no longer depends on family members alone but must be defended by a larger collective. As I argue in the next section, family becomes the symbol for a broader collective struggle based on a relational strategy that links individuals to each other in the family, families to communities, and communities to the nation.

THE NATIONAL FU CAMPAIGN

Since LFLU's initial years of activism and the Elvira Arellano case (2006 and 2007), the focus on family has acquired a broader resonance among several social and political actors. In the 2007 and 2008 marches, family motifs were much more visible in activists' literature and signs. Spanish-language television programs ranging from *Don Francisco* and *Cristina* to *Veredicto Final* covered several cases of family separation. Human Rights Watch and the National Council of La Raza (NCLR) published reports on the effects of raids on children and families. The New Sanctuary Movement was created as a national, interdenominational coalition of faith-based groups and organizations designed to assist families facing deportation and defended the importance of family in its major events and publications. At the local level, in 2008, shortly after the Postville,

Iowa, raid, which galvanized immigrant rights activists throughout the country, LFLU and CSF, as well as youth organizations Zooalo and Batey Urbano, played a central role in founding Ya Basta, a coalition of more than forty immigrant-serving Chicago organizations that demanded a moratorium on deportations in order to end family separation.[6] In October of that year, the Chicago City Council unanimously approved a resolution to support a moratorium against all raids and deportations, after hearing moving testimonies in which family separations were emphasized.

Finally, in November 2008, shortly after Barack Obama's election, First District congressman Luis Gutierrez, in conjunction with the Ya Basta coalition, initiated a campaign in several churches in Chicago to collect petitions from citizens willing to adopt a relative or friend who is undocumented and then deliver these petitions to President Obama, who had promised to push for congressional reform in his first 100 days of office. The first rally was held in Saint Pius V Church in Pilsen on November 1, where approximately 250 people attended. While this was about one-third of the capacity of the church (this first event was not widely publicized), the significant crowd led organizers to be hopeful about the potential for subsequent events. This hope came to fruition in the next rally held on December 6 of that year at El Rebaño Evangelical Church in the Humboldt Park neighborhood: over 2,000 people attended. The common area was filled to capacity, and those who did not arrive early had to watch the video in adjacent rooms. The successful attendance and enthusiasm of the participants encouraged organizers to plan a national tour. By February 2009, the FU campaign, now sponsored by the Congressional Hispanic Caucus, had gone national in an attempt to present President Obama with thousands of individual petitions as well as to obtain media attention as each event occurred, pressuring for a moratorium on deportations and advocating comprehensive immigration reform (CIR). Bilingual rallies were held in twenty-two cities and fifteen states (four alone were held in the Chicago area) in mostly (but not exclusively) Latino churches and with Latino audiences between November 2008 (Chicago) and June 2009 (Denver). In the period after the marches, this campaign was the most important set of actions to call attention to the deportation issue. Importantly, while the marches were primarily organized by networks of local activists and organizers in each city, the FU campaign required more extensive coordination across cities, facilitating the creation of a national network that would prove especially useful for the execution of the national March for America held in Washington, D.C., on March 21, 2010.

This analysis of the campaign is based on the collection and study of videos, audio recordings, and/or field notes of a sample of eight of the rallies that I or my field research assistant, Vanessa Guridy, personally attended. Our sample includes three events in Illinois, including at El Rebaño Evangelical Church in

Chicago (December 6, 2008); Chicago Cathedral (March 21, 2009); and Our Lady of Mercy Catholic Church in Joliet, Illinois (March 21, 2009); as well as events in Nahbi Christian Ministries (nondenominational) in Homestead, Florida (March 29, 2009); Iglesia de Dios Pentecostal in Orlando, Florida (March 28, 2009); Jesucristo es mi Refugio (Evangelical) Church in Dallas, Texas (March 14, 2009); and Iglesia del Pueblo (nondenominational) in Mission, Texas (March 15, 2009). Additionally, I analyzed media reports as well as videos of several other rallies and conducted interviews with some of the main organizers as well as several participants and volunteers.

The campaign's purpose was to hold large rallies in churches of different denominations throughout the country, inviting religious leaders, local and national politicians from each respective district, and community members to rally together for families facing deportation, performing a national enactment and validation of the family, and family unity, as a main rationale for the struggle against deportations and for legalization. In each event there would be families bearing witness who had been separated or were about to be separated by the deportation of an undocumented member, usually a parent. Additionally, there would be prayer, music, and moving speeches by religious leaders and national and local politicians. In addition to pressuring Obama to act, the campaign asked local elected officials (congressional, state, and city representatives) to participate and pronounce themselves publicly in support of legalization.

Perhaps one of FU's most important achievements was creating the opportunity for religious leaders to own the issue by helping to organize and coordinate the event, publicly carrying the banner in front of their own constituencies as well as in their growing advocacy in Washington, D.C. While religious leaders of different denominations had been supportive of humane immigration reform for several years, this was an opportunity for them to do so in a broader platform, beyond their religious constituency, and to link arms with the secular sectors and political actors of the immigrant rights movement. While pressuring Obama and other politicians as well as other religious leadership (beyond the already supportive Latino religious leadership) was a key goal, addressing and persuading a general (usually religious) Latino audience were equally as important. The creation of a "we" that included not only the undocumented and their family members but also legal immigrants as well as native-born citizens in massive support for legalization was a work in progress. The concept of family and the importance of its preservation and unity in a context of increased deportations became the main theme or frame that anchored the campaign. While there clearly was an overlap (as many of the organizers and some of the audience members were also longtime movement participants), the events attracted crowds that might not have participated in or have been likely to participate in marches and do not self-define as political, but are likely to mobilize for something that is linked to their sense of spirituality and moral responsibility. The next section discusses the shared structure and content of these rallies.

STRUCTURE AND THEMES

At a rally at El Rebaño Evangelical Church, Pastor Eddy Santiago incited the crowd:

> Are you ready for a revolution? Are you ready for a revolution? Are you ready for a revolution? [cheers and applause]. Jefferson says each generation needs a revolution and this generation demands a revolution. How do we initiate a revolution? Letting people know that their voice must be heard. You have not come to any political event. You have come to an event where your voice will be heard. We must educate our people because they are the only assurance for the preservation of our liberty. . . . We want to create a revolution. Today history is in the making. Our children and their children will hear what started one day in Chicago with people in Chicago, the pastors, the bishops, fathers, political leaders, and the community is why we take seriously this grave situation of immigration. Because we know what it is to be a stranger. As believers we are Latino families united in one voice. Say it with me. It's time for a revolution. [crowd repeats] It's time for a revolution. [crowd repeats] Say it louder: it's a time for a revolution. [crowd repeats]

This statement alone refers to some of the important themes raised consistently in the FU events, including privileging the sacral over the political (even while being political in a broader definition of the term), appealing to a broader Latino identity, and calling for an alliance or unity of voices. A detailed analysis of the shared themes and structures of the event provides key insights into the goals and achievements of this campaign.

The seven FU events analyzed in this section reveal important differences even as they follow a predetermined structure. The shared structure of the rallies (although sometimes in varying order) usually included a welcoming prayer, a speech by a hosting religious leader and briefer speeches by one or more invited religious leaders (which could be of the same but also different denominations), a speech or two by local politicians (although none in some cases), and in most but not all occasions a longer, culminating speech by Luis Gutierrez. The rallies' importance as opportunities for religious leaders' ownership of the issue, however, meant that on a few occasions religious leaders predominated over politicians, and in a couple of cases when politicians attended, they were not encouraged to speak. The advance negotiations over the balance between the podium time of religious and political leaders, as well as the balance between religious leaders of different denominations under the roof of a specific church, were somewhat delicate and varied significantly in each site. Perhaps one of the most important examples of this was the negotiation between a high-level Catholic leader who did not want a national politician who was pro-choice to attend an event in a Catholic church. In the final agreement, the politician attended but did not speak. And an Evangelical church pastor gave the closing prayer in an attempt to symbolize interdenominational unity despite other differences.

In addition to the speeches and music, there were usually three or four testimonials from family members whose undocumented relatives had been deported or were scheduled to be deported. Sometimes accompanied by children and other family members and sometimes alone, those bearing witness were always citizen spouses, relatives, or older children of the undocumented person. In no instance did an undocumented person speak, a purposeful decision of the campaign. In instances in which the undocumented member had not yet been deported, he or she would stand next to the speaker and other family members, but would never speak. Frequently, the families that had borne witness would be surrounded by religious leaders who would pray and/or lay their hands on them. Finally, the filling of petitions followed the performances. After the talks, people who were citizens and who wanted to petition for a relative worked with volunteers to fill out a petition. In May, when the campaign officially ended, Representative Gutierrez and the Congressional Hispanic Caucus delivered thousands of petitions to President Obama.

Although the events varied in some of the ways described above, they had important common themes. While obviously cross-cutting, the themes that can be distinguished are: appeals to the higher order of God or a higher law; appeals to community identity and collective behavior (through a combination of positive collective self-definition, promotion of truly Christian behavior toward neighbors, direct comparison to other oppressed communities, affirmation of group worthiness, or calls to unity and action through political work); and an emphasis on the role and importance of leadership (as mediators for the collective, vessels of God, and subjects of prayer).

A Higher Law

Many speeches and prayers alluded to a higher order in which all people were understood as God's children, their dignity and humanity to be placed above the laws of "man" or the state. In this view, religious leaders frequently stated that the work of the church and the community was to uphold this higher law as part of their commitment to God's benevolence and justice. For example, Freddy Santiago, pastor of El Rebaño Evangelical Church, stated the following when invited to speak at a rally at Our Lady of Mercy Catholic Church on March 21, 2009:

Why are we here? Because Jesus has said a Good Shepherd lays his life for his sheep and as good shepherds we must stand together on this issue and demand change on immigration reform. The Bible says that for everything that God made God saw and said that it was good. There was one thing that he saw was wrong. He saw that man was alone and said it is not good for man to be alone. God understood that man should be in a community, that man needed a wife, that God needed children, that man needed a family. . . . We believe in the Father, we believe in the Son, and we believe in the Holy Spirit . . . and we believe in the husband, in the wife, and in children and that they should be together. And what God has established can't be separated, father from mother, or children from parents [applause] and so we stand on this issue together and we demand change.

This view was reflected in the politicians' speeches as well. For example, in most of his presentations, Representative Gutierrez referred to his courtship and marriage with his wife to illustrate the existence of a higher law that must be respected. He would mention meeting his in-laws and learning to follow their rules on courting their daughter. Next, he would mention their decision to marry and would rally the crowd by asking, "Do you think if Zoraida and I had gone to city hall and gotten a piece of paper and I had brought that to my in-laws and told them that we were married they would have said ok?" "No," the crowd would usually shout. "Of course not," he would state. In order to be married, his in-laws believed that he had to do it in the house of God, and after several months of sacramental preparation. "So I learned," Gutierrez would follow, "that what God has united no government [no man] can separate."[7] The audience usually responded with thunderous applause and loud cheers. In the rally at El Rebaño Evangelical Church on December 6, 2008, Gutierrez stated: "With the community and with the power that exists in our churches, there is no representative or senator who will be able to stop this movement. If you arrest these parents, if you separate this woman from her husband, there will come the time when you will have to take me in chains because where you go I go. Where the most vulnerable of our community goes we all go." Hence, in these speeches, in one stroke Gutierrez would generally both refer to the higher moral authority of God (recognized by good people of faith such as his in-laws as well as the responsive audience) and specifically address the moral illegitimacy of separating people who were married in the church (relying on the general assumption that most of those present as well as most immigrants were married in the church).

In Gutierrez's view, because a higher law had been violated, immigration reform had become a moral issue, not just a political issue. Thus, not only are people compelled to move on this issue for moral reasons, but God is called upon to right this wrong. Appeals and prayers to God often involved asking God to intercede to rectify the wrongs of the United States, which had turned its back on God and was in a moral decline due to its immigration policy. However, political leaders did not always use religious language to allude to the decline of the nation. For example, at an FU event in San Francisco on March 7, 2009, then Speaker of the House Nancy Pelosi stated: "Raids that break up families in that way, just kick in the door in the middle of the night, taking [a] father, a parent away, that's just not the American way. It must stop."

In addition to confirming a national decline, several religious leaders in these rallies stated that in order to right this wrong, God's intervention seemed not only indicated but necessary in view of the difficult odds. In Orlando, the first pastor to speak stated:

> God is the one who can provide total victory. Only God has the control and the power to make things change and make men think differently. We believe Lord that you are the one who can make justice. You are the one who can change minds. You are the one who can act in people's hearts to provide mercy to the families that are being damaged. . . . I ask that you intervene Father and that this nation can begin a new phase that will be its own blessing.

Many political leaders spoke in messianic tones, predicting that 2009 would be the year in which legalization would happen and God's justice would prevail. For example, congressional representative Lincoln Diaz Balart, speaking in Homestead, recalled his experience sponsoring the Nicaraguan and Central American Relief Act (NACARA) to explain how nothing is insurmountable:[8] "I have seen miracles in my life. Do you remember the NACARA law? They said it was impossible and yet we were able to obtain legislation that legalized 500,000 of our brethren. We have been able to obtain medical insurance for immigrant children. I have seen miracles. That is why I believe in them."

Collective Identity and Action

In addition to referring to the will of God, people were encouraged to support this issue as a way of fulfilling their social responsibility to all members of the community. This meant the creation of a collective that involved four key aspects: the representation of Latinos as social and political actors with shared identifications and sensibilities, the identification of immigrants and the broader Latino community with other oppressed communities, the affirmation of group worthiness through an emphasis on family values, and the moral justification of the struggle as the fulfillment of a basic religious principle. Together, these four dimensions helped to create an imagined community that while first made visible in the megamarches of spring 2006, was reinforced in this campaign, which additionally invited new participants who, while not likely to organize for what they perceive as political reasons, might support it for spiritual reasons.

If the key external goal was to pressure President Obama to initiate legalization legislation, the key internal goal was to build a coalition among Latino community members that would cross political parties, religious affiliation, nativity, and immigration status. This involved the work of creating an internal "we," in which Latinos of different conditions would recognize others facing deportation as part of that "we." This is a very important distinction from the religious discourse of many other supportive religious groups and organizations that focus on biblical references to "welcoming the stranger" as a rationale to argue for humane immigration reform, World Relief and the Catholic Campaign for Immigration Reform being only two of many notable examples.[9] Very rarely was the notion of "welcoming" the stranger used in the rallies. In fact, the only use the author witnessed was one in which Pastor Freddy Santiago of El Rebaño Evangelical Church stated, "We know what it is like to be the stranger." In contrast, the FU campaign utilized notions of "us," "our community," "our people," and "our neighbors," and not "the stranger," to refer to people who are vulnerable and facing deportation, suggesting a shared Latino racial identification.

This discourse on unity helped create a link between the native- and foreignborn, highlighting the discrimination and oppression all Latinos experience regardless of legal status. One of the important tasks at hand was to underscore that this issue affected citizens and legal immigrants as well. Testimonial after testimonial highlighted the effect of deportations on native or naturalized citizens. This allowed audience members who were not undocumented but had immigrant relatives to relate to the issue and view it as their own. Even in cases in which members of the audience did not have family members facing deportation, the issue was worded in terms of support for the community. In addition, the sole use of citizens in testimonials was a way of communicating to the press and politicians in attendance that voters and future voters were deeply affected by, and organized around, this issue.

Additionally, heavy emphasis was placed on interdenominational unity. With very few exceptions, most events had religious leaders from various denominations as invited speakers. Representative Gutierrez highlighted this unity in his discussion on several such occasions. For example, at the Homestead event he proudly described the Detroit event as one that was held in an African American church located in a Latino neighborhood and had a Catholic bishop initiate the evening with a prayer. He also mentioned the rally in the Chicago Cathedral:

Evangelicals and Catholics sharing one altar like when Cardinal George said at the altar that deportations and separations are immoral and must stop. On that same altar the pastor of El Rebaño Church closed the event with a prayer. I have never seen a cardinal witnessing that. That demonstrates our commitment. And do you know why that is? Because the only institution, the only place where the immigrant has always been welcome and has been protected is the church.

This public linking of religious institutions with the issue was crucial because most contemporary churches have a growing Latino base and an important immigrant base, many of them undocumented. According to the Pew Hispanic Center, Latinos have higher levels of religiosity than the white population. Sixty-two percent are Catholic, and 19 percent are Protestant. The majority of these Protestants are Evangelicals. (The breakdown of the Protestant 19 percent is 13 percent Evangelical and 6 percent mainline.) While Catholicism predominates among immigrants, Protestantism rises as we look at second and third generations. Additionally, Latinos are more likely to attend religious services than non-Latinos (43 percent versus 36 percent). Moreover, 61 percent of Latinos say religion is important in their lives (compared to 58 percent of the general population), the highest numbers going to Evangelicals, 92 percent of whom stated religion was very important in their lives. And Evangelicals are as likely to be foreign born as native born.[10] Freddy Santiago stated at the Dallas event that 38 percent of his church membership was undocumented. Several pastors in the rallies mentioned not only their undocumented congregations but undocumented pastors, some of whom had also been detained and even deported. Many religious leaders made direct links between their work with, and responsibility to, their parish members and their campaign for humane immigration reform.

In addition to unity across religions, interpartisan unity was also considered necessary, as the issue is considered broader than partisanship and is especially so for Latino Republicans. In Homestead, Florida, where Representative Luis Gutierrez spoke immediately after then Florida congressional representatives and brothers Lincoln Diaz Balart and Mario Diaz Balart (Republicans),[11] he stated:

> And I think that same unity of Lutherans and Methodists, Evangelicals and Catholics and Baptists, Muslims we have seen, all of them unite to defend our families. And if they can leave aside their differences for this campaign, we can also leave aside our political differences. When people speak of this campaign they will speak of Catholics and Baptists and Evangelicals but they will also speak of Latino Democrats and Republicans defending our migrant community as Lincoln Balart and his brother have done here today.

This moral rationale for immigration reform allowed speakers to argue that this issue was considered above political differences. In fact, this sense of shared morality, and not politics (understood as partisanship), should guide decisions to support or oppose specific individuals in the voting booth. At that same event, in his closing prayer a priest stated: "Let us not be afraid to pressure politicians just as Jesus came to preach to those who were mistaken. The system is wrong. We must say good-bye to any political party or any political discussion that goes against our values. Our values go above any politicians. Above any identification is the compassion that must govern the church of Christ in these times."

A second theme that emphasizes the collective is the identification of immigrants as oppressed peoples, occasionally with African Americans but most noticeably with Jews as an oppressed people in their enslavement and flight from Egypt. At the Homestead event, Rabbi Mario Rojzman stated:

> The history of my people is the history of a group of immigrants seeking a better life. But the ones who were most needy we were called potential enemies. A potential enemy, does the story sound familiar? [loud clapping and cheers] . . . We must stop seeing the migrant as the problem because [the migrant] can be the solution. This is not a political problem. It is a religious problem because as long as we mistreat part of our people the blessing of God will be incomplete.

Evangelical pastor Freddy Santiago made powerful use of the comparison to Jews in his own church, El Rebaño:

> Moses was a man of God, and that is what we need in these times, men of God to rise up who have spent time battling different enemies. And when Moses went to Pharaoh he said powerful words. He said let my people go. He said let my people go. Today we are that generation that demands reform for our Latin families, and all the spiritual families in Chicago will rise in a revolution and tell Washington let our families go because we are all immigrants. We know the Bible mentions immigrants. Ephesians 2:19 says for God you are no longer strangers. We know what it is to be a stranger, what it is to be rejected, what is not to be part of our family . . . but Ephesians says we are part of the family of God. We have our rights to a family, and since we have all the rights in the heaven Ephesians tells us we have all the rights in heaven. And because we have all the rights in heaven we have all the rights in the world. How many here want it to be here on earth as it is in heaven? We are part of the family of God. Churches are made up of families. Our communities are made up of families. Our nation is made up of families. And our families cannot be separated. Our families need to remain to be united. . . . We are the generation that is victorious that stands before the Pharaoh of this decade and says "ya basta," enough is enough, enough is enough, let my people go. We will not allow our families to be threatened or oppressed . . . we have one voice as one people of God, united.

Santiago uses the Jewish example to highlight the similarities and validate the notion of immigrants, but also refers to all Latinos, regardless of nativity or legal

status, as a "we" consisting of persecuted and oppressed people who must struggle for their own liberation. By stating "we know what it is like to be a stranger,"
he is connecting the experiences of Latinos who are "othered" because they are
immigrants or ethnically and racially distinct with those of the undocumented.
He is using the term "stranger" in a broad way to create a bond among all Latinos, suggesting that one can be a stranger due to legal status, but also because of
other conditions that everyone in the audience has experienced. "Our families"
can only survive if the collective "we" assumes an emancipatory role.

Another way in which the events involved a collective racial affirmation was
through the positing of "we" as a valuable people whose families are worthy. All
the self-presentations of families as hard-working, loving, and patriotic are very
similar to the self-representations of LFLU family members discussed earlier in
the chapter. Youth who testified spoke of being outstanding students and having big dreams that were threatened with the deportation of a parent. Citizens'
spouses spoke of their devotion to their spouses and the difficulties in caring
alone for their children as well as addressing everyone's trauma. They spoke of
their hard work, upstanding citizenship, and commitment to family. Several
explicitly countered the stereotypes of immigrants as criminals or threats and
reiterated that "we" are a valuable, worthy people. However, because all those testifying were residents or citizens, their representations of worthiness were clearly
not restricted to the one undocumented member, but to the citizen members as
well, and by extension to the entire family in this collective construction of worthiness. At the same rally mentioned above, Pastor Santiago stated: "We Latinos
are not terrorists, we are deeply spiritual and love our Father and know the issue
we are standing for—we don't just want to be consumers, we all want to be part
of the dream of America." The use of "we Latinos" is not an accidental slippage,
but attests to a shared sense of a "we" based more on a shared racialization than
on legal status. Despite or rather because of this racial subordination and lack
of power, they seek to reassert their worthiness as noble "family-loving" and
"church-attending" people. Much of the discourse in the rallies is a reaffirma-
tion of these self-understandings. At the Orlando rally, Evangelical pastor Xavier
Villacís stated: "We do not have money nor resources, only the power of Christ.
They may say what they want but we are family-loving people, we are people who
work, we are people of God. We have come here to work. Perhaps the church does
not have gold or silver but we tell the United States in the name of Christ, rise Jeho-
vah." This "we," which can refer to the undocumented but also to immigrants and
Latinos, is a flexible category that allows the broadest group to identify with
and draw connections between each other even when there are important differences in denomination, political affiliation, and legal status.

Finally, a fourth key collective theme engages moral responsibility. Once the
need for unity among heterogeneity and the identification as oppressed peoples

(via comparison and identification with other oppressed groups) are established, a moral and spiritual rationale is summoned to encourage people who are not directly affected to support this cause. This refers not only to how God wants the world to be (the previously mentioned higher law that sustains human dignity and liberty over governmental law) but also how he wants his children to behave. The idea that is frequently repeated by religious leaders as well as by Representative Gutierrez is that one should follow the Golden Rule. Those who follow the rule identify fully with the people bearing witness, and would do everything in their power to prevent the separation of their families. Gutierrez stated in Mission, Texas:

> You know it is interesting as we look at our nation, what is something that is the fundamental underpinning, what should be sacrosanct, something of ultimate importance? What is the foundation of our nation? It is families, it is marriage, it is people coming together, to build a bond, to have children and build that marriage. And we are asking the government not to destroy the very foundation of the United States of America, of its families. [applause after which he switches to Spanish] They teach us two basic things. To love God above all things and to love our neighbor as we love ourselves. Think about what it means to love your neighbor as yourself. If you are a citizen of the United States imagine that the government takes away your wife, that early one morning Immigration would come calling and take her away, would take her away from your house, from the hands of your children. Think about that because that happens every day in this country. If you are a woman think about your husband going to work one day and getting a call telling you that your husband has been deported from this country so that you cannot see him again. If you are a young person imagine that you wake up one day and your mom and dad are no longer here. What commitment would you have to your husband or wife and your children so that they may return to your home? What would you do to ensure that the husband you love returns to your home? So that your wife could return to the arms of your children? Think for a moment, the most cynical among you, what would you do if you really love and went before God to get married? What would you do? I am sure you would take all the money you have in the bank and would deposit it to have your wife or husband returned to those children. You would lose your house, you would lose everything you have in terms of material wealth. You would call your congressman. You would call your president, councilman, minister, the pastor of your church. Now think about the most fundamental thing you are doing here tonight. Because if you truly love your neighbor as you love your child then you have the responsibility that you are fulfilling here tonight of doing everything possible so that others may have their wife, so that others may have their husband, so that they do not suffer. Because you are going to do everything possible so that those people may return to their

homes. And that is the fundamental message, [switches back to English] to love my neighbor like I love myself I am going to make sure I double my energies, I am going to vote, write [and] I am going to march, I am going to organize. I am going to talk to my church. I am going to talk to my pastor to make sure that all families are sacrosanct in this country.

In this and other speeches at the rallies, immigrants are again not considered strangers, but neighbors, and the audience is asked to assume responsibility for the life and well-being of their neighbors. This sense of responsibility, this obligation to love the neighbor as oneself, is supposed to compel all attendees—not only those with immigrant family members, but all members of a parish—to work for the rights of their fellow neighbors, parishioners, and community members. In this context, immigrant rights activism is considered morally necessary and equated with spiritual duty and moral responsibility.

Responsible Leadership

Finally, the third important theme emphasized at these rallies (in addition to the higher law and the collective identity and responsibility) is the role of leadership, both political and religious. Leaders are considered vessels representing the will of a people who clamor for immigration reform, and therefore as representatives need special insights, talents, and support through prayer. At the rallies, they are both thanked for the work they have done and commissioned by the audience to continue their work with mass moral support. At most of the events a call is made for God to guide the elected representatives present and other politicians in their attempt to persuade President Obama to move toward immigration reform. These leaders are assumed to have not only understood but also to have committed to the higher moral struggle of the people. For example, in the final prayer in Homestead, a Catholic priest stated:

And a very important thing is the agreement of these congressional representatives who do not represent parties, but represent the people, all those of us who have suffered and know this goes beyond parties. It's a commitment to God. [switches to English] . . . Lord, thanks for them [Gutierrez and the Balart brothers] here today. In a humble way we offer everything we have. This is a poor community; this is a humble community. This is a community victimized by many situations including the immigrant deportation drive. But Lord they [the politicians] are here because you brought them here, and you brought them here for a purpose. You brought them because here we can tell that we are altogether the children of God, and we don't represent a particular party, a particular faith. We are all denominations. We pray for them. They are leading the struggle. They are representing us, because us altogether, if one member of our community suffers we all suffer. And Lord we pray that you give them wisdom so you might give them the determination to go before the president and refresh his memory that he was elected by Latino voters that made a difference in his campaign because he did a commitment with us. I pled with him for commitment to legalization and he told me in a year you will have it. And to refresh his memory we send you these messengers so you may refresh his memory, stopping all deportations, bringing families together, and giving us legalization and a path to citizenship to all those who are paying taxes, working hard, and raising families. We send them with a blessing wherever they go. That this meeting will keep their mind fresh, that they have a commitment with this community to make this bill happen.

In El Rebaño, Pastor Wilfredo de Jesus, of the Church Nueva Vida, read a letter to Obama signed by pastors and priests of many denominations and invited the pastors and priests present to add their signatures. After the signing another Evangelical pastor stated:

And that is why I tell all my fellow pastors—this is a job we must do with integrity. We are not politicians, we are servants of God. And we must support politicians who have integrity, who use their political capital, who take risks with their own colleagues, with their own political parties. Our prayer today will be that Luis Gutierrez receive the peace of God in his heart, receive the joy of God, and that what has started here in this congregation we may imitate in other cities, we take to other cities. That we may start working with Obama with this document [the letter].... God, please control the mind of each congressman and you would grow in their hearts.

These political leaders, as representatives of a collective voice, are charged by religious leaders and all the attending community to continue and intensify their work. While at some of the events the focus of the main prayer was on the elected representatives to enlighten Obama, in others it was a prayer for Obama himself to follow the course. Obama is discussed both in terms of empathy and accountability. In terms of empathy, Obama, as a loving family man, is called upon to think of his own family and relate to the families that have faced or are facing deportation. Marta Sanchez, who spoke of the case of her deported niece (a mother of three young girls) at the Mission, Texas, rally, responded to the question of what message she would like to give to Obama:

Well what I see is that he is with his family a lot. He spends time with his daughters and they have the best. I would say there are other separated families who also want to be with their daughters [thunderous applause] and who should also have the opportunity to be able to grow as a family as it should be. This immigration reform has hearts and stories, and we all want to be good parents for our families. Give us the opportunity to be with them.

On other occasions Obama is discussed in terms of accountability, as having been the benefactor of Latino votes, and even of having won due to Latino votes. More than once, different leaders spoke of their collective investment in the Obama presidency and about his promises and commitment to them on this issue. Representative Gutierrez stated in Mission: "Seven million [Latinos] voted in 2004 and in 2008 it was 10 million. This is a main reason why he is in the White House. Not only because he received three million more votes but because our community voted for him. It was our investment."[12] And in Homestead he told the crowd: "We'll let him begin his work now so that he can fulfill his promise. [Crowd chants "Yes we can."] We have to be very clear. We have deposited in the bank of the presidency a bunch of money and deposits and now we are writing a check, and we are asking for a halt to the raids and deportations and immigration reform."

In addition to the focus on political leadership, FU became an important site for the affirmation and consolidation of religious leadership on this issue. While the Catholic Campaign for Immigration Reform (Justice for Immigrants) had existed since 2004, it was important in Chicago, for example, that an event was held in Our Lady of Mercy Catholic Church, with Cardinal Francis George hosting, in addition to the earlier one in Saint Pius V Church, a primarily Mexican congregation in the Pilsen neighborhood. Methodist, Muslim, and Jewish religious leaders were invited speakers at several of the events, endorsing the campaign. Most strikingly, Evangelical pastors of primarily Latino congregations took a leadership role. Using the case of Chicago as an example, pastors from two churches, spouses Freddy and Lynette Santiago and Wilfredo de Jesús, assumed local and national leadership. Pastor De Jesús accompanied Luis Gutierrez on several trips, including a visit to the site of a raid in Postville, Iowa, where he claimed to have been deeply moved and renewed his dedication to the cause. In fact, he led a discussion at the 2008 Democratic National Convention focusing on the Postville raid. At the Rebaño event he read a letter signed by dozens of pastors that was sent to Obama to formally endorse an interdenominational (although primarily Evangelical) call to Obama for reform. Pastor Freddy Santiago and his wife, Lynette, not only led the event at El Rebaño in Chicago but also played a leading role in the events in Dallas and Mission, Texas. Additionally, Santiago was the Evangelical leader selected to say the final prayer at the Chicago Cathedral event, an important moment of interdenominational unity.

Santiago and De Jesus are not alone, but are part of a new Latino Evangelical leadership with growing Latino and immigrant congregations that are part of a broader coalition of Latino Christian leadership embodied in the National

Hispanic Christian Leadership Conference (NHCLC) created in 2001, which self-reports as serving 18,000 churches and close to fifteen million Christians (De Jesus is its vice president for social justice). In 2006, the NHCLC commissioned an immigration task force, the National Latino Evangelical Coalition on Immigration. Today, the coalition functions as a subsidiary of the NHCLC committed to working with other ethnic faith groups, community development organizations, government agencies, and civic partners in the pursuit of immigration reform. The NHCLC includes an increasing number of Latino pastors working with a quickly growing constituency arguing for a place in the national Evangelical conversation advocating on behalf of Latino issues, most important among them, immigrant rights. This advocacy has not only been directed to the president and other elected officials at all levels; they also lobbied the National Evangelical Association, which in 2010 made a rare public policy endorsement supporting just immigration reform.[13] If the FU campaign was by no means the beginning of Evangelical pastoral involvement in this issue, it was a moment of consolidation and public ownership, of creating bridges between different churches of one denomination as well as different churches of many denominations, and between politicians and immigrant advocacy organizations and religious organizations. While not all the denominations have made the public pronouncements of the Catholic and Evangelical churches in favor of CIR, there are many ministers and representatives of other religions who actively support reform, are engaged in national and local efforts and campaigns supporting immigrant rights, and participate in rallies such as the FU ones.

SIGNIFICANCE OF THE FU CAMPAIGN

While neither Obama nor congressional leaders followed through on a viable effort toward immigration reform legislation after the FU campaign, it would be an error to judge the campaign's worth solely on the basis of direct policy outcomes. The FU campaign was a key occasion for consolidating the family frame, as well as bonding among different immigrant rights supporters (advocacy, social service, religious organizations) and between them. Through the emphasis on a higher law, a collective identity and responsibility, and the role of leadership, the rallies emphasized and performed a moral and communal dimension that provided participants and audiences with another rationale or window (besides the human rights framework) from which to view the issue and be moved to action.

The FU campaign was also a site of crossovers, of intermingling of two realms, of sacralizing the political and politicizing the sacral. One would hear political speeches from religious leaders who quoted Jefferson and Lincoln in their discussions of equality, fairness, and justice, as well as increasingly religious speeches from political leaders like Gutierrez. What was clear to both sets of leaders and the audience was that the church, and more specifically the Latino church, of any denomination was a source and site of power and resistance on the side of those who were considered the most vulnerable.

Additionally, the campaign was a site for creating a collective identification among all Latinos, making the issue as equally relevant to citizens as it was to those who were not. The basis for this shared identification was the need for the already enfranchised to protect the most vulnerable, even if their immediate families were not directly affected. This role was assigned to those who were the least vulnerable in terms of legal status. Luis Gutierrez reaffirmed the role of citizens in his speech in Homestead: "We are asking for the most vulnerable in our communities, for those who have less of a voice. And I am so happy that those of us who are citizens of the United States will go to any institution and demand what is just and necessary."

The creation of this model in which those with the most power work for and protect those with the least, and in which families who are not at risk struggle for the rights of those who are, pushes the family frame beyond the privatized limits of the nuclear family. While the nuclear family is what is performed in these testimonies, these family stories are followed by calls to the collective (among them many citizens) to act because they value families, follow a higher law, share a racial and ethnic identification with those affected, and follow the Golden Rule. In this context, "families" are both specific families and no family in particular, representing an essentialized vision of "the Latino family" as the most basic, sacred unit whose violation affects not only the specific individuals in it but also an entire community that is racialized.

Hence, there is an ethical, relational, and racial dimension to this shared identification, which not only states "you are like me," but my life, my values, and my respectability and dignity are linked to you and therefore lead me to struggle for your rights. In this view, the families bearing witness and all the families facing deportation are not in any way nuclear, privatized families that can survive on their own resources or abilities (what would be a more neoliberal notion of family), but depend on the collective, which symbolically assumes its moral and social responsibility in these rallies.

Ironically, however, in this protection of the most vulnerable also lies a key limitation of the campaign, which is the disappearance of the agency of the undocumented. In the carefully thought-out plan about who would be allowed to give public testimony about his or her case, only citizens or legal resident family members were allowed to speak. There were not even any instances of a brief introduction by an undocumented member, such as the one made by LFLU's Raquel Jimenez, cited in this chapter's opening. Despite the important variations across these rallies, what remained constant was the absolute silence of the undocumented person in question and the emphasis on the effect that this absence or threat of absence has on citizen relatives. The citizen as agent becomes both proxy and ventriloquist for the undocumented—the citizen's suffering is the subject of the bearing witness, and it is his or her voice that is heard. This is not a departure from dominant state practice of "erasing" the undocumented immigrant but rather helps to sustain the practice.[14] While the undocumented immigrant inspires concern and compassion, in the model the suffering of the citizen is highlighted, and it is the suffering of the citizen that ultimately matters. Conversely, it is only through the agency and power of the citizen that any change can happen. Citizens become proxies for those who have no voice. The hyperagency of the citizen, in this instance, becomes a form of ventriloquism that relies on the silence of the undocumented. Hence, while the model of speaking for the most vulnerable seems laudatory in an environment of fear, detention, and deportation, it appears to require the absence of the voice, perspective, and agency of the individual facing deportation.

One image from the FU rally held in Joliet, Illinois, exemplifies this model. A family approached the podium to tell their story of imminent deportation of the undocumented father. The daughter, son, and Puerto Rican wife of a Guatemalan immigrant, a Mr. Torres, a pastor's assistant, narrated in moving ways the terrible consequences of a possible family separation, experienced already once before. The daughter described the pain of not having a father present to dance with her in her *quinceañera*, or to share her first excellent grade on a report card, and not wanting her younger sister to go through the same experience. As the wife spoke they all held hands, huddled together, her husband in the center, his face with a moving expression, remaining completely silent. Afterward, they drew in a circle as they received a religious blessing. All the 1,000 people in the audience raised their arms during the blessing, coming a little bit closer to the family, in a symbolic effort to protect this family and prevent its separation. In this very powerful presentation, there were not many dry eyes in the crowd.

This moving moment symbolized the protection of the vulnerable by the collective mentioned in all the rallies. The relational identification of the family in the movement was no longer only about blurring the lines between undocumented and documented individuals within the nuclear family (in order to render the family a political subject) but also was about tangling them together, blurring or complicating the lines of distinction between the undocumented and documented in the broader immigrant and Latino community, rendering the family a main axis of moral, social, and political identification.

However, this very same image shows how this model based on the protection and defense of family unity by citizens can erase the agency and voice of the undocumented, and perhaps even requires it. The disappearance of the undocumented spokespeople and the practice of citizens speaking for them appeared to be a condition of this specific antideportation and legalization struggle. How was this strategy consolidated? The LFLU's experience in its early years consisted of a family advocacy that, while predominantly using citizen speakers (among them children), included both documented and undocumented members speaking and advocating (status mattered less than the ability of the family member to be articulate). However, Elvira Arellano's sanctuary broke with this model. As a undocumented single mother who spoke out against her own deportation (singling herself out from more conventional LFLU families), she became quite controversial. The lessons learned from this negative backlash led CSF leaders (who were Gutierrez's main collaborators in the design and implementation of the LFLU campaign) to opt to exclusively choose citizen speakers.

Another important factor in the selection of the families and stories shared in the FU campaign related to an important aspect of the early LFLU strategy: demonstrating worthiness. While they did not speak, the undocumented members of the families who would bear witness were selected with special care. They could not have criminal charges or records, and their legal case needed to be in some kind of legitimate process (usually thwarted by a missed interview or an unethical lawyer). Very young citizen children were usually not allowed to speak, whereas teenagers were (again a lesson likely learned from the Arellano case). Cases that were considered most compelling include those in which the spouse was a white American (Dallas), a case in which someone who cared for a young man with a disability was about to be deported (Mission), and the case of the wife of a veteran who was detected and deported after she reported on her sister's spouse for domestic violence (Orlando). Additionally, the weekly circulation of new testimonies and new cases created a multiplicity of voices, of onetime testimonies, fluid, to be retained by the press only until the next set of testimonies the following weeks, and far less subject to the scrutiny and critique of the Arellano case.

RENDERING THE FAMILY COLLECTIVE AND VALUABLE

This chapter has argued that the family as a political subject has played an important role in shaping the forms of self-representation that undocumented immigrants create in response to the decline in their opportunities for legal self-representation and the questioning of their right to political agency. As a plural entity that groups undocumented parents and citizen children and spouses, the relational family subject emphasizes the inextricable ties among family members who are being separated by deportations, countering dominant representations of the undocumented as "illegal" individuals, and questions a liberal political model that posits the polity as a mere aggregate of individuals.

However, this comparison of the LFLU and FU campaigns has attempted to show that the work of "the family" in the immigrant rights movement goes even further. While LFLU was a group of families gathered together to make their plight more public, in the national campaign the collective scenario or stage preceded and justified bearing witness, making an explicit connection between the family and the collective by highlighting what the decline of the family does to a community. If Benjamin shared in his individual interview what the deportation of his wife could potentially mean for his local community and his children's ability to grow up and become responsible members of society, at the FU rallies the attending crowds were in a sense bearing witness to the bearing witness of the families—the community is already, always recognizing the importance and place of this family. In so doing, it is tying family not only to a religious collectivity and a broader community but also to the nation. And the audience, people who are part of a community emulating God, are assuming the moral responsibility of bridging the survival of these families and the health of the nation, in order to shake the United States out of its moral decline and help it fulfill its destiny. Hence, for those not directly affected, this struggle is not only about compassion or solely about justice but is about moral responsibility as well—in opposing deportations and advocating legalization, people are fulfilling their responsibility to God, community, and country. Nowhere is this more evident than in Representative Henry Cuellar's (from Texas's Twenty-eighth Congressional District) call to the audience during his speech in Mission:

> There is a saying that we have to be ready for our country and for our family. So if we say ready you have to respond "for the family and the country." . . . Ready? Ready? Ready? [in unison with crowd]: For the family and the country. Ready? [in unison with crowd]: For the family and the country. Ready? [louder, in unison with the crowd]: For the family and the country. So I ask you this: the people that are here will go out and vote for the families that cannot vote.

While FU takes the LFLU strategy to a collective stage, both of their approaches are more or less similar (a focus on the mixed-status family, on the rights of the citizen, and on the moral worthiness of families). The effectiveness of this framing lies in simultaneously relying on the notion of family values (values to which Latinos purportedly adhere) and noting the contradictions between those supposedly American values and the policy realities of hundreds of thousands of deportations and family separations. Just like the Mothers of the Plaza de Mayo in Argentina who used the same norms of the patriarchal state to show how their traditional reproductive role had been interrupted by the repressive state, the immigrant movement questioned the reach of the family values rhetoric of the Right, not the rhetoric itself. "Are not our families also valuable?" both campaigns ask. This family frame, which allows for secular (human rights, social justice) and religious rationales to sustain it and even converge, has also helped to create bonds in a fragmented movement with communities that do not easily have a shared collective identity, and to build key bridges with other political and social actors, making allies out of politicians, other social movements, media, and religious leaders.

This coalescing around family unity has grown stronger since the FU campaign, becoming evident in moments such as different grassroots organizations' marches and rallies for family unity, and the national March for America, in which thousands of people converged in Washington, D.C., in March 2010, with prominent signs and chants for family unity while religious leaders prayed for families, as well as the movement's first civil disobedience action in Broadview, Illinois, on April 27, 2010, in which twenty-three immigrant rights, civil rights, labor, and religious leaders wearing large placards on their chests with pictures of a family facing deportation impeded the way of a bus heading to the airport to deport detainees. The coalition that came together at Broadview represented a very diverse set of actors that have not convened in that way before or since, united around the family issue. Additionally, a number of state and federal legislative efforts initiated in recent years (with varying levels of success), as well as a 2011 prosecutorial discretion memo, are also designed to prevent unnecessary family separation.[15]

In a few short years, the defense of family had now expanded beyond LFLU and FU and penetrated most major organizations and activities so that it is almost no longer possible to distinguish certain organizations as based on family rights from others that are not. It would be more accurate to describe the family issue as one that has been assumed and internalized by most secular and religious sectors of the immigrant rights movement. As one organizer of the Illinois Coalition for Immigrant and Refugee Rights (ICIRR) told me during the Broadview vigil in April 2010 when I mentioned how interesting it was to hear even members of a new business coalition for immigration reform repeatedly mention the importance of keeping families together during their inaugural event: "Well, everyone and everything is about family now."

However, on what concept of family do LFLU and FU rely? As I argued in the introduction, conforming to traditional family roles and expectations has been a key way in which Latinos in general, and undocumented immigrants specifically, have claimed their worthiness as U.S. citizens or potential citizens. Clearly, the families bearing witness in the FU rallies, like LFLU families, presented themselves as conventional heteronormative and model families—attending church, abiding by the law, and contributing to their communities. They were carefully selected by local organizers together with CSF leaders who oversaw the family selections in each city to make sure they conformed to the campaign's standards. The problem with this family frame is that it places immigrant rights activism in an increasingly tighter straitjacket, as conforming to state- and society-sanctioned concepts of what is a worthy family leaves a large number of nonconforming families out of the equation, and even forces families who may not conform on all accounts to create a fictive representation of themselves. The bridging of the secular and religious in the FU campaign also required adhering to a fairly traditional and ever more religious perspective on personal and family morality, especially in light of new religious allies. As chapter 4 explains, however, this vision would be challenged in 2011 and 2012.

In sum, this family frame and its related discourse has had important and powerful effects. It has challenged the individualization of the undocumented immigrant, creating the family as a political subject in which the rights of citizens and the undocumented are inextricably linked; used discourse of family values to point to state contradictions; and played a powerful role in both bonding and bridging within the movement. I have also argued, however, that it has important limitations a well. This heteronormative discourse of worthiness does not necessarily challenge the existing constructions of citizenship worthiness or laws that lead to the exclusion of undocumented immigrants, but argues instead for the mixed-status family that is deemed worthy as an "exception." Finally, I have attempted to show how, taken to the extreme, this family strategy aimed at "protection" can lead to the erasure of the agency of the very undocumented people who are the object of protection. Despite these limitations, the family discourse also does important political work. It relies on (and reproduces) conventional meanings and understandings of family to challenge racism, exclusion from the polity, and the individuation of immigrants in order to render them less or more deportable.

This analysis of the family approach of LFLU and FU begs the question of whether a focus on the family always leads to these potential limitations, or whether it can be constructed in different ways, using other expressions and strategies. Does defending the family and family unity require, by necessity, maintaining heteronormativity and erasing the agency of the undocumented? In the next chapter, I argue that "family" can actually be framed differently, as new actors emerge and new political events and moments suggest different directions for the movement. The following chapter underscores the polyvalent notions of family within the movement and points to new directions for understanding the work of family as well as the emerging agency of the undocumented as political actors.

4 · OUR YOUTH, OUR FAMILIES
DREAM Act Politics and
Neoliberal Nationalism

When our immigrant youth are under attack what do we do? Stand up,
    fight back
When our families are under attack what do we do? Stand up, fight back
    —Chants during a rally organized by the Immigrant Youth Justice League
    (IYJL) to stop the deportation of the Mathe family, August 2, 2011

As the members of the Immigrant Youth Justice League (IYJL) chanted and walked in a circle outside the U.S. Immigration and Customs Enforcement (ICE) offices in the summer of 2011, a bystander might have viewed this as another immigrant rally designed to stop a deportation, an ordinary occurrence in a movement that had mobilized for over five years. But a closer examination would reveal that this is an unusual crowd, not consisting of the usual combination of middle-aged activists, some children, and a few youths present in most rallies, but mostly of youths under the age of twenty-five. Moreover, most of these youths were part of a national undocumented youth movement that had primarily been advocating passage of the DREAM Act (a bill that would legalize youth who attend college or do military service for two years), while other sectors of the movement had been advocating comprehensive immigration reform (CIR) that would halt the deportation of thousands of more family members such as the Mathes.

Why was this rally significant? The previous specialization of activism (youth organizations) appears to have been dissolved as youth began to cross over and organize actions that were not exclusively youth-oriented but about the defense of family. Additionally, the rally reflects an important power shift. The IYJL youth did not merely join a rally organized by other sectors in the movement, but organized the rally themselves. Later that month six youths representing Chicago-based IYJL, Nuestra Voz (Melrose Park and adjoining suburbs), and the more recently created Latino Action Youth League (LOYAL, based in the suburb of Addison in DuPage County), engaged in civil disobedience outside a union hall where a Secure Communities hearing was being held. While several IYJL youth had engaged in acts of civil disobedience in other cities, this was the first one in Chicago. Moreover, the action was not about youth rights exclusively, but called for the termination of the Secure Communities program, which affects all immigrants and tears apart immigrant families.[1] The signs and posters used by the participating youth referred specifically to the effect of Secure Communities on immigrant communities and families.

As I argued in chapter 3, the concept of "family" in the analysis of the immigrant movement has gone beyond the organizing of families as families, and includes other sectors and groups that are also engaging with the notion of family as a signifier for a broader, collective, and relational subjectivity that informs the political identity and strategy creation of activists. The evolving ways in which youth organizations like IYJL and Nuestra Voz articulate and express their distinct family issues and concerns signal not only the increasing and more autonomous role of youth within the larger immigrant debate but also the key role the family claim can play in interrupting a neoliberal frame that has shaped the advocacy for the DREAM Act and the representations of DREAM-eligible undocumented youth. In juxtaposition to a neoliberal framework that posits undocumented youth as highly talented potential individual producers, a relational framework relies on drawing connections between the youth and their families and communities as a rationale for their worthiness. Since 2006, family has been the main point of reference for a relational identity in the movement and one that the youth have made, either because their struggle is not only for them but also for their undocumented siblings and, indirectly, for their parents, or because their own deportation would lead to their separation from their families. However, in a quest to demonstrate the "worthiness" of youth, this relational subjectivity was put aside and played a minimal role in the formal advocacy for the DREAM Act carried out by politicians, civic leaders, and youth themselves in 2010 as well as in earlier campaigns.

In this chapter, I explain how this neoliberal model has shaped the advocacy for and politics surrounding the DREAM Act, and how the 2010 advocacy for DREAM as well as the subsequent failed DREAM vote led to the direct juxtaposition of the neoliberal and relational frames within the movement, as well as a postvote repositioning of the undocumented youth on questions of strategy. While these challenges have not undermined the neoliberal framework, they have served to solidify the standing of "family" as a basis for cohesion and have led to the integration of youth and family issues within the movement. It has also, for the youth, further unveiled the promises and limits of the DREAM Act as the main anchor of their activism and led them to pursue new directions.

TWO MODELS: THE NEOLIBERAL AND THE RELATIONAL

The analysis of immigrant family policy requires not only discussing the thousands of families that have been separated and the millions that face the possibility of separation under the current immigration regime but also the trend in immigration debates and policy to move from a prioritization of family reunification or unity as the leading rationale for entry and legalization to one that would prioritize talent, intelligence, professional abilities, and experience in order to help the United States maintain its place in the world. The last few attempts at legalization aimed to curtail family rights by decreasing the categories of relatives and increasing visas for professionals.[2] This trend replaces a relational logic with one based on an ideal of global competitiveness that looks at individuals in terms of their productive ability to succeed in high-end jobs. It is important to note that this logic does not stand alone, but is buttressed by contemporaneous racialized fears of the demographic growth of the Latino population that find expression in the cultural nationalism of some nativists or restrictionists. However, if this cultural nationalism does indeed inform policy, the more utilized and "acceptable" counter to it (crossing party and ideological lines) is the claim that attracting the best brains, and not the family relationships (what immigrants can do for us, and not who they are for their U.S. citizen or resident family members), should increasingly be the basis for the granting of visas. The labor that the majority of immigrant family members produce, concentrated more in the low end of the service realm, is not only undervalued but erased from this juxtaposition. Interestingly, while both a "brain-visa" labor rationale and a nativist one would aim to decrease the number of family-based visas, the first rationale has been key in arguing for the legalization of DREAM-eligible youth.

For many immigrant movement advocates, the past fifteen years of struggle have involved the defense of the relational logic both in maintaining rights to reunification as well as advocating for the rights of undocumented and mixed-status families that are already here.[3] Since the option to legalize family members in the United States without setting off a ten-year bar from returning disappeared in 2000, increasingly the legal as well as movement strategies to remain in the United States have emphasized the importance of family ties over the worthiness of specific individuals for their own sake. Away from the courtroom, in movement politics the worthiness of individuals lies in what they represent for other family members (who may or may not be citizens) and their social roles in raising responsible children, caretaking, and emotionally and economically supporting the family (see more in chapter 2). In both the legal and movement strategies, strategies that stress relational worthiness have taken precedence over strategies that stress individual worthiness apart from the role the individual plays in the family.

This is quite distinct from the main strategies used to advocate the legaliza-tion of youth, which are based on a neoliberal perspective that looks at people's individual capacities and makes claims about their worthiness based on each indi-vidual's productive potential. Neoliberalism emphasizes the competitive, individ-ual entrepreneur, and has a tendency to underscore the protagonistic role of the unfettered individual (de facto minimizing or privatizing the collective or famil-ial upon which that individual's "success" may rely). It is in this context that we must understand the DREAM advocacy that posits undocumented youth as ideal protocitizens who cannot only compete effectively in the marketplace, but upon whom the future competitiveness of the United States may depend (the future inventors, doctors, scientists, and so forth).

This neoliberal perspective subsumes the familiar (and liberal) ideology of meritocracy that would claim that in the United States, an individual's hard work will lead to rewards. This "pull yourself up by your bootstraps" philosophy (Hora-tio Algerism) undergirds the notion that anyone can make it in this country, how-ever fictitious this idea may be. Another metaphor for this myth of unfettered individual success is the not uncommon "immigrant success story." This is used for different political purposes, at times to single out specific individuals, ethnic groups, or historic migrations as successes (rendering the nonsuccess stories more questionable or laying the responsibility for their lack of success on individ-uals alone) or to paint an image of America as a nation of immigrants who have helped to make this country great (erasing the history of nativism and related conflict). As Tamara Nopper has argued, the myth of immigrant success is a myth precisely because it privileges human capital explanations and ignores the state's role in promoting the integration of some immigrants over others:

> Unless we explicitly trace how the state collaborates with ethnic institutions, we end up coming back to what's presumably particular about ethnic groups—as if ethnic contexts flourish outside the purview of the state. In the process, we ignore the ways state institutions assist immigrants in their quest for socioeco-nomic mobility *after arrival*, albeit to differing degrees. . . . We need to consider how the state actively promoted and promotes immigrant economic assimilation after arrival. To ignore this reality is to reproduce myths about human capital that impact how we address economic disparities between ethnic and racial groups, some of whom may not be immigrants.[4]

However, as Wendy Brown (2003) explains, it is the myth of unfettered human capital that neoliberalism aims to reproduce. So while this notion of unfettered human capital is historically inaccurate, this "immigrant success story" fantasy serves an ideological purpose that is congruent with the market rationality of neoliberalism.

Additionally, to the extent that we can conceptualize a neoliberal national-ism, it would be a form of nationalism that gauges American greatness by its economic competitiveness—hence the value of those who are meritorious and rise to the top lies not exclusively in their success for their own sake but in their capacity to make the United States globally competitive.[5] This neoliberal nation-alism both relies on and reinforces the idea that the United States is an individu-alist meritocracy that ensures that the best talents rise to the top to help improve U.S. global competitiveness. This sustained competitiveness, in turn, will ensure the economic growth that will continue to allow the United States to be a land of opportunity and social mobility. If the state needs to intervene in order to pro-duce and sustain this "unfettered competitiveness," intervene it will.

Neoliberal nationalism weds classic ideas about America as a beacon of light, a land of opportunity, and a site of immigrant success, on the one hand, with a strict market rationality designed to boost the engine of global competitiveness, on the other. In this view, migrants' worthiness depends on a combination of their ability to supposedly succeed on their own with no state assistance and on their ability to make and keep America competitive. The relationships between talent and rewards or economic growth and real opportunity are not problematized but simply assumed, despite the existence of social and economic structural inequalities that deeply complicate these relationships. However, to the extent that formal barri-ers are viewed as impeding this unfettered individualism, the state plays a key role in creating policies that are believed to liberate this unfettered subject and create ideal conditions for U.S. competitiveness in the global market. Selective attention can be paid to obvious forms of legal exclusion (and therefore policy targets) that must be addressed because they are viewed as obstacles to Ameri-can global competitiveness. Financial deregulation in the 1990s and 2000s is one example. Another one is the changing of immigration policies that impede the recruitment of the top global talent or the advancement and mobility of the top homegrown talent.

So while the contemporary nativist movement that has opposed the legaliza-tion of undocumented immigrants draws from cultural nationalism and neocon-servative discourse on morality and criminality, neoliberal nationalism claims that an immigration policy that is inclusive of all those who can make the United States economically powerful and keep it competitive is what is best for the United States. This tying together of the hardworking American, the immigrant success story, and global competitiveness is exemplified in President Obama's speech on immigration in 2010:

So this steady stream of hardworking and talented people has made America the engine of the global economy and a beacon of hope around the world. And it's allowed us to adapt and thrive in the face of technological and societal change.

To this day, America reaps incredible economic rewards because we remain a magnet for the best and brightest from across the globe. Folks travel here in the hopes of being a part of a culture of entrepreneurship and ingenuity, and by doing so they strengthen and enrich that culture. Immigration also means we have a younger workforce—and a faster-growing economy—than many of our competitors. And in an increasingly interconnected world, the diversity of our country is a powerful advantage in global competition.[6]

Obama develops this idea further in his 2011 discussion of legalization as a priority for his administration in a speech in El Paso on immigration: "That's how we'll get this done. That's how we can ensure that in the years ahead we are welcoming the talents of all who can contribute to this country and that we're living up to the basic American idea that you can make it here if you try."[7]

But merely willing neoliberal nationalism does not make it so. Just as socialist nationalism required what Che Guevara called a "new man," neoliberal nationalism relies on the creation of neoliberal subjects that are characterized by ideas and behaviors that confirm and reproduce a specific mode of belonging in the United States. According to Brown (2003), neoliberalism involves the following:

> Neoliberalism casts the political and social spheres both as appropriately dominated by market concerns and as themselves organized by market rationality. That is, more than simply facilitating the economy, the state itself must construct and construe itself in market terms, as well as develop policies and promulgate a political culture that figures citizens exhaustively as rational economic actors in every sphere of life. Familiar here are the many privatization and outsourcing schemes for welfare, education, prisons, the police, and the military, but this aspect of neoliberalism also entails a host of policies that figure and produce citizens as individual entrepreneurs and consumers whose moral autonomy is measured by their capacity for "self-care"—their ability to provide for their own needs and service their own ambitions, whether as welfare recipients, medical patients, consumers of pharmaceuticals, university students, or workers in ephemeral occupations.... Neoliberal political rationality produces governance criteria along the same lines, that is, criteria of productivity and profitability, with the consequence that governance talk increasingly becomes market speak, businesspersons replace lawyers as the governing class in liberal democracies, and business norms replace juridical principles.

Three main nodes of neoliberal rationality are used to advocate the worthiness of undocumented youth and specifically of undocumented students: first, the central role of productivity and competitiveness, in which the worth of a human lies primarily in his or her role in market transaction, either as producers or consumers; second, their individuation, that is, the extent to which they can separate out and differentiate themselves from other undocumented youth; and third, their potential for self-care and self-responsibility, that is, the extent to which they can create or make themselves without any state assistance.

The first feature is the positing of DREAM-eligible undocumented youth as outstanding talents who are the potential producers that will help keep America great and competitive, as well as potential consumers who will make the DREAM Act more than pay its own way in the long run. The second involves a rhetorical separation and social distinction from family members as well as other noneligible immigrants who purportedly do not occupy or have the potential to occupy the same location in the marketplace. This both confirms and reproduces this individualization upon which their claim to distinction in the marketplace rests. The third feature, the self-claiming of responsibility, while common to other undocumented migrants (who are denied any state benefits), has specific implications for undocumented youth, as it targets primarily the educational realm and lays the success or failure of their promised rise squarely in their laps.

These rationalities are not always openly articulated, but are the bases for specific ways of imaging and messaging DREAM advocacy. These images of DREAMers as exceptional, as innocent, and as American (discussed in more detail in the next section) are not mere frames or representations but also reflect subjectivities that inform the ideologies and actions of undocumented youth and their supporters. In other words, I am not claiming that the politicians have merely manipulated the youth to say what will "sell" (although some of this does occur, and some of the messaging has been viewed as problematic by activist youth in recent years) or that the youth have a false consciousness that involves the uncritical embracing of neoliberalism. I am attempting, instead, to underscore the ways in which neoliberal rationalities may be shaping and even constituting youth advocacy. That is, neoliberalism has not only become a way of understanding and organizing our social world (in and of itself an important cultural and political critique) but the main filter or optic through which undocumented youth can claim a right to belong in a hostile anti-immigrant context in a world in which, according to Brown, notions of public good, universal equality, and collective rights have been undermined by the market rationality of neoliberalism.

It is important to note that undocumented youth have alternative sources of rationality that informs their claims of worthiness. As Coutin (2000a), I (Pallares 2010), and others have discussed, worthiness is often gauged by morality—that is, a self-presentation of individuals as upstanding protocitizens with no criminal records, a history of community and/or church service, and an idealized family life. Undocumented youth are not exempt from these expectations, as they are expected of all the undocumented who seek exemption from deportation (either through legal or political means) and are usually built into any bill designed to legalize a larger population. Alternative positions from legal or social movement advocates have relied on more collective axes of political subjectivity such as community and family or rationales such as fairness and equality. In the eleven years since the DREAM Act was introduced, while undocumented youth have articulated some of these other positions and some politicians have tried to include them in legislation, they have been excluded or disregarded, while the neoliberal rationality has prevailed.

It is also important to note that there are other ways in which neoliberal rationality can be used to discuss the regulation of migrant labor: the notion of a temporary workers program that would ensure flexible, adaptable labor also obeys a market rationality that sees humans only as capital and not in a more holistic manner. However, this chapter focuses specifically on undocumented youth who are viewed as potential "heads," and not "hands"—that is, as they potentially fit in the higher ranks of the segmented and highly differentiated labor market, and therefore rely on the specific neoliberal rationality outlined above in their claims-making.

In the following three sections of this chapter, I analyze the framing of DREAM advocacy, paying particular attention to how neoliberal rationalities have shaped claims, informed the debate, and modified different versions of the bill; explain how the undocumented youth movement shifted the struggle for DREAM from a legislative advocacy process to one of mass resistance, challenging differences within the movement as well as existing representations of the DREAMers; and discuss how this moment of empowerment and the loss of the DREAM vote in the U.S. Senate has deepened the cracks between neoliberal rationality and undocumented youth advocacy while giving new relevance to a relational strategy in which family plays a central role.

THE DREAM ACT AND THE "WORTHINESS" OF UNDOCUMENTED YOUTH

The DREAM Act was first introduced by Senator Dick Durbin in 2001. It was reintroduced in 2003, 2007, and 2009 and has also been included as a component in different bills for immigration reform. None of these efforts was successful in getting the bill passed, although the closest it came was in 2010, after a positive House vote on December 8 and a subsequent negative Senate vote ten days later in which the bill failed, by five votes, to obtain cloture. While they shared the same general goal of legalizing undocumented youth who have attended college or served in the military for two years, each version of this bill was different, as earlier, more generous provisions were challenged and dropped and new restrictions were created, narrowing the parameters of subsequent bills. By the time the bill introduced in 2009 was voted on in the 2010 Senate, modifications made in order to squelch possible Republican opposition had already narrowed it further than previous bills. This is why many youth who advocated for it in 2010 understood it as far from perfect, but the only option available.[8]

Despite these differences among the versions of the bill, the three main points used to support the DREAM Act have remained consistent: the youth are exceptional; they are innocent; and they are already American.

They Are Exceptional

There are at least a couple of important components to the claim of youth exceptionalism: the idea that they are independent and resilient, capable of achieving on their own without any government help, and the notion that they are the brains, part of the future heads (and not hands), the talent that, if gone to waste, will not only be detrimental to them individually but will be a loss to the country. Since the DREAM Act was first introduced, a number of exceptional students have testified at congressional hearings. Politicians advocating DREAM usually utilize cases of outstanding students, and for years several undocumented students have participated in press conferences and other events as well as testified before different government bodies, highlighting their own stories to advocate DREAM. In most of these cases, the students mention their academic excellence and potential as well as the hardships they have overcome, including things such as traveling to the United States as children alone without parents, lifelong economic hardships, and different examples of exclusion and restriction from educational, work, and travel opportunities available to residents and citizens.

In the 2003 Senate Immigration Committee negotiations, some Republican senators were willing to vote for DREAM to be considered by the full body of the Senate on the basis that it would provide rights for good, hardworking students who were not "to blame" for being undocumented ("Marking Up the Dream"). However, they were disturbed by two things: the possibility of any state taxpayer expenditure on financial aid for these students (the undocumented are regularly perceived as not paying taxes, even if multiple reports show that most of them do), a concern shared with some Democrats; and the possibility that the undocumented would have access to something that citizens would not get, which would then be considered a privilege. So the incorporation of the undocumented, to be acceptable by most, could not be on equal terms as citizens. Since the original bill had allowed DREAM-eligible students to have access to grants and loans, a key amendment introduced and passed in the committee stipulated that the youth would have access to loans but not grants. This amendment enabled Senator Durbin to get the majority he needed in the committee to move it to a vote of the entire Senate. However, the bill was trapped for three months as members of senators' staff had difficulty reaching an agreement on the language of the final bill. By the time the bill was drafted, the political opening for the vote had closed, and the Senate never voted on the bill ("Marking Up the Dream"). Every new version of the bill since has excluded grants. In addition, the bill that went to a vote in 2010 excluded the youth from any health benefits until they were eligible for legal residence, after several years.

Even though the assumption that immigrants somehow made it in this country with no state assistance is a myth, it has powerful consequences when it is used not only to construct a false and romantic notion of the United States as a melting pot of people who succeeded based solely on their human capital (laying the responsibility of those who do not succeed solely on themselves) but also to shape policy that imposes these assumptions on young immigrants. They will have to perform the myth. They will have no recourse but to be enactments of self-reliance, to sink or swim without receiving any benefits eligible to citizens. Hence the "good" immigrant is not only the morally outstanding one of neoconservative discourse (as outlined in the introduction) but also someone who is completely self-reliant, demonstrating that capacity for self-responsibility and self-care that Brown highlights as a key element of neoliberal subjectivity. In neoliberalism, whether as producers or consumers, the onus is on individuals to be self-propelled, to care for their bodies and souls and achieve their own economic viability, exempting the state and private industry from social support (Mascia-Lees 2011).

This is not only a state discourse though, but one in which immigrants more broadly, and not only undocumented youth, have actively participated. Leo Chavez (2008) has argued that immigrants marching in 2006 displayed signs that said "we are not criminals," "we pay taxes," and "we are hard workers," presenting themselves as ideal neoliberal subjects who were responsible for themselves and embodied the kind of workers needed in today's competitive labor market able to survive without government support.

The second aspect of the exceptional claim is that DREAM-eligible students are increasingly valued as potential boosters of U.S. competitiveness. This claim is present in the 2007 House hearings on DREAM and became noticeably more prominent in the 2011 hearings in the Senate. For example, in a 2007 House hearing Jamie P. Merisotis, president of the Institute for Higher Education Policy, testified on behalf of the DREAM Act by describing nonaction as a loss of investment:

> The investment already made in these students' primary and secondary education has no chance of paying off for the nation. If you consider what our national workforce needs are in the specific sense of human capital, it is clear we are looking at an enormous shortage of educated workers in the not-too-distant future. Already we are seeing corporations recruiting overseas in critical workforce

sectors like technology, and by 2020 we will be looking at an employment gap of about 14 million people needed to fill jobs that require a college education, according to Census Bureau projections. Investing in those who are already here is our best hope for remaining competitive on a global scale. Congress can address these deficiencies in educational and economic competitiveness by making comprehensive immigration reform a reality and by passing the DREAM Act.[9]

Diana Furchgott-Roth, a senior fellow and the director of the Center for Employment Policy of the Hudson Institute, stated:

The DREAM Act would allow students who graduate from college to use their degrees in the fields that education prepares them for. This makes the educational investment worth it both for the students, but more importantly for the rest of us. It will help us as well as them because we have more productive citizens who fill needed job openings and who can pay taxes. And the United States needs these young workers, who are presently prevented from working through no fault of their own. Our global competitiveness is enhanced by attracting bright young people such as the ones we have heard from today. We live in an open global economy, and we are continually competing against other countries. We want firms to locate and expand in the United States, creating jobs here rather than going offshore. In order to do that, we want to keep the smartest entrepreneurs and workers here.

Referring to the undocumented youth who had just testified, she added: "As all of you wind down your lengthy negotiations and start the process of making a law on immigration reform, you should keep one question in mind. Why send the Martine Kalaws, the Tam Trans and the Maria Gonzalezes of the world back to their countries to compete against us here?"[10]

In the years between the 2007 House hearing and the 2011 Senate hearing, this position only strengthened and became more clearly represented. For example, while the students that Firchgott-Roth mentions were mostly in the humanities and social sciences, at the 2011 hearing most of the testimonies came from students from the science, technology, engineering, and mathematics (STEM) disciplines. Secretary of Education Arne Duncan referred to DREAM-eligible youth in the following way:

With a college education, they can fill important jobs in fields today facing critical shortages, such as engineers and nurses and teachers. And today it's important for folks to really understand that in these very tough economic times, our country still has about 3 million unfilled jobs open today. By 2018, we'll need to fill 2.6 million job openings in the fields of science, technology, engineering, and mathematics. Let me say that again: 2.6 million openings in the STEM fields alone. The students who will benefit from the DREAM Act will absolutely help to fill those jobs. . . . According to a 2010 study from UCLA, those who would benefit from the DREAM Act could generate between $1.4 trillion and $3.6 trillion in income over their careers. With those extra earnings, they will purchase homes and cars and other goods to drive our economic growth. . . . All told, the Congressional Budget Office, the CBO, estimates that the DREAM Act would generate $1.4 billion more in revenue than it would add in cost over the next decade. And collectively, as we strive to reduce the deficit, we simply can't afford to leave that kind of money, those kinds of resources on the table.[11]

Later in the hearing Duncan replied to a question from Senator Durbin about whether the bill would generate revenues or simply be an expense:

They are going to contribute. And, again, according to CBO's numbers, this will lead to deficit reduction. To not take advantage of this as a country is simply nonsensical to me. This is an investment, not an expense. . . . And we need people who are going to be the creators, the entrepreneurs, the innovators who are going to create the next generation of jobs, the next Google, the next Facebook. I've seen numbers that show that of all the startup companies that are coming out of Silicon Valley, about a fourth are started by immigrants. We need that talent. We need them to drive our country forward. They are—they can be the fuel to our economic engine. So to not give them opportunity, we hurt our country. And that's what I simply can't get past, I can't understand that.[12]

Duncan was then asked a question by Texas senator John Cornyn:

CORNYN: Well, do you know—do you know for a fact that—that the young men and women here in this room who—who seek passage of this authority would, in fact, qualify for those 3 millions of jobs that are unmet right now?

DUNCAN: I don't know all these young people intimately here. So I'm here today. But I will tell you there are many young people in this room and around the country, in your home state and mine, who when we talk about almost 2 million unfilled STEM jobs, and we know that's the future economic engine of our country, could many of the young people in this room and around the country help to fill those jobs and drive the economy? No question in my mind. Absolutely. I've worked with many of them in the Chicago public schools. Extraordinarily talented.[13]

This is not to imply that Duncan and other politicians and educators do not mention issues of fairness or justice. They do mention them briefly, but they spend most of their hearing time relying on economic arguments because these have become the primary justification for the bill.

They Are Innocent

One of the most prevalent claims used by politicians and other civil society supporters, and to some extent by some youth advocates during the first years of lobbying for the bill, is the idea that DREAM-eligible youth are innocent because they were brought here when they were very young and did not knowingly break the law. In their narration of specific individual cases, politicians frequently emphasize the very young age of the individuals when they migrated and their lack of knowledge that they were breaking any law. They also like to emphasize the fact that many youth did not learn until much later in life that they were actually undocumented, further emphasizing their innocence.[14] Here is where politicians are most likely to mention fairness, as they often state that the youth should not pay for the crimes of their parents. For example, Senator Charles Schumer from New York, a supporter of the act, stated in the 2011 hearing:

> First, the DREAM Act comports with basic American traditions of enforcing the rule of law and holding individuals accountable for their actions. Unlike other individuals who might fall under the category of being an illegal immigrant, the DREAM Act only applies to young persons who made no decision to come to America. None of the young people who would benefit from the DREAM Act broke the law when they came here. They had no intent to break the law, and there is no law they can be prosecuted for breaking. This is an undisputed fact. The best thing about America, the thing I'm proudest of, is that we each stand on our two feet. We're not judged by who our parents are, what our parents did for a living, or when, why or how our parents came to this country. We're judged by our own actions. And the deal we all abide by is that, if we work hard and play by the rules, the American Dream is available to each and every one of us. But too many still say we should punish people not for their own actions but for actions of their parents. Well, that's un-American, and it violates the very spirit of our Constitution, which specifically says that "there shall be no corruption of blood," meaning our founding fathers specifically endorsed the concept that children should not be punished for the sins of their parents.[15]

Schumer is not alone, as several politicians who support DREAM make a similar point. As other scholars have discussed, this claim values the youth by basically criminalizing their parents (see Abrego 2011; Gonzales and Chavez 2012). The impediment or obstacle to the youth's success is the criminality of the parents and not the actions of the state that, instead, steps in as a compassionate savior.

There is no questioning of the social construction of illegality or of the criminality of undocumented migration (Ngai 2004), but rather the making of an exception for these youth by absolving them from the choices of their parents, in the process enabling them to unharness all their potential.[16]

This process of separating the youth from the parents requires a performance of their individuation as the sole authors of their destiny. In many of the youth's testimonies in Congress, little if any mention is made of their parents' contribution to their success or even of their relationship to family members. What gets emphasized is the individual story of struggle, innocence, talent, realization of their status, and lack of ability to fulfill their potential. Until quite recently it was rare to see a parent or other family member appear next to the youth. One obvious reason was protection, as family members and especially parents are usually undocumented as well, and many have not publicly come out as such. However, it also serves to protect the claims of the youth as exceptional deserving and unattached individuals.

While youth advocating for DREAM in 2010 were far more likely to mention their parents in spaces outside of congressional testimonies, and, more recently, in coming out events to supportive crowds, they hesitated to mention their families when doing public advocacy to a general public. IYJL activist Reyna Wences stated:

> It depends on who I am talking to. When I talk to people who are more supportive or potential supporters then I feel like I can bring up my family. And I say things like "Yeah, I am a DREAM act–eligible student but this is the reason why, because of my family" and I go into why we came to this country and that the fear that it means to be undocumented, but not just for ourselves but for people we consider our families. And when I speak to people who I do not know if they are supportive or not or that may not be then I don't.[17]

What Wences's comment implicitly refers to is how opponents can make use of these associations with family members. This is the reason why even supporters and advocates who make no explicit reference to the supposed "crimes" of the parents opted to exclude parents from their narratives. This exclusion serves a purpose. Many politicians who supported DREAM, especially the more moderate Democrats and Republicans, did not question the criminalization of the undocumented, but claimed that the youth should be an exception. The opponents, by contrast, often mentioned and reinforced the association with their families to invoke future flow whenever possible. The family ties of the youth were used to signal future chain migration. DREAM opponents claim that DREAM would create an incentive for more parents to migrate and bring their children, as well as lead to the legalization of the parents who are criminalized.

While these concerns have been addressed through the years by modifications of the bill that do not make future migrants eligible, and create large time lags and obstacles for the parents of DREAM-eligible youth to become legalized (it would have taken twenty-one years in the 2010 bill), they were still raised by senators opposed to immigrant rights during the Senate debate in December 2010.

Because most undocumented migration is criminalized, separating the youth from their families in both rhetoric and policy serves a dual purpose: it dissociates them from their parents who are held responsible for their situation, and it differentiates them from the collectivity of families out there who are viewed as constantly expanding, increasing the flow and creating chain migration. It distinguishes them from the foreign bodies that have been so collectively vilified not only as workers but also as bearers of reproductive power. Moreover, these fears are also revealed in opponents' increasing insistence on limiting the pool of DREAM-eligible people by cutting the age limit further. While the initial bill had no age restrictions for DREAM-eligibility, as long as someone migrated before age sixteen and had been in the country for a lengthy period, later versions created age limits, the 2010 bill lowering it to age twenty-nine from thirty-five in the 2009 version. This would in effect mean the ineligibility of thousands of youth who have aged out even if in every other way they have met the requirements.

The innocence argument also serves to victimize the youth as products of the "bad" actions of their parents. As victims, they are viewed as needing protection and being politically helpless, while, ironically, still expected to help themselves in the economic and educational market. So their political agency is minimized, as they were expected only to provide narratives of their life stories, plead their cases, and testify to governmental bodies, performing conventional actions of advocacy that do not in any way challenge or complicate their image as innocent victims. This would change in 2010.

They Are American

One of the most powerful claims that is repeated by both youth and politicians is that undocumented youth are essentially American in every way. This gets reinforced in narratives equally made by youth and their advocates about youth having barely any or no memory of their lives in their land of origin and being lost if sent back, and in claims that this is the only country they know as home. Dominant representations of the Americanism of youth are those that focus on cultural assimilation and military patriotism.

Advocates claim that fluency in English and the cultural practices of youth already make them American in every way. Youth speak of the values they acquired, such as the promise of the American Dream, usually defined as the notion that if you study and work hard, you will make it. Politicians point to the hard work of the students as evidence that they have embraced American values, confirming that they are part of us, not strangers, "the other" that Bonnie Honig (2001) refers to. This de facto Americanism is a key way in which DREAM-eligible students are differentiated from immigrants who came as adults, have difficulty with English or speak with an accent, and are less familiar with American popular culture and values.

Additionally, while undocumented people cannot join the military, politicians and military officials testifying on behalf of DREAM frequently mention the patriotism of immigrants who are permanent residents, and their willingness to put their lives on the line. According to Hector Amaya (2007), there are approximately 42,000 permanent residents who constitute 2 percent of the military and 17.7 percent of those who directly handle weapons. Since 2004, not only is their citizenship expedited when they enlist, but since 2001 permanent residents have been granted posthumous citizenship in case of death during service (Perry 2012).[18] Politicians also mention cases of youth who have been in Reserve Office Training Corps (ROTC) programs and who dream of serving the military in their desire to give something back to the country they so love.

Taken together, these notions of exceptionalism, innocence, and Americanism work to present DREAM-eligible students as ideal actors for boosting U.S. global competitiveness: the youth are presented as exceptional in their talent and self-resilience, innocent individuals separated and even freed from their families and communities, interested in their own advancement but devoid of a more collective consciousness or political agency. They are viewed as Americans who are culturally assimilated, loyal, and patriotic, willing to help increase the productivity and place of the United States in the world. During the 2010 struggle for DREAM, however, this representation would simultaneously become more utilized and come into question by the youth it was designed to protect.

IYJL AND THE 2010 STRUGGLE FOR THE DREAM ACT

In November 2006, after the megamarches had eliminated the possibility of the 2005 Sensen-Brenner bill becoming law, the Democrats won the House and Senate.[19] This political shift as well as the momentum from the megamarches led movement actors to view this as a window of opportunity to get immigration reform passed. President George W. Bush's agenda had involved an immigration reform bill that included a guest worker program; it was supported by several members of the Republican Party who wanted to ensure a flexible and low-cost labor supply. However, both bills in the House and Senate failed to gain approval, and since June 2007 there has not been a successful effort to arrive at a compromise bill. Between 2007 and 2010, however, the immigrant movement continued to pursue a relatively unified strategy for CIR with the understanding that an inclusive bill that guaranteed some form of legalization for most of the eleven million undocumented was the option that would offer relief to most people. In exchange for broad reform, some of the main advocacy organizations realized that they would have to concede on enforcement, as most congressional representatives would not vote for a legalization bill that did not include enforcement measures. The extent of enforcement concessions and the extent and depth of legalization options were issues over which different sectors would struggle, but the general understanding was that CIR was the main goal and would be the focus of strategizing, messaging, and agenda creation. Strategies included advocating CIR, marching, and electoral strategies that would support CIR supporters in Congress and the presidency. Obama's victory in 2008 had created great expectations, as he had campaigned in support of immigration reform and committed to addressing the issue early in his first term. However, by early 2010 it was becoming increasingly clear that CIR would not be introduced in Congress, and movement activists had begun to lose hope.

In the meantime, fall 2009 and all of 2010 were a time of resurgence of youth activism within the movement. While activism for the DREAM Act had existed for practically a decade, in the years after the megamarches it was understood by both tacit and overt agreement that CIR would be prioritized over the DREAM Act. Youth had focused on activism around individual deportation cases, such as the case of Rigo Padilla, a twenty-one-year-old University of Illinois at Chicago student who was facing deportation in December 2009. Padilla's case gained national attention, and during the fall of 2009 youth activists, several immigrant organizations, educators, and religious and community leaders participated in an intense petition and action campaign to stop his deportation. At the very last minute, his deportation was stopped, constituting a success and leading local undocumented youth organizers of the campaign to realize that they could be effective.

Near the end of this campaign, several of these youth, including Padilla, founded the IYJL, an organization of undocumented youth based in Chicago. After Padilla's stay, IYJL pursued a strategy of undocumented youth coming out to each other, in meetings on campus and in community settings. After a couple of these events, they began to develop the idea of coming out as a public action that would have a wide attendance and media coverage. In their view, it was important to increasingly take an open and public stand as undocumented youth, meaning coming out openly and publicly as undocumented, even if it meant facing the risk of possible deportation. They wanted to pursue it as a national strategy as well, as they considered overcoming the fear of showing oneself a necessary first step to assuming political agency in their struggle. Coming out publicly not only would provide a distinct and different face to the undocumented for a broader public but also would encourage other undocumented youth to have hope in a shared future and become involved in the struggle. Since IYJL was at that time a member of United We Dream (UWD), a national umbrella organization organizing for the rights of undocumented youth, it proposed to UWD a "Coming Out of the Shadows" week in which youth organizations in several cities would participate. Despite the reluctance of some members, UWD did finally vote to support this plan. While some local organizers also questioned the safety of this strategy, IYJL was able to gain the support of several grassroots organizations in addition to the Illinois Coalition for Immigrant and Refugee Rights (ICIRR), and, with legal advice, planned the event with seven members who were willing to assume the risk.

On March 10, 2010, seven youth came out of the shadows in front of Federal Plaza, where Senator Dick Durbin's office is located. After marching from Daley Plaza to Federal Plaza, they stood on a stage, and each person stated his or her name, followed by "I am undocumented and unafraid," and explained, in her or his own words, the effect of their legal status on their lives. This was not like the testimonies where students tried to prove how outstanding or deserving they were, but instead they expressed their simple desires to live freely, study, and love without obstacles, interruption, and pain. Their moving stories led many of the hundreds gathered to tears. They discussed how their legal status shaped their lives in the most basic of ways, such as not allowing them to drive, to have a library card, to work. They talked about their love of the United States but also expressed their anger about the hardships endured, creating, for the first time, a public safe space to be critical. Tania Unzueta stated, "I believe that we have only one life and that we are not free. In this country we are not free." They stressed the relational dimensions of their identity, emphasizing not only their dreams but also how staying here meant fulfilling their parents' dreams, making their parents' sacrifice worth it, and how being deported would be intolerable because it would mean being unable to see their parents again. One youth, Nicolas Gonzalez, stated that his mother's death from cancer after working in toxic conditions in a factory made him want to stay so that his mother's sacrifice would be worth something. Another speaker, Ireri Unzueta, expressed that her main reason for wanting to stay in the United States was her love for her family:

> But the thought of not being able to come back and laugh with my parents and sister keeps me here. The thought of not being able to kiss them or see them when I miss them or they miss me or when we miss each other, that keeps me here, so I stay. . . . I am done holding myself back. I am done feeling like I have to choose between my family and the life that I want. I choose both. I choose to fight for both. Choose to fight with me. My name is Ireri, I am undocumented and not afraid.

Still hoping for CIR with the DREAM Act included, the youth encouraged Senator Durbin to work toward passage of the DREAM Act and CIR. This

Coming Out of the Shadows action, the first held in the nation, was repeated by undocumented youth organizations in several other states that month, consolidating the youth movement and increasingly gaining more strength and support from the broader immigrant movement.

With this new momentum and increasing power and visibility in the movement, the youth took two important steps in the months that followed. First, with CIR increasingly less viable, they began to organize toward the possibility of pursuing the DREAM Act as a stand-alone bill. In addition to viability issues, they maintained that a DREAM-alone bill would not include additional enforcement, something any CIR bill would contain, and that witnessing the criminalization of their communities, they were not willing to support any bill that increased enforcement and criminalization. IYJL, with some internal division, voted overwhelmingly to support a DREAM-only strategy, joining other DREAM advocacy organizations as well as youth organizations that had made a similar choice. Second, they opted for a strategy of civil disobedience, a dramatic change designed to call attention to the issue in a novel way. Both of these decisions challenged immigration politics as usual and created tensions within the movement and with politicians.

Several immigrant rights organizations had mixed views on this strategy, and therefore while supportive, were not necessarily prone to putting their force behind this position. The arguments opposed to the DREAM-only strategy can be grouped into two main positions: the practical argument and the ethical argument. The practical argument was visibly articulated by Illinois congressman Luis Gutierrez and supported by most of the Congressional Hispanic Caucus as well as the Reform Immigration for America (RIFA) campaign and many important national immigrant rights organizations.[20] The basic claim was that in a somewhat hostile political environment, the passing of the DREAM Act would mean no possibility of a majority vote for CIR, as very timidly supportive legislators would claim they had already done enough to support immigration. The strategy was to continue to hold off on DREAM, since CIR would include DREAM anyway, or to advocate for that included DREAM. This argument stood, however, on the possibility of there being any opportunity to pass CIR in the upcoming years, something that seemed increasingly questionable by the spring of 2010. It also was anchored on a comprehensive policy model as opposed to an incremental or gradual model. This was also an object of criticism from some advocates, who believed that comprehensive change in the United States was extraordinarily difficult to push through successfully (the recent health care bill being the most obvious reminder). In response to this argument, IYJL and other youth nationwide argued that CIR was no longer feasible, and that DREAM was a policy that stood a chance. To anchor DREAM to CIR would mean, at that political moment, the death of both.

The ethical argument was anchored on the importance of the family, as a stand-in for a broader, more inclusive constituency for immigration reform. The claim was that the DREAM Act excluded or did not do anything for families that were facing separation, primarily due to the deportation of undocumented parents who were not DREAM-eligible. This was a powerful critique at a moment when family had become consolidated as one of the two main frames that anchored the movement (work being second but less powerful at this point). Between 2006 and 2010, the threat and dire consequences of family separation had become the main humanitarian issue that had bonded different sectors of the immigrant movement, the rationale that religious, civil rights, labor, and community leaders could agree upon as they witnessed cases of family separation.[21] The position sustained by those who opposed DREAM-only was that it was not inclusive enough and would do nothing to stop the deportations. In March 2010, Reverend Walter "Slim" Coleman, of La Familia Latina Unida (LFLU), wrote a widely circulated letter warning of the dangers of straying from CIR to adopt DREAM as a stand-alone bill:

> There is another danger: The bait dangled before the movement by the Democratic Leadership, the bait of isolated legislation for the Dream Act and/or for [agricultural] jobs is being swallowed by people desperate to deliver some relief to some of the people. We must be clear that the price for limited legalization is the same as the price for legalization *Para Todos* [for all]. To pay that price and leave 10 million people without any protection, to unleash the dogs of I.C.E. on them, is unacceptable—ask the ten million and the twenty-five million that are part of their social, economic, and religious lives![22]

Youth leaders responded by stating that they were part of families too, and that if the DREAM Act stopped them from being deported, it would already be preventing family separations. They also stated that if legalized, they would continue the struggle to legalize their parents, something that was not a given with the DREAM Act. Many of them had frank conversations with their parents, and all of the activists I interviewed stated they had their family's unequivocal support. In a personal interview with the author, Reyna Wences commented on her mother's response:

> My mom said, "You do whatever it takes. Don't worry about us, worry about yourself. If the DREAM Act is going to help, go for it." She said, "I understand things are really rough right now." . . . She was not going to blame me. She was not going to feel forgotten. . . . She said, "I understand, I know, think about yourself, think about your brother." . . . I knew that if my family was ok with it . . . we had our conversations with our parents so we were like, "We have our community,

screw what you are saying. We are the undocumented ones here, these are the undocumented families . . . this is what we are doing . . . we have the ok."[23]

The parents of the youth also played a critical role in defending the DREAM-only position. A few of them made public statements in support of the DREAM Act. Arguing that they had migrated primarily to provide their children with a better life, they emphasized that the legalization of their children was not only their children's dream but their own dream as well. Activist Rosi Carrasco, Tania and Ireri Unzueta's mother, stated in an interview: "I am fine with them legalizing and not us because we came for them, and we are only suffering because they suffer. And number two, because I am absolutely confident that [after their legalization] they will keep struggling for us, and we will fight together for the parents."[24]

In an effort to pressure for the DREAM Act, the youth embarked upon a civil disobedience campaign that picked up on an immigrant rights civil disobedience campaign initiated in the spring by supportive citizens and permanent residents, but was fundamentally different in that undocumented youth participated directly, risking possible deportation after their arrest. This made the stakes much higher, as the previous civil disobedience actions had purposefully only included U.S. citizens. A few of the citizen participants in the earlier civil disobedience actions whom I interviewed expressed this as a key opportunity to be able to do something meaningful on behalf of those who could not risk arrest. While the undocumented youth I interviewed expressed gratitude, the acts of civil disobedience also prompted discussions among them about the importance of assuming their own agency by risking arrest and deportation. Even before Arizona Bill HB1070 was passed, IYJL leaders had been focusing on Arizona as a possible site for their first act of civil disobedience.[25] On May 20, 2010, IYJL participated in an action in which four youth refused to leave Senator John McCain's Arizona office and were arrested. IYJL member Tania Unzueta played a key role in organizing the event as well as participating, but was not one of the four arrested. Three of the arrested had deportation proceedings initiated against them, although they were eventually not deported. This action was followed by successive acts of civil disobedience in summer and fall 2010.

Undocumented youth activists, however, had different positions on the civil disobedience strategy. While a loose coalition of activists had initiated the civil disobedience actions and continued to stage such actions in different locations (what would become the National Immigrant Youth Alliance [NIYA]), some of the UWD organizers were not supportive of these actions, concerned that they would taint the positive image of DREAM-eligible youth they had worked so hard to build. Several of these actions were planned by UWD member organizations without telling UWD leadership first, as they believed UWD would disagree. In a Washington, D.C., civil disobedience action in August 2010, UWD had planned for a mass "graduation" in which DREAM-eligible youth would don their caps and gowns, give speeches, and perform a graduation ceremony. The youth who were planning to engage in civil disobedience during that event kept their plans from UWD, adding the surprise element to the act. When it became apparent that they were going to get themselves arrested, Congressman Gutierrez, who was engaging in civil disobedience himself, argued with a couple of the IYJL youth, trying to convince them to desist, without success. Additionally, UWD leaders proposed other less controversial strategies instead, such as blood donation and food drives organized by DREAM-eligible students in their respective states, to show the broader public that they were solid, contributing "citizens." Wences, frustrated about UWD's insistence that the youth do this instead of pressing civil disobedience or advocacy work in the face of an imminent vote in upcoming weeks, stated:

> United We Dream was taking a completely different route from what we were going for, from what the sit-ins had started. The different route was more pacifist, more compliant, highlighting "look at these poor DREAM Act students, they are willing to donate blood." . . . It was November, we were so close, we still needed a lot of phone banking and here you have one of the most recognized and powerful networks for undocumented youth saying "we need to show them how American we are by donating blood and doing food drives for Thanksgiving." It was ridiculous. I didn't want to plan that.[26]

Finally, as the DREAM Act vote approached and Democrats modified the bill to make it more palatable to Republicans, rumors spread that while the youth had not been officially consulted, a member of UWD had actually been the only youth who had held conversations with the legislators on the changes. The accommodationist strategy of UWD seemed to get them closer to Congress but drove a wedge between UWD and IYJL and other organizations in the undocumented youth movement that wanted to pursue more contestatory strategies.

The civil disobedience strategy had several audiences. One was clearly the at-large public and congressional representatives, to raise awareness and support for DREAM, but there was also the audience of the broader immigrant movement and Latino politicians supportive of CIR who were initially reluctant to support DREAM only. The civil disobedience risk did bear fruit. The increased visibility, sympathy, and power gained by the youth and their ability to use more dramatic pressure tactics led to new conversations and a change of position of many policy leaders and politicians, as well as the Congressional Hispanic Caucus, which, by mid-fall 2010, was fully supporting DREAM. Chicago's IYJL was a key player in this shift, as the two politicians most important for the introduction of and support for DREAM were from Illinois. Senator Dick Durbin, the original sponsor since 2000, had stated to the youth and several other organizations that summer that he would reintroduce it but only if the broader movement supported it, as it needed all the support possible to be viable. Congressman Luis Gutierrez had stuck to his CIR strategy and remained reluctant. While the broader movement wanted to openly pressure Durbin and challenge Gutierrez, IYJL played a key intermediary and diplomatic role, attempting to persuade both politicians to move forward. When it appeared that Gutierrez was not budging, IYJL planned for an act of civil disobedience in his office. Activists in other immigrant organizations strongly advised against it, concerned that the movement would look divided and that Gutierrez, the strongest advocate for immigration reform in the House, would be viewed as a movement target. As plans moved ahead, last-minute conversations with his staff finally led to a meeting with a group of the youth. In this meeting, Gutierrez committed to considering the issue. Shortly after, Gutierrez openly started supporting DREAM, albeit framing it as a step to a larger reform that would keep families in mind. The Congressional Hispanic Caucus and RIFA soon followed in their support. By late fall the debate had been resolved and an impasse avoided, and a broader movement was in full force for DREAM, collecting as many sponsorships as possible, including the support of Janet Napolitano, then head of the Department of Homeland Security (DHS). However, this was not enough to garner the necessary votes, and despite passing the House, the DREAM Act failed to achieve cloture in the Senate by five votes.

POST–DREAM ACT VOTE: BEING UNAPOLOGETIC

The loss of DREAM was a very intense moment for those active in the undocumented youth movement. Battling feelings of loss, pain, anger, and depression, IYJL members, after a short break, reflected on the process that preceded the December vote. They believed that while they had increasingly gained collective power, media attention, and popular support, their voices were not included in the actual bill design and legislative strategy. One consequence of this was that the content of the bill, altered to squelch Republican opposition (such as an extraordinary delay in petitioning parents and new age limits), was something they did not fully support but had struggled for nonetheless. Moreover, to do so, they had both reinforced the individualistic and neoliberal discourse in ways with which they were no longer comfortable. Shortly after the vote, IYJL member Alaa Mukahhal wrote for the organization's blog:

> We pushed aside the fact that we would still be marginalized as conditional residents: we will pay more taxes but we get no financial aid, no federal loans, no healthcare, and we will have to pay fees so high, it was as if the country was

mocking us. It didn't make sense; how were we supposed to finish school if we qualified for nothing? Not to mention, if you were above the age cap, you would not qualify. And one felony meant we're out of the country. Then there are finger-prints, biometrics, and selective service. Big Brother was going to be breathing down our neck. . . . Is that what we were fighting for?! Was this an act to pave the way for future intellects, doctors, architects, lawyers, teachers, nurses, and lead-ers; or was it an act paving the way for future laborers? . . . No person with any self-respect would even consider what we were trying to pass, no person would accept all the limitations, the conditions, and ridiculous restrictions. But we were so desperate, so hungry, and it was so close that we thought, this must be it! This is victory, we can taste it! Just one more push. We've made so many concessions because the reasoning went, the more we yielded the more likely it will pass. But now we know better. We now know we cannot compromise justice. We cannot compromise liberty. We cannot compromise human dignity.[27]

Their reflections touched on all three of the themes discussed above: the youth are exceptional, they are innocent, and they are American. Increasingly, the youth I interviewed had started to distance themselves from the image of the ideal or idealized youth and from the label of DREAMer. Some of them expressed that the actions in which youth dress in caps and gowns were not about showing that they were different from other immigrants, but were about putting a positive face on undocumented immigrants, different from the typi-cal stereotypes of immigrants, to show that undocumented immigrants could be just like, or as good as, any student. While they viewed the idealized view of the youth as something that has been necessary to construct in their quest for DREAM, many stated in interviews that they do not consider themselves more worthy than other undocumented youth, even if they are honor students. One of the strategies they have adopted to question this exceptionalism is to work on cases of youth facing deportation who are not ideal honor students.

They have also questioned the idea that they are solely responsible for their success and have pointed out the critical role of the political and economic struc-tures that impede their progress, with particular attention to the role of the state. This is what Wences refers to when she rejects the DREAMer label:

Using the word DREAMER for undocumented people is not addressing and not letting other people see. . . . I mean it sounds nice, and it's not addressing the fact that it is systematic. Undocumented says that you have a person that is undocumented and using DREAMER is not letting people see that we are undocumented. . . . And so it feels very hypocritical, and I think that is one of the reasons why in the past few months when we were able to get out of the whole DREAM Act that happened last year we have been more unapologetic about what we say and how we say things and the way that we frame it, which is not about blaming our parents. It's about blaming the system or trying to find solutions for that. And the fact that we're not DREAMERS. That word has gotten me so worked up lately because I don't want to be a DREAMER. I don't want the legislation to define who I am. . . . And it doesn't allow for us to open up the debate about our families because if we keep using DREAMER then people are just going to have this notion of what a DREAMER looks like. And when we start growing up, when the DREAMERS start growing up and nothing happens, then are we going to be the DREAMERS with a family, then are we going to be the ex-DREAMERS? It's just ridiculous. Hiding behind the label DREAMER is just not wanting to acknowledge it, not wanting to take on the fact that you are undocumented, it's like denying it. . . . DREAMER is something that the politicians put on us. When I hear DREAMER I know here comes the argument, "it wasn't their fault, it was their parents' fault." "They were brought here really young" and no, that just doesn't go with me. I don't want to be a DREAMER, I want action.[28]

Wences's comment addresses the problems some youth activists have with the special status assigned to DREAM-eligible youth, symbolized by the common practice of calling them DREAMers. She views it as a false differentiation from other undocumented individuals as well as a personalization and privatization of their condition that absolves the state by laying the responsibility for their status on their parents.

IYJL, LOYAL, Nuestra Voz, and other youth organizations have challenged and attempted to reverse the criminalization of their parents. On March 10, 2011, youth from IYJL and Nuestra Voz carried out the second Coming Out of the Shadows Day, in which they now stated after their name: I am undocumented, unafraid, and unapologetic, a term coined by Alaa Mukahhal, who used the word in a December 2010 action prior to the vote to convey that she would not apologize for being who she is or for her parents. When she came out in the March 2011 action, Mukahhal stated: "I will no longer live like this. I will not allow anyone to be ashamed. There is no shame in tears, no shame in dignity, no shame in pride. I with my head raised high can finally look at my parents in the eyes and tell them I don't blame you. I don't blame you."[29] Arianna Salgado, of Nuestra Voz, explained to me in an interview in June 2011 what she meant by "unapologetic": "I am unapologetic because I am not sorry that my parents brought me here, and for being here and wanting to stay in this country." Youth interviewed explained that the most difficult thing for them to tolerate during the advocacy was to hear politicians blame their parents, and that now, with no possibility of DREAM and nothing to lose, they had no reason to tolerate it. When I asked how she feels when she hears people blame her parents, Wences responded:

I heard it from Durbin, from the media. From the president, from people on the phone, strangers. I hear it everywhere . . . before last year I really didn't pay attention to it. I knew it was wrong but at the same time last year was so tied to the legislative calendar and all these people that we had no control over. It was something that we had to kind of like ignore. But after all that happened I had to laugh, like here we go again. There are so many jokes online, among undocumented people, organizers, that whenever we hear it and we tweet it and we go "ha ha ha there we go again." But it is also very bitter. . . . We are using undocumented humor basically to deal with the fact that this hurts. And personally I get angry [pause] but at the same time I almost tell myself to not get angry. Because at this point I don't know what we could do to get them to change their mind. Because even though we are trying to be more outspoken about "don't blame our parents, don't blame our parents," we hear it everywhere. We are the only ones that are saying that. I do worry about whether the social movement is going to fizzle or actually be a sustainable thing because I see the divisions that have been created by policy makers and the government in terms of defining what a good immigrant looks like and what is not an immigrant, who should be allowed to stay here and who should leave.[30]

Salgado explained that one of the strategies youth have pursued is a plan to be careful about their language in any future coming out events. They did this, for example, by saying, "I came with my parents," not "My parents brought me here." Moreover, they have embraced the relational in a more public way. Since 2011 they have been staging actions and coming out events in which they emphasize their relationship with their parents, have parents or siblings together speak at events, and are developing their own relationship to the familial frame that had prevailed in the broader movement.

Finally, while the youth still embrace America and Americanism, they tap into different ways of thinking and performing Americanism than the assimilationist modes discussed above. While they agree that their socialization and cultural formation make them as American as somebody born in the United States, they do not see it as something they need to prove or to earn, but that already is. In the IYJL blog, IYJL member David Ramirez stated in 2011 in a reflection on his exchange with a reporter: "I'm not even sure I feel comfortable with 'immigrant.' I was a year and half old when we moved to the United States. How is my brother, who was born in the United States only a bit after we had moved here, any more or less of an immigrant? I've spent all of the life I can remember in this spot, and I was raised by TV just as much as you were. How are you any more or less of an immigrant than me?"[31]

Additionally, they have tapped into different American values that are not about their productive potential but about their political potential by using a political agency that Linda Bosniak (2008) explains is often denied to the undocumented. The youth have openly articulated the ways in which their coming out strategy was inspired by Harvey Milk and the gay liberation movement, and the civil disobedience strategy from the civil rights movement. While they do not see themselves as disconnected from the global struggles of immigrants, they use American social movements as their reference point. Other civil rights leaders have recognized their relationship to these traditions, and have granted them awards for their courage in the struggle. Another example of this recognition was evidenced in the warm reception that African American prisoners gave them when they were jailed in Montgomery, Alabama, after an act of civil disobedience in November 2011. The prisoners offered them the best beds and specifically mentioned that their actions had reminded them of the actions held in Alabama during the civil rights movement.[32] They have made it clear that they are also unapologetic about assuming this agency, which they see not only as a strategic need but as their right. As Mukahhal explained in the second Coming Out of the Shadows Day on March 10, 2011: "We believe enough in the democratic system and we have faith enough in the democratic system to know that we can change it. And we know that we are Americans and that the only way to give back is to be allowed a path. I want the chance to be allowed a path."

The assumption of this agency, as Americans following in the footsteps of American activists, strays significantly from the image of passive victims waiting to be rescued from the crimes of their parents and to be deemed worthy of legalization. It is very different from the far more disciplined acts or scripted narratives that tapped into all the points the politicians were most likely to use to prove that the youth were worthy. Moreover, it reverses the order of responsibility by not putting the onus on the youth to prove that they are worthy, but on the state to prove that they are not. Since the acts of civil disobedience started, no youth who has participated in these actions has been deported, even when deportation proceedings have been initiated. This led one youth to comment shortly after the Georgia arrests in spring 2011 that it seemed like the best protection against being deported was to engage in civil disobedience.

REVISITING THE FAMILY—A NEW RELATIONAL STRATEGY

While questioning their own exceptionalism as DREAMers, rejecting the criminalization of their parents, and representing their struggle as intimately linked to American social movement ideologies, the most important post-DREAM-vote shift I want to underscore is the way in which IYJL and other organizations have sought to link their own plight to others who lack their purported privilege, by challenging the use of exceptionalism in the exclusion and potential deportability of all the undocumented.[33] Ways in which they do this include participation in campaigns to stop the deportation of immigrants (youth and nonyouth) who are not always ideal poster children, underscoring the humane reasons why they belong in the United States as much as anybody else. (They first did this in collaboration with DREAM Activist and NIYA; since early 2012, however, several youth organizations grouped under the umbrella organization Undocumented Illinois have created Organized Communities against Deportations [OCAD], a network that focuses on Illinois cases working with immigrants of all ages.) Another tactic is the use of acts of civil disobedience against deportations, most recently participating in the "Not One More Campaign," organizing three local civil disobedience actions in 2013 and one in 2014 as well as engaging in civil disobedience against Secure Communities (2012), state laws in Arizona (2010) and Alabama (2012), and educational policies in Georgia (2011).

A third important way in which the Chicago undocumented youth have changed direction is the introduction of a new family emphasis into their activism that is both novel for the youth and distinct from other ways in which family has been articulated in the movement and in policy. First, beyond not blaming their parents, they have begun to include them in their actions as a way of both highlighting their parents' presence in their lives and support in their struggle (moving away from the individuation that hides the parent) but also as equally struggling for and deserving of recognition of their own belonging. In this way the parent acts as both a medium that links the youth to the larger, older undocumented community and as a representative of that community, which outside of the youth and a few workers' movements or individual cases, such as Elvira Arellano's, has not organized as undocumented.

Perhaps IYJL member David Ramirez presaged this new turn of events in spring 2011 in an interview held after his release from custody for engaging in civil disobedience in Georgia: "If it had been my father he would have been deported." With the new Deferred Action for Childhood Arrivals (DACA) discretion announced in summer 2012 (creating a process by which undocumented youth can apply to get a work permit and avoid deportation for at least a two-year period), the youth responded in two ways. First, they continued to engage in civil disobedience even while realizing the new rules may have clipped their wings by minimizing their claim of risking deportability. Second, they upped the stakes by inviting their parents, who do not share their purported state protection, to engage in civil disobedience. The question then becomes whether the state will deport these parents or extend its protection of youth who engage in public civil disobedience to their parents.

The first test occurred in Montgomery, Alabama, on November 15, 2011, where two parents of undocumented youth were arrested for engaging in civil disobedience along with the youth. One of the arrested parents was Martin Unzueta, the undocumented father of IYJL founders Tania and Ireri Unzueta. Both parents were released two days later after paying fines and dealt with charges in February 2012, and ICE made no attempt to contact them or initiate deportation proceedings. Finally, on March 13, 2012, Martin Unzueta and Estela Cuellar, another undocumented parent of a Chicago-area youth who is a member of Nuestra Voz, came out as undocumented and unafraid in the first Coming Out of the Shadows action in DuPage County. They were the first parents in the nation to do so. In a personal interview with Martin Unzueta in March 2012 , he expressed hope that other undocumented parents who attended the DuPage event might become more active as they continue to organize more intensely in the movement, not autonomously but as needed by the youth and specifically mobilized as parents of the youth. Here is another way in which the relational subject, discussed in other chapters of this book, is deployed by new actors in novel ways, challenging the myth of the individualized deserving student who is somehow separated from his or her origins and relationships as a condition for his or her inclusion.

The creation of DACA only justified even further the focus on parents and other older immigrants. Since the government's deferred action memo was announced in June 2012, IYJL's strategy has been to continue to pressure to stop the deportations of many people still detained and/or in deportation proceedings; to inform and educate on the memo and its limits while continuing to pressure for a DREAM Act or its equivalent; and to emphasize the parents and families as a next point of pressure once youth gain deferred status. The launching of the "undocubus" in August 2012, carrying over thirty undocumented immigrants from Arizona to the final destination of North Carolina for the Democratic National Convention (four of them IYJL members), also reflects this change. The undocubus carried older immigrants, emphasizing their status as workers, as well as youth and parents, some of them members of the same family. As it was actively organizing the undocubus, someone in IYJL wrote on its Facebook status report July 2012:

> In 2010 we started calling ourselves "undocumented, unafraid" as part of a campaign to pass the DREAM Act, but really as demand to be acknowledged as people with stories, hopes, dreams, and fears. Then we added "unapologetic" speaking from our experience about not blaming our parents, or apologizing for being here without documents. Little by little, we have seen others outside of undocumented youth begin to think about coming out of the shadows too, regardless of the risk. Now it is our parents, our aunts and uncles, our older relatives and friends who are also talking about being "undocumented & unafraid," or "*Sin papeles y sin miedo.*" We are no longer the only ones who have to be unapologetic about our parents; they are speaking for themselves.

It is important to note that the notion of family that the youth have articulated is different from the heteronormative, citizen-centered model displayed in the family campaigns discussed in chapter 3. This different way of
articulating the family was exemplified on March 10, 2012, in the third Coming
Out of the Shadows action at Daley Plaza. For the first time a young couple
explicitly stated that they were coming out as an undocumented and unafraid
family. Fanny Lopez, an undocumented member of the suburban youth organization LOYAL who had been arrested for engaging in civil disobedience
protesting Secure Communities in August 2011, spoke of her fears and wor-
ries as the undocumented wife of a U.S. citizen veteran. While she qualified
as a DREAMer, having been in the United States since childhood and being
an exceptional student, Lopez was opting to emphasize her relationship as an
undocumented spouse over her DREAM eligibility, revealing the actual intersectionality of these seemingly different identities and the inseparability of
DREAM-eligible youth from their relationships with others. Her coming out
placed undocumented youth squarely in this social imaginary of the family
from which they had been excluded in the past.

Her husband, David Martinez, spoke of his anguish while serving in Afghani-
stan of not knowing if his wife could be deported at any moment. In one poignant moment he stated: "Our love is no different than any undocumented
love." This statement represents a marked difference from the strategy adopted
by LFLU, whose main claim, as members of mixed-status families, was the right
of the undocumented who have citizen relatives to be recognized. Their imaginary excludes the entirely undocumented family. Martinez instead not only
points to his second-class citizenship given that his wife's status is extended to
him (implied when he compares them to "any undocumented love") but also
includes the entirely undocumented couple in the social imaginary of those who
suffer and deserve justice. While one could state that the two claims are simply different sides of the same coin or equation, it is an important political difference to stress one or the other. While LFLU focused on the special status of
the mixed-status family to make a particular claim of exceptionalism, the Martinez family focused on undocumented love to claim that being of mixed status
is actually no different than being an entirely undocumented couple. Instead of
separating the undocumented from the mixed-status families, it places them in
the same condition, challenging the exclusions and exceptional categorizations
that have characterized the movement and the state's relationship to immigrants'
claims. Relationships in one context are not better or more deserving than in
the other case. They are both worthy and deserving, and they have both been
devalued and threatened by current immigration policy. And relationships and
the relational, it appears, will only continue to be emphasized in fundamental
ways as the undocumented youth movement generates new ways of belonging

that simultaneously use but also challenge prevalent notions of their individual exceptionalism.

Additionally, the use of the term "love," and not "wife" or "husband," marks the inclusion of nonheterosexual relationships. In stating "we are just like any other undocumented love," Martinez was not only equating the undocumented and citizen, but the homosexual or bisexual or pansexual with the heterosexual. As Martinez made this statement, I could see Wences (who helped him finalize the statement) and Salgado, an undocumented queer couple who were very visibly moved, listening almost in tears as they stood together. Even if it was not the moment for the coming out of an undocumented GLBT couple or family, it was clear that Wences and Salgado felt included. Three months later, Wences came out as undocumented and queer in a stakeholder's meeting at an ICIRR event, although that type of coming out has yet to occur at a mass public rally. As the "undocuqueer" identity becomes increasingly politicized and becomes a larger presence in the movement, a more open inclusion of undocuqueer voices within the larger movement (they are already very present and among the main leaders of IYJL as well as the national youth movement) and the related expansion and transformation of the "worthy" family seem imminent.

INHABITING THE EXCEPTION *AND* THE MARGINS

Two statements made by different IYJL members capture the two main themes of this chapter. Questioned by a reporter about why the youth were being given special consideration, David Ramirez stated: "We're not cute. We're organized. Our activism is the reason you believe the administration is easy on us."[34] Additionally, during the first Coming Out of the Shadows Day, Hugo Esparza stated upon coming out: "We've already won, for living under the radar has not kept us from living in love. But remember love is the starting line from which we will smash the radar and claim what is ours."[35]

Taken together, the statements convey IYJL activists' awareness of their agency and voice in creating their own movement, building their own power, emphasizing their humanity in its relational dimensions, and articulating their own reasons for their activism. They continue the path that Elvira Arellano initiated, claiming the right of the undocumented to speak and act. However, as this chapter has explained, they, along with all the other undocumented youth, have faced the challenge of creating a space of articulation in a policy context characterized by a form of neoliberal nationalism that reduces them to their economic and professional potential in a competitive global environment.

In his immigration speech in El Paso in May 2011, President Obama attempted to appeal to a Latino audience to display his support for immigration reform while not delivering any concrete policy proposal. After only a brief mention of

America not being a country that should break up families (with no accompanying narrative of a specific person or family), Obama ended his speech with a reflection on José the astronaut, a young man born in the United States (whose siblings were not, although their legal status is unclear), worked in the fields, studied hard, and eventually fulfilled his dream of going to space. José sounds like a perfect example of the neoliberal subject who, through education and hard work, achieves the American Dream.

How was the story of a U.S.-born citizen used in a presidential speech to describe an immigrant story? How is this slippage possible? Why does the undocumented person, once again, get erased? Clearly, this focus on this native-born individual "dreamer" provides a broader racial appeal to all Latinos, and to those who aspire to the opportunities provided by education. It is hard not to cheer for José. But the problem with being a "dreamer" is that while it has broad appeal, it can also be easily and problematically appropriated. Everyone who "makes it" was a dreamer once. José's success does nothing for the life chances of thousands of undocumented youth who cannot afford to study and, until DACA, were not allowed to work. And in this appropriation the undocumented youth and their stories, and, most important, their need for legal reform, are erased.

This replacement exemplifies a serious disconnect between the actual structural conditions faced by DREAM-eligible youth and the continued ascent of the neoliberal frame utilized by state actors in the name of immigrants. The speech reproduces the myth of a self-reliant individual replete with human capital while completely ignoring the legal restrictions that allow citizens like José to fulfill their dreams while undocumented students cannot. How, then, can movement actors fit the stories of the undocumented within the framework of the American Dream, the historical immigrant origin of most Americans, and the increased need for competitive individuals in the global marketplace, and yet not disappear as individuals lacking status, members of families and communities, and actors claiming a political voice? How can they hold the state accountable for the legal obstacles that render them permanent dreamers, never astronauts? As Leisy Abrego (2011) has explained, while other immigrants' success is shaped by the support of co-ethnics as well as the context of reception, for the undocumented it is primarily the context of reception—and within that, legal status—that most affects their opportunities. No amount of self-care, responsibility, brilliance, and talent can do the job of the state. The youth cannot legalize themselves.

Within the movement the youth faced challenges as well. The DREAM/CIR debate was a contested and uncomfortable moment in the immigrant movement, as it pitted two policies in a way that posited the youth against families. But the reality, as usual, was far more complicated. There is clearly an overlap of these constituencies as the youth come from undocumented or mixed-status families. Moreover, the difference between a family with younger children and a family with DREAM-eligible children is only a matter of years. In fact, since the DREAM bill had first been introduced, many formerly younger children have become DREAM-eligible, and many of the previously DREAM-eligible have aged out. Ultimately, as this chapter has explained, the continued empowerment and leadership of the youth ultimately won over the support of the rest of the movement for the DREAM vote and has led to continued collaboration since. The youth are no longer at the margins, but a central part of the movement, and are seen by many as its most imaginative agents. Post–December 2010 we can no longer speak of a DREAM/CIR division, but of a broader position that embraces both the youth and the family and is interlinking or supporting both issues and constituencies in novel ways.

But this is not a narrative of simple transition from a neoliberal to a relational strategy. On the one hand, the CIR/DREAM debates and failure of DREAM in the Senate have led to significant reflection among the movement and the youth. New bridges have been built between the previously conflicting perspectives, as exemplified in Luis Gutierrez's most recent Familias Unidas (FU) campaign (2011), which emphasized both family and youth. As described above, the youth have been actively challenging and attempting to reverse the criminalization of their parents and emphasizing the relational through their activism for the families. However, this neoliberal framework, so present in the hearings, speeches, and congressional debates, remains prevalent among political elites. To get any future version of the DREAM bill passed, the youth will still very much depend on this individualistic frame to obtain legalization. And in performing this exceptional innocent American, they render others unexceptional, ordinary, criminals, and non-American.

Where, then, in this scenario lies the potential for this agency that undocumented youth have sought with such perseverance? Social theorists and social movement scholars have taken great care to point out the structural constraints of social activism, following in part Marx's claim that people make history but not of their own choosing. Perhaps it lies precisely in the youth's contemporaneous distinction and nondistinction from other undocumented immigrants, in the blurring of lines that they create between the performance of exceptionality and the reminder that undocumented immigrants are no different than citizens, in their straddling the neoliberal and the relational while questioning, challenging, and reinventing what is actually meant by exceptional, innocent, and American.

In her discussion of undocumented migration, Mae Ngai (2004) makes the historical argument that illegality is constructed, as different lines have been drawn between legal and illegal migration in different periods. An analogous claim could be made about the lines being drawn among undocumented immigrants in the contemporary politics of legalization. With the possibility of a more general amnesty discarded, differentiation among the undocumented has become a basis for claims for legalization, as different groups try to demonstrate their worthiness. Groups advocating for the rights of citizen children have argued that parents of citizen children should be spared from deportation (a claim that, by definition, excluded undocumented immigrants who do not have citizen children). Likewise, bills proposing exceptions for agricultural workers have also been introduced. DREAM-eligible youth are another such category.

Hence, while Nicholas De Genova (2005) is right to claim that deportability is what renders undocumented immigrants vulnerable, differentiation may mean that they are not equally deportable and therefore not equally vulnerable. More vulnerable groups include undocumented families with no citizen children; LGBT immigrants who are not married or whose marriage is not recognized by the federal government for immigration purposes; immigrants not eligible for the military; immigrants not able to study; and adults who have aged out of DREAM. The Obama administration's order in August 2011 to allow prosecutorial discretion in deciding the cases of over 300,000 immigrants currently in deportation proceedings reinforces this differentiation logic, creating a number of specific categories describing cases that are most likely to receive prosecutorial discretion (although as individuals, not collective claims). Youth who have been in the United States since early childhood are high on the list.

However, despite this under-enforced administrative order, none of these claims of differentiation has achieved the legalization sought. And despite DACA, which can be reversed by a future administration, undocumented youth, like the rest of the undocumented, continue to be in a state of liminality. In addition to claiming the relational, through family and community, they continue to point out the systemic conditions that block them from improving their life chances. No amount of study, talent, entrepreneurship, or self-care makes up for the consequences of their lack of legal status, a condition that renders them in the most important of ways no different than any other undocumented immigrant. When Arianna Salgado stands next to Illinois governor Pat Quinn and Chicago mayor Rahm Emanuel giving a moving speech prior to the signing of the Illinois DREAM Act (in August 2011) one week, and then two weeks later joins five other youth to get arrested and risk deportation in a civil disobedience action against Secure Communities, she is performing her exceptionality and marginality, claiming both her difference and similarity. Most important, she is claiming that her difference does not erase the most basic similarity she shares with all the undocumented or her relationship to that community. She is engaging in the tactic of crossing, blurring the line between the "deserving" youth and the "undeserving" older undocumented immigrant.

And here is where the relational serves to interrupt the neoliberal, and also why, in claiming that the youth do not care about families, Walter "Slim" Coleman gets it wrong. It is not that the youth did not care about families before, but that they were by necessity linking to a discourse that required individuation and differentiation to advocate for a bill that, however imperfect, appeared achievable at the time. Their multiple rallies, antideportation campaigns, and civil disobedience actions for families from 2011 to the present are not about proving that they now care for families, but to challenge this notion of differentiation based on individuation and to claim identification with other undocumented people who are and are not like them. Moreover, through the growing activism of parents as "undocuparents," the "coming out" of a family that, while mixed-status, called itself undocumented, and the inclusion of parents in the undocubus that highlighted the plight of undocumented families, the youth are framing and performing the family in ways that challenge the divisions and categorizations of the state as well as other sectors of the immigrant movement. These changes, moreover, are not unique to IYJL, as integration of family and youth issues and the creation of multiple organizations of undocumented parents in the last two years have occurred throughout the nation.[36] Once again, "family" became a site for the construction of political identities and strategies in which immigrant rights activists, and increasingly more undocumented activists, coalesce, negotiate, and articulate new directions and goals.

CONCLUSION
Moving Beyond the Boundaries

I am an act of kneading, of uniting and joining that not only has produced
both a creature of darkness and a creature of light, but also a creature that
questions the definitions of light and darkness and gives them new meanings.
—Gloria Anzaldúa, *Borderlands/La Frontera*

In July 2013, a meme circulated on Facebook with a picture of Congressman Luis Gutierrez stating that reform cannot only include youth—that is,
it also has to include the parents. This was a direct reference to a debate in the
House over whether nonyouth should have a path to legalization and an existing
Senate bill that would include over half of the undocumented, but would render others ineligible. In the context of policy discussions in which all amend-
ments were seeking to enforce more and curtail legalization as well as provide
no significant expansion to family visas, Gutierrez's statement sounded progressive, inclusive, and urgent, a reminder to many in the movement that the struggle
was for a much larger universe than what Congress was willing to consider—a
push for more inclusion. Several activists, many of them youth, posted this
meme that particular week, as it became clear that the battle in the House for
any broadly inclusive legalization would be extraordinarily difficult, and that,
at most, there would be some version of the DREAM Act that included only
youth. "Parents" in this instance represented the push for the inclusion of a larger
undocumented community.

Barely three years earlier, this meme with its exact wording would have been
viewed as oppositional by youth activists who were seeking passage of the
DREAM Act in a context in which a bill for comprehensive immigration reform
(CIR), while promised by President Obama, was clearly not politically viable.
The youth had been waiting since before Obama's election, as the larger, more
established immigrant rights organizations organized in Reform Immigration

for America (RIFA) requested that the youth trust the process and advocate CIR and not the DREAM Act only. When undocumented youth initiated civil disobedience actions in the summer of 2010, part of their goal was to pressure the more mainstream organizations and Democratic politicians like Gutierrez to drop the pipe dream of CIR and support the more realistic effort of passing the DREAM Act. They also rejected some opposing activists' claim that being for DREAM only was antifamily, promising they would never give up on the struggle for their parents, who supported their quest for DREAM only. For these youth activists, statements very similar to this meme represented the nonrecognition of their plight, their exclusion from decision making, the negation of their vision and role in the movement, and the pursuit of a path that was so hopeless that it would not benefit anybody. "Family" in this instance represented paralysis.

The difference in political meaning of this meme in three short years reminds us of the different political positions, goals, and strategies that can be embodied in discussions of the family in different moments. This book has attempted to show how family has not remained a fixed and static construct in an eight-year period of intense immigrant activism. As different groups pursue different visions and strategies, they emphasize different dimensions of what the family is and what family unity could look like. As a polyvalent concept, family can be both conventional and emancipatory—sometimes in the same act or event, sometimes in different ones. I have also argued that while the defense of the family or family unity is something that has been key in the framing of and performance of worthiness, in some ways reinforcing conventional, heteronormative ideals of supercitizenship, it has also challenged racism, exclusion from the polity, and criminalization that have justified undocumented immigrants' deportability, subordination, and ultimate exclusion through deportation. In its different manifestations, family acts as a powerful basis for the creation of alternative meanings and political mobilization. It represents that which is considered the most essential, basic, and solid unit of association but also, despite apparent rigidity, is flexible and porous enough to signify different things to different groups and to be represented in different ways. Simultaneously rigid and nonrigid, a source of great passion and emotional attachment as well as a site of flexible messaging, in this movement "family" has become a frame and shared identifier, glue, and source of contention all in one.

This dynamic political dimension of family is best explained or understood through the analysis of the relationship between meaning and political action. The questions that have guided my research are: What does family mean in a specific context and why? What is the work that this specific articulation of family does in a specific political action or moment? What do these different ways of relying on the family teach us about immigrant rights activism? Addressing these questions led me to conclude that family operates in three related but distinct ways, as a political subject, as a relational strategy, and as a source of collective identification.

The notion of family as a political subject interrupts narratives and representations of undocumented immigrants as individual deviants transgressing sovereignty and links them in powerful ways to citizens and residents who love them, who live with them, and whose future well-being depends on them. The family as a political subject also challenges elite and state discourses that claim to uphold family values, underscoring the race, class, and status dimensions of exclusion, pointing out that not all families are valued or viewed equally.

Family as a relational strategy has been deployed by different actors with different purposes. For organized mixed-status families, the mobilization of families and children has highlighted the "worthiness" of the families, conforming to dominant understandings of what a good family is, underscoring their idealized values, and highlighting the pain caused by separation. For youth individuated by a neoliberal DREAM Act politics, family as a relational strategy was a way of opposing mainstream understandings of their worthiness as exceptional, innocent American individuals and stressing their relationship to family members who had been vilified in the same discourse. As chapter 4 explained, by bringing parents in actions and acts of civil disobedience, they challenge this exceptionalism, showing that they did not spring out of nowhere but came from somebody who may be undocumented but also has worth. Today, there are several workers' and parents' organizations organizing nonyouth in protests, antideportation campaigns, and civil disobedience actions, claiming their own value, challenging the dominant notions that only youth, or only parents of citizens, are worthy of citizenship. Two notable examples are Dreamer's Moms, a national organization associated with United We Dream (UWD), and Mothers Against Raids, Enforcement, and Deportation (MADRE), based in New Orleans.

Additionally, family has become a site of collective identification, bonding communities that do not easily have a shared collective identity, creating bridges, making allies out of politicians, other social movements, media, and religious leaders. This ability to be a bond, however, can also become a source of dispute when activists align themselves on different sides of a specific debate. The concern with "caring about the families" is alluded to by activists defending specific positions, not only CIR versus DREAM in 2010 (described above) but also by those upholding two very different positions on the 2013 Senate bill that failed to move to the House: those who opposed the Senate bill claimed that it would be more punitive toward families who do not qualify, while those who defended it argued that it would stop the separation of the families that will qualify. Both sides defended their positions as being in the best interest of families. Aligning oneself with the family cause, identifying with family unity as a central claim enables cross-racial, cross-ethnic, cross-status coalitions and alliances.

Performing family in testimonials, narratives, marches, and protests has become a main part of most political actions, whether organized by civic, religious, or youth organizations. As my analysis in chapter 3 of the national Familias Unidas (FU) campaign explained, it is a form of collective identification based on a shared value and not necessarily a shared condition. It is not necessary to be undocumented or have a close undocumented relative to share the value. Family is performed during an action, and most of those present connect and relate.

The three dimensions of family are connected in a number of ways. While relational strategies perform and reaffirm the family as a political subject, they are also conveying a broader collective identity that goes beyond those in undocumented or mixed-status families. Moreover, relational strategies must be understood in their complex dimension; in some cases they are referring specifically to family members, in others they are using family to represent the broader undocumented community beyond youth. For example, one Immigrant Youth Justice League (IYJL) activist and I were discussing a national gathering in which the youth attending the event all voted on moving forward with CIR and not only DREAM because CIR would include their families. As I discussed this conference with this IYJL activist, he mentioned a young woman attending the conference who was interviewed on television and how frustrated he was when he listened to her. "She was talking about not wanting her aunt to be deported. But she meant her real aunt," he said. "And for you it is not just about her real aunt, no?" I hinted. "Of course not," he said. As I discussed in chapter 4, for many of the youth activists relying on relational strategies, family is a way of bridging with the broader undocumented community, of challenging the categorizations of deserving and undeserving by blurring the previous boundaries, and of representing a more inclusive community of all the undocumented.

In addition to explaining these different dimensions of family, this book has also aimed to explain how family politics sheds light on undocumented immigrant subjectivity, specifically on the politics of motion discussed in the introduction, and its tactics involve tangling, intersecting, and crossing. Their personhood always in question, their right to citizenship denied, immigrant activists tangle by underscoring their relationship with citizen relatives, as Elvira Arellano and other members of La Familia Latina Unida (LFLU) did, or with noncitizen relatives, as youth often do when they discuss their attachment to their families. They also intersect, highlighting other dimensions of their lives that show that they are not only their status, articulating their dignity and worth as full human beings, whether it is families claiming they are hardworking and religious, or youth emphasizing their community work and their studies.

As conventional as some of these advocacy efforts stressing worthiness may seem to outsiders, we should keep in mind that they can still disrupt and elicit staunch rejection. This is evident in the recent visit of a group of families linked to the Resurrection Project (a coalition of Latino Catholic churches in Chicago) who had attempted a meeting with Congressman Dan Lipinski and been denied several times. Lipinski is a Democrat who has consistently voted against immigrant rights and appeared to not be supportive of immigration reform in the House. Finding it impossible to meet with him personally, this group of families attended one of his Willow Springs town hall meetings on September 5, 2013. As soon as they began to talk, they were booed and heckled by others who were attending the meeting. Alma Silva, of the Resurrection Project and Saint Pius V Church, described the event:

> This is the second time we went to a public meeting. The last time was a bit worse since somebody said they should deport us all and kill those who refused to leave. But last night we took children, since one of them is suffering because of the separation from his dad. We wanted Lipinski to listen to him. When we asked Lipinski to listen to this child, the people there started to heckle him and scream that they did not care to listen to him, and that we should get out, that nobody cares about reform, that we should all be deported, that we are all criminals, that we might not like to be called illegals but that is what we are. . . . One man told Lipinski to throw us out and to give Americans our jobs because we came to rob them.[1]

Silva shared this description of the event with me after I asked her what had happened that night, since she had posted a memorable Facebook post on the incident the morning after the meeting. She posted:

> It's incredible how still today there are people who continue to call us illegals with such hatred . . . without recognizing that we are UNDOCUMENTED and it is not our fault. We entered this country without permission because there is no other option but we are not thieves, assassins, nor criminals. We are people who came seeking a better future for our children just like they, or their parents or grandparents did at some moment. We follow the law as much as we can. . . . Yesterday we were at the receiving end of so many humiliations and insults that they made us cry. But well, what is left for us to do is to pray for those people and ask God not to forget us and our families. For him nothing is impossible.

In this post Silva expresses many of the claims made by families relying on a worthiness appeal, the need to support children as an explanation for migration, the law-abiding behavior and noncriminality. She also draws parallels between their experiences and the migration history of those in the room and their ancestors. And finally she appeals to a higher power. Nothing of how they presented themselves was controversial or radical, yet their very presence, their desire to speak and articulate their position, generated rejection, confrontation, and mockery from others, creating a traumatic experience.

Silva's and her group's recent experience is a reminder that despite some significant advances in the movement, the rejection of the undocumented immigrant's political voice and agency, described in chapter 2's discussion of Elvira Arellano, remains a persistent problem. It also reminds us that even when they appear to be engaging in the least threatening and most conventional of worthiness politics, in certain restricted contexts they are also (like Arellano and IYJL) "crossing," and thus perceived as challenging and subverting dominant modes of power by stepping outside of "their place," in the process creating a new space for themselves where none existed. Their presence and narrative in an immigrant protest at a public plaza in Chicago would be quite common and accepted. The very same actions (or attempt to engage in these actions) in an oppositional space make them transgressors.

Hence, both despite of and because of this rejection and exclusion, undocumented immigrants will continue to cross, whether it is Elvira Arellano seeking sanctuary, Alma Silva and other immigrants crashing Lipinski's town hall meeting, or the multiple examples of crossing of youth described in chapter 4—from Arianna Salgado's performing the role of "civil advocate" and then engaging in civil disobedience two weeks later, to the "exceptional" youth getting arrested with their parents challenging the categorizations that define "worthiness," to Fanny Lopez and David Martinez coming out as an undocumented family and stating that their love is "no different than any other undocumented love."

A more recent example of crossing outside the scope of this book is the act of the DREAM 9 youth, three of whom crossed the border from the United States to Mexico in order to attempt to cross into the United States again (one of the youth was Lulú Martinez, a former IYJL member). In this crossing, the DREAM 9 were detained for two weeks, shedding light on their case in order to expose the situation of all the undocumented who were crossing the border. But they were also challenging the state's categorizations, since most of them qualified as the DREAM-eligible youth the state had claimed it would not deport. If the state had said it would not deport DREAM-eligible youth, then would it deport them when they were caught returning to the border? Could it possibly deport them and uphold its own rhetoric? The state's decision to release the DREAM 9 and consider their asylum claim attests to the power of "crossing" in turning the state's own categories of worthiness on their head, in the process challenging them.

More poignantly, in March 2014 Elvira Arellano crossed back into the United States with a third group of immigrant returnees organized by the National Immigrant Youth Alliance (NIYA) (Dream 9 in July 2013, then Dream 30 in September [mostly youth], and finally, in March 2014, the Bring them Home 150, also supported by the National Day Laborer Organizing Network [NDLON] and IYJL and consisting of several families). In her work supporting both Central American immigrants crossing through Mexico and deportees and their families who had lived extensively in the United States prior to deportation, she had supported an LFLU family from Michoacán who crossed with the Dream 30. She was supporting other LFLU families planning to cross in March when she decided to cross with one of the groups, joined by her fifteen-year-old son, Saul, and her five-month-old son, Emiliano, who is not a U.S. citizen. She was detained for two days and was released after her petition for a humanitarian permit was accepted. Awaiting her court date in September (when she will go before an immigration judge who will decide whether she will be deported or remain), she flew to Chicago, where she awaits her trial living in the same apartment above the church she stayed in while she was in sanctuary.

In distinction from her sanctuary year, she is free to move and attends protests, rallies, and speeches, where she advocates for the right of deportees to return legally to their families, claiming that members of families deported from the United States are at higher risk for violence and kidnapping by drug cartels (who believe they have access to funds from citizen relatives in the United States) and that U.S. citizen children living in Mexico and Central America are especially at risk of kidnapping. For her own case, she claims she has received death threats due to her activism in Mexico, and she fears for her safety and that of her children. In her first speech in Chicago, she recognized the initiative of NIYA in planning for these public returns and claimed that she is not the voice of the immigrants, but one of many, and wants others to claim their voices and engage in the struggle for their families. This public return has become a new strategy in the movement that highlights not only the profound long-term effects of deportation on families but also their increasing politicization, as parents were willing to risk their long-term detention and the detention of their children (most of them detained separately), possible placement of their children in foster care, and another deportation for the slightest opportunity to be granted legal entry into the United States via asylum or a humanitarian visa. In her speech, Arellano emphasized the noncriminality of her act, explaining that she and the other families did not enter surreptitiously but through an entry point, where they were met by immigration officials. Defining herself as a transnational activist who works in both countries, she asserted that her activism and that of others does not end at deportation: "The fight does not stop when a mother is separated from her son. The fight stops when we don't want to be part of it. As long as the immigration politics of President Obama do not change, we'll continue to see this kind of activism in favor of families so they can return home."[2]

Through tangling, intersecting, and crossing as they embody and perform the family, undocumented immigrant activists are both relying on existing forms of worthiness and creating new ones. In doing this, they are engaging in a politics of motion that enables the creation of a new space where there was not one, in their ever-present quest for voice and agency. They are also interrupting the categories of the state, blurring the lines between the mixed-status and the undocumented family, the DREAMer and the non-DREAMer, the deserving and the undeserving immigrant. Through this process they have questioned and challenged the ways in which they are viewed and categorized by mainstream society and the state, and also critiqued the dividing lines that include some immigrants and exclude others. Living in the borderland of status, they are challenging these categorizations from what Gloria Anzaldúa called a third space, as they seek to create a new world in which their agency is recognized and their personhood is not denied.

This political work and consciousness-raising of the past seven years, this ever-moving but also ever-expanding notion of who are deserving families, helps to explain the differences among immigrant groups as they debated the possibility of a now-failed Senate CIR bill in 2013. It would be a mistake to think that the division is merely one between "practical" activists who will take what they can get (even if millions of families do not qualify) and idealists who want perfect reform with no enforcement. Those who have continued to advocate reform, despite its intensified enforcement and exclusion, do so with the ambiguity and pain of knowing that some families would be sacrificed. Those who did not openly support the bill also did so with feelings of ambiguity, acknowledging that the bill would indeed benefit many, but still felt unable to fully support it. The questions of which and how many families would qualify and the understandable reluctance to subject immigrant communities to revamped standards of worthiness are in direct tension with the urgent need to stop deportations and the suffering they cause. Additionally, the intensified enforcement provisions that would apply to families who do not qualify are "collateral damage" that many are unwilling to accept.

This discomfort with the CIR strategy led to the Not One More Campaign in 2013. Spearheaded by NDLON and supported by a number of organizations nationwide, the campaign has engaged in numerous national and local actions to shed light on the two million deportations by the Obama administration (a record obtained in April 2014) and demand that the president issue an expedited order granting a deferred action that would include most of the undocumented. While this may seem to some like a temporary solution that does not achieve long-term legalization, its advocates underscore its possibilities in halting a reign of fear, family separation, and social death. Its focus on reprieve and disconnection from intensified enforcement represents a different possibility than the legalization for enforcement trade-off present in every CIR bill crafted since 2007. For some of its advocates, while imperfect and temporary, this policy alternative would buy some time, allowing the movement to work toward an alternative political environment that would be more supportive of a more socially just solution than current versions of CIR.

While the movement has persevered in creative ways, there are no easy options. The greatest challenge for undocumented immigrant activists is the creation of a new world, a new politics in which their personhood takes precedence over their "merit" in a context in which merit appears to be the only yardstick that matters. Most activists, by contrast, yearn for a country that is far more inclusive, that stops criminalizing and punishing immigrants and starts recognizing their personhood, and that provides undocumented people with a place in the struggle but also a place to rest.

NOTES

INTRODUCTION

1. In some cases ideological and strategic differences have led to organizers taking different routes.

2. "Nation as house," argues Santa Ana, has been a metaphor used since the 1800s, making "immigration as dangerous waters" a metaphor that is therefore interwoven in a complex of other metaphors such as "nation as house" that help to make it commonsensical, resonate with a broader public, and a dominant view.

3. The memo to ICE field officers states that in the case of nursing mothers, absent a national security threat, mothers should be released; or if necessary, the nursing child should be housed with a mother in detention. See Immigration and Customs Enforcement, "Memo for All Field Office Directors and All Special Agents in Charge from Julie Meyers, Assistant Director of ICE, Regarding Prosecutorial and Custody Discretion, November 7, 2007," http://www.ice.gov/doclib/foia/prosecutorial-discretion/custody-pd.pdf.

CHAPTER 1: FROM REUNIFICATION TO SEPARATION

1. The Immigration and Naturalization Act of 1952 (McCarran-Walter Act), U.S. Department of State, http//www.state.gov/r/pa/ho/time/cwr/87719.htm.

2. After the Supreme Court found section 3 of the Defense of Marriage Act (DOMA) unconstitutional in July 2013, U.S. embassies and consulates started adjudicating visa applications that are based on a same-sex marriage. Same-sex spouses of U.S. citizens and LPRs, along with their minor children, are now eligible for the same immigration benefits as opposite-sex spouses. http://travel.state.gov/visa/immigrants/types/types_1306.html; http://travel.state.gov/visa/frvi/frvi_6036.html. However, implementation is complicated by the fact that the marriage must be recognized in one of the two jurisdictions where couples reside; and the investigation process for the spouse residing in another country may result in an involuntary "outing" that may have detrimental personal consequences for the applicant. http://colorlines.com/archives/2013/09/lgbt_immigrants_could_face_hard_road_in_applying_for_marriage-based_visas.html. Also, in October 2012 DHS issued written guidance to its field officers indicating that long-term same-sex partners should be considered as family members and therefore as a positive factor in exercising discretion. http://immigrationequality.org/issues/couples-and-families/prosecutorial-discretion/. This memo "defines same-sex relationships which qualify as family relationships for purposes of prosecutorial discretion as those in which the individuals: 1) are each other's sole domestic partner and intend to remain so indefinitely; 2) are not in a marital or other domestic relationship with anyone else; and 3) typically maintain a common residence and share financial obligations and assets. . . . The October 2012 memorandum also makes clear that a legal marriage is not necessary for the relationship to be considered." http://www.livesaymyers.com/prosecutorial-discretion-same-sex-couples/.

3. "Family Migration: Repairing Our Broken Immigration System," Immigration Policy Center, January 15, 2010, http://www.immigrationpolicy.org/just-facts/family-immigration -repairing-our-broken-immigration-system.

4. Patricia Hatch, "US Immigration Policy: Family Reunification," League of Women Voters, LVUWS Immigration Study: Background Papers, http://lwvlacrosse.org/files/immigrationstudy _familyreunification_hatch.pdf.

5. Ibid.

6. "Family Unification, Employer Sanctions and Anti-Discrimination Under IRCA," Hearing before the Subcommittee on Immigration, Refugees, and International Law of the Committee on the Judiciary, House of Representatives, 100th Congress, 2nd Session on Family Unification, Employer Sanctions, and Anti-Discrimination under IRCA, August 23, 1988, Serial N. 83, http://www.loc.gov/law/find/hearings/pdf/00005124906.pdf.

7. While PRWORA also had an effect on families in cutting access to federal aid, I do not focus on it because it has less of a direct bearing on undocumented migration and deportation patterns.

8. For more on the three-year and ten-year bars, see "So Close and Yet So Far: How the Three- and Ten-Year Bars Keep Families Apart," Immigration Policy Center (2011), http://www .immigrationpolicy.org/justfacts/so-close-and-yet-so-far-how-three-and-ten-yearbars-keep -families-apart.

9. In *Moran v. Ashcroft*, Circuit Judge Betty Fletcher stated that in a previous case, *Gonzalez-Gonzalez v. Ashcroft*, "the cancellation of removal statute must read 'to cross-reference [the relevant concepts] in [other] statutes, rather than statutes as a whole.'"

10. U.S. Department of Homeland Security Report, January 12, 2009.

11. The discrepancy between the 73 percent and the 82 percent figures is explained by the fact that many mixed-status families have both undocumented and citizen or LPR children. "Removals Involving Alien Parents of United States Citizen Children."

12. "Forced Apart: Families Separated and Immigrants Harmed by United States Deportation Policy," Human Rights Watch 2007, http://www.hrw.org/reports/2007/us0707/.

13. Ibid.

14. Jin Lee Kyung, "U.S. Deportations Double over 10 Years," Medill Reports Chicago, http:// news.medill.northwestern.edu/chicago/news.aspx?id=157904.

15. "Immigration Enforcement Actions," Department of Homeland Security, 2011 (published in September 2012), http://www.dhs.gov/sites/default/files/publications/immigration-statistics/ enforcement_ar_2011.pdf.

16. While the Obama administration announced a prosecutorial discretion that asked ICE officials to thoughtfully review cases involving parents, this program has not fulfilled its directive. According to a recent study by Syracuse University, only 1.9 percent of pending deportation cases have been closed because of this program. See TRAC Immigration, "ICE Prosecutorial Discretion Program: Latest Details as of June 28, 2012" (Syracuse, N.Y.: Syracuse University, 2012), edu/immigration/reports/287.

17. Ramah McKay, "Family Reunification," Migration Policy Institute's Migration Information, http://wwww.migrationinformation.org/feature/print.cfm?ID=122.

18. The Universal Declaration of Human Rights states that "family is the fundamental and natural unit of society and is entitled to protection by society and the state" (UDHR, Adopted December 10, 1948), G.A. Res. 217A(III), U.N. Doc.A/810 at 78 (1948), art. 16 (3). The Convention on the Rights of the Child (CRC), which the United States signed but did not ratify, requires that "States parties shall ensure that a child shall not be separated from his or her parents against their will, except when . . . such separation is necessary for the best interest of the child." Convention on the Rights of the Child (CRC), adopted November 20, 1989, G.A. Res

44/25, annex 44 U.N. GAOR Supp (No. 49) at 167, U.N. Doc A/44/49/(1989), signed by the United States on February 16, 1995, http//www.ochcr.org/English/countries/ratification/11 .htm. For more discussion of the right to family, see Honohan 2009.

CHAPTER 2: A TALE OF SANCTUARY

1. Conavigua was founded in September 1988. See the link for a description: http://conavigua .tripod.com/cuales.html. Comadres was founded in December 1977: http://www.comadres .org/main_english.html.

2. Elvira Arellano, press conference transcript, recorded on August 17, 2007.

3. For more on the 1980s sanctuary movement, see Bau 1985; Golden and McConnell 1986; Tomsho 1987. For more on the role of Chicago, see Crittenden 1988; Lorentsen 1991.

4. Elvira Arellano, press conference, August 15, 2006. Author's translation.

5. "Deportation Lawsuit Takes New Turn," *Chicago Tribune*, September 8, 2006, http://articles .chicagotribune.com/2006-09–08/news/0609080339_1_elvira-arellano-deportation-citizen -children. See also the interview with Arellano's attorney, Chris Bergin, December 2006.

6. In distinction from the sanctuary movement of the 1980s, which was more effective at providing sanctuary for immigrants, the new sanctuary movement has focused on addressing the raids, detentions, conditions in detention centers, and fairness in legal procedures, as well as calling for a national moratorium in coalition with many other immigrant advocacy groups.

7. While Montgomery, Alabama, had a 1900 municipal ordinance that allowed bus drivers to segregate riders by race, it also stated that no passengers would be required to stand up or give up their seats if no more seats were available. However, bus drivers' standard practice was to order blacks to give up their seats when the bus was full in order to allow whites to sit down. Rosa Parks was seated in the "colored" section and refused to give up her seat to a white person once the bus was full. Technically, she did not break the Alabama law, although she did break with custom. For this she was arrested and charged with violating Chapter 6, Section 11, of the segregation law of the Montgomery city code, despite the fact that she technically had not taken up a whites-only seat, but had been in the "colored" section. For more on this, see Hawken 2007, 79.

8. The only exception to this occurred in the years following the *Silva v. Levi* case, which was filed in the district court in Chicago in the 1970s to recapture unused visa numbers. If a family had a citizen baby, they could file under the lawsuit. The case allowed undocumented immigrants who had a child born before 1977 to self-petition to obtain an unused visa number. Once parents were certified and their turn came up, they could travel to a city on the Mexican side of the border (Tijuana or Juarez usually) and get a visa and return as residents. However, by the early 1980s the deal was scuttled, as the remaining visas were assigned to Cubans arriving in the Mariel boatlift in 1980 and 1981, and many of the Silva cases were placed in deportation proceedings. *Silva v. Levi*, No. 76-C4268 (N.D. Ill. March 10, March 22; amended April 1, 1977), final judgment order entered as *Silva v. Bell*, No. 76-C4268 (N.D. Ill. October 10, 1978); communication with Diego Bonesatti, February 4, 2010.

9. When Zorn consulted with an immigrant rights activists about the term, he learned that many considered it dehumanizing. Other complaints include that nativists have used the term to describe children of legal immigrants or even citizens. For more details on Zorn and the anchor baby controversy, see Eric Zorn, "Sinking 'Anchor Babies,'" *Change of Subject* (blog), August 18, 2006, http://blogs.chicagotribune.com/news_columnists_ezorn/2006/08/sinking _anchor_.html. The term continues to be a subject of debate since the Zorn incident. In 2007,

Mexican American columnist Ruben Navarrete wrote about recently being called an anchor baby, although he and his parents were born in the United States.

10. Eric Zorn, "Immigrants' Rallying Point: Right to Dream," *Change of Subject* (blog), May 2, 2006.

11. As discussed in this book's introduction, our survey of the May 1, 2006, march in Chicago revealed that 73 percent of our respondents were citizens.

12. "Sanctuary for Now: One Illegal Immigrant Battles in the Public Eye," *Milwaukee Journal Sentinel*, February 9, 2007.

13. "Demonstrators Demand Amnesty for Illegal Immigrants," *People's Daily Online*, http://english.people.comcn/200609/04/eng20060904_299243.html.

14. I say this because if Arellano had a partner, this person's participation in these actions would have probably led to an alternative scenario in which Saul would have acted next to his father and therefore not necessarily be viewed as being manipulated—as happens with many other dual-parent families facing this situation—or his father would have acted and spoken instead of him.

15. This was witnessed by the author, who attended the migrant parliament of 2007 in Mexico City.

16. While "you are wearing the pants" conveys having courage, or having what it takes, it is also a gendered expression, since the proper wearing of pants is associated with masculinity.

17. "Updates from Chicago," *Mothers Against Illegal Aliens*, http://www.mothersagainstillegalaliens.org.

18. "Declaracion de Flor Crisóstomo," declaration during hunger strike outside of Representative Rahm Emanuel's office, November 2007, unpublished document. Author's translation.

19. "Lo que Hillary and Barack no dijeron: Declaracion sobre el gran Debate Democratico desde el Santuario por Flor Crisóstomo, Familia Latina Unida e Iglesia Adalberto," unpublished press release, February 1, 2008.

CHAPTER 3: REGARDING FAMILY: FROM LOCAL TO NATIONAL ACTIVISM

1. This and other names of LFLU members in this chapter are pseudonyms, with the exception of Elvira Arellano.

2. The Personal Responsibility and Work Opportunity Reconciliation Act (PRWORA) of 1996 added work requirements for recipients and stricter conditions for food stamps and welfare eligibility. It also reduced the already limited welfare assistance for documented immigrants. The Defense of Marriage Act of 1996 (DOMA) defines marriage as the legal union of a man and a woman. This means that until DOMA was struck down in 2013, for all federal purposes same-sex marriage was not recognized by the federal government, regardless of whether it was recognized by a state. In a 5–4 decision on June 26, 2013, the U.S. Supreme Court ruled Section 3 of DOMA to be unconstitutional, declaring it "a deprivation of the liberty of the person protected by the Fifth Amendment." Since the ruling, some same-sex couples have been able to legalize the status of the noncitizen spouse.

3. In terms of the citizen children rights angle, no court has ever agreed that citizen children have a constitutional right to remain with their parents, as federal immigration law tends to trump state-level family law. Nor has any court agreed that deporting a parent is a de facto deportation of the child, as this child is purportedly free to stay in the country or to return at a later stage. Courts have repeatedly established that undocumented immigrants cannot use the citizenship of their own child to prevent their deportation. While immigration law has historically favored family reunification, it is based on the parent's right to use his or her status as a means to legalize the child, and not vice versa. Children's rights are derivative of their parents'

rights, and to complicate things further, they are not recognized as having legal agency in their own right, but as being under tutelage of their parents. For a more extensive discussion of the legal angle, see Thronsonn 2008 and see also chapter 2.

4. Some of these strategies include a legal case filed by Saul Arellano, which was dismissed by a judge in 2006; a collective lawsuit, "4 Million Kids," filed by several children throughout the country; marches and demonstrations staged by citizen children; and the Citizen Children Bill sponsored by Congressman José Serrano in the current Congress.

5. For a more extensive discussion of this, see chapter 2.

6. The Postville, Iowa, raid occurred on May 12, 2008, in a kosher slaughterhouse called Agriprocessors. Five hundred workers (mostly Guatemalan) were arrested, and 400 of those were convicted of identity theft. Most were deported after several months of detention. Postville was considered particularly egregious by immigrant rights and human rights activists because of the conditions under which the workers were detained and the collective charge of identity theft, which had never been used in this way before.

7. While I am quoting some of the exact language he used in the Homestead Rally on January 29, 2009, he told this same story with very slight variations in the language in five of the seven events we recorded or observed.

8. NACARA provided some Nicaraguans, Central Americans, Cubans, and nationals of former Soviet states with asylum claims relief from deportation and access to permanent legal residency.

9. The notion of welcoming the stranger was a principle frequently mentioned to me in interviews by religious leaders of different faiths, including Catholic, Evangelical Protestant, and mainline Protestant, as one of the key rationales for many religious communities' support for this issue. There are several passage in the Bible that refer to welcoming the stranger, the most mentioned one (in interviews and literature of religious supporters of immigration reform) being Matthew 25:35: "For I was hungry and you gave me something to eat, I was thirsty and you gave me something to drink, I was a stranger and you invited me in."

10. Pew Hispanic Center 2011 National Survey of Latinos; Pew Research Center for the People and the Press, Aggregated January, March–December 2011 surveys. Cited in http://www .pewhispanic.org/2012/04/04/v-politics-values-and-religion/.

11. During the Homestead event, both brothers were congressional representatives. Lincoln Diaz Balart represented the Twenty-First Congressional District between 1992 and 2011, and Mario Diaz Balart represented the Twenty-Fifth Congressional District from 2003 to 2011. When Lincoln retired from Congress in 2011, Mario was elected to replace him as representative of the Twenty-First Congressional District.

12. This claim begs the question of whether those three million additional Latinos voted for Obama, and even if most of them did, if they were voting in states where their vote actually made a difference. And it also begs the larger question of whether Gutierrez's claim can actually be supported (although widely believed). According to the postelection report of the National Association of Latino Elected Officials (NALEO), there was an 11.5 percent increase in Latino voter turnout between the 2004 and 2008 elections and one in every six Latino voters was voting for the first time in 2008. Among overall Latino voters, 72 percent said they voted for Obama, and 25 percent reported voting for Senator John McCain; second-generation children of immigrants and Spanish speakers showed the strongest support for Obama, nearly 80 percent. http://www.naleo.org/downloads/Post-Election%20Survey.pdf. Since Latinos were one of many groups who supported Obama, it is not clear that their vote made a significant difference outside of battleground states like New Mexico and Nevada, where margins were so narrow that it would not have been possible for Obama to win without

the Latino vote. It is somewhat of an overstatement then to claim that Obama won the presidency because of the Latino vote, although it is something that many Latino activists believe. Increasingly, Latinos are making a bigger difference in the outcome of key and close congressional races, such as the case of the election of Senator Harry Reid in Nevada.

13. The resolution, approved overwhelmingly by voice vote of the National Association of Evangelicals board, called for the government to safeguard national borders, recognize the importance of family reunification, and establish an "equitable process toward earned legal status for currently undocumented immigrants." http://www.christianitytoday.com/ct/2009/octoberweb-only/140.51.0.html.

14. The state mode is most noticeably reflected in the replacement of the legal mechanism of suspension of deportation for cancellation of removal, in which an undocumented immigrant's right to appeal a deportation that was previously based on the hardship to the immigrant if deported is changed exclusively to the hardship to citizen relatives.

15. Also known as the Morton Memo after then ICE director John Morton, this refers to two memos issued on June 17, 2011, that addressed the use of prosecutorial discretion in immigration matters. The memos state that the agency has the authority to not enforce immigration laws against certain individuals and groups. This includes noncitizens who have military, education, and family ties in the United States, as well as victims and witnesses to crimes and plaintiffs in lawsuits. Prosecutorial discretion, however, has not been widely implemented, and individuals in several of those categories continue to be deported.

CHAPTER 4: OUR YOUTH, OUR FAMILIES

1. Secure Communities is a Department of Homeland Security (DHS) program with the goal of identifying immigrants being held in jails who are deportable under immigration law. Participating jails submit an arrestee's fingerprints to a database, which then gives ICE access to information on these individuals.

2. This trend started with the 1996 Illegal Immigration Reform and Immigrant Responsibility Act (IIRIRA), which did not change the categories but barred the readmission of family members who had overstayed their visas. Since then, every bill proposed has created more limits to family criteria while expanding the number of visas for immigrants with specific skills.

3. For example, after IIRIRA movement activists struggled to extend section 245 I of the Immigration and Nationality Act, which allowed people to petition family members who are present in the United States without having to leave the country. However, 245 I was renewed only once and was no longer an option by April 2001.

4. Tamara Nopper, "The Myth of Imported Immigrant Success," Everyday Sociology Blog, July 21, 2009, http://www.everydaysociologyblog.com/2009/07/the-myth-of-imported-immigrant-success.html.

5. Neoliberal nationalism may sound contradictory, since it has frequently been viewed as an ideology and practice directly tied to a globalization process that is often seen as eroding state capacities and sovereignty. Hence, neoliberalism is often equated with the declining power of states and the increasing power of private authority and transnational corporations. Nationalism, as an axis of identity closely tied to the notion of the nation-state, is understood as going through important challenges, as supranationalism and subnationalism (subregional or local forms of nationalism) take hold. The ability for nationalism to survive in a context of globalization has been questioned—however, others have claimed that nationalism persists through change and economic transformation. The forms that nationalism may take,

however, may vary and be transformed in some ways, but be reinforced in others. For a discussion of national identity and globalization, see Hall and du Gay 1996. For an analysis of neoliberal nationalism, see Davidson 2008.

6. Remarks by the president on CIR, July 1, 2010, American University School of International Service, Washington, D.C., http://www.whitehouse.gov/the-press-office/remarks -president-comprehensive-immigration-reform.

7. Remarks by the president on CIR, May 10, 2011, Chamizal National Memorial, El Paso, Texas, http://www.whitehouse.gov/the-press-office/2011/05/10/remarks-president-comprehensive -immigration-reform-el-paso-texas.

8. For a detailed look at the legislative history of the DREAM Act, see Olivas 2010.

9. Hearing before the Subcommittee on Immigration, Citizenship, Refugees, Border Security and International Law of the Committee on the Judiciary, House of Representatives, 110th Congress, 1st sess., May 18, 2007, Serial No. 100–36.

10. Ibid.

11. Transcript of Senate Judiciary Subcommittee on Immigration, Refugees and Border Security Hearing on S 952, Development, Relief, and Education for Alien Minors (DREAM) Act of 2011. Hearing held on June 28, 2011.

12. Ibid.

13. Ibid.

14. No youth I have interviewed have stated that they did not know they were undocumented, and other ethnographers I have consulted who work with undocumented youth have told me that those cases are rare. However, the fact that this is often mentioned as something common is relevant, as it appears to assign even more innocence and therefore more credence to the plight of undocumented youth. What is much more common to hear is that they knew they were undocumented, but did not understand what it really meant until they were adolescents.

15. Transcript of Senate Judiciary Subcommittee on Immigration, Refugees and Border Security Hearing on S 952, Development, Relief, and Education for Alien Minors (DREAM) Act of 2011. Hearing held on June 28, 2011.

16. This absolution of the children of the "crimes" of their parents is not a given, as shown by cases of citizen children who have been charged out-of-state tuition due to the undocumented status of one or more parents (see Olivas 2010) or as reflected in the current debates about changing birthright citizenship so that children born in the United States of undocumented parents would not be automatic citizens.

17. Reyna Wences, interview with author, April 2011.

18. Since an Executive Order in 2002 that expedited citizenship, 83,000 immigrant soldiers have become citizens. Also, by 2012 there had been 144 immigrants who had received posthumous citizenship since 2001. http://articles.latimes.com/2012/dec/07/local/la-me-citizen -posthumous-20121207.

19. The Sensen-Brenner bill is the common name used to refer to Border Protection, Antiterrorism, and Illegal Immigration Control Act of 2005, or HB 4437, passed by the House on December 16, 2005, by a vote of 239 to 182. The bill would have criminalized all undocumented immigrants and the people who assisted them. The immigrant marches helped to prevent the bill from being considered by the Senate in 2006.

20. RIFA is an umbrella organization that consists of several regional organization including ICIRR, CHIRLA, Casa de Maryland, and so forth.

21. For example, during a civil disobedience action in Broadview in April 2010, labor, religious, and civic leaders who sat on the street to stop a bus from taking deportees to the airport each had a picture of a family hanging from their chest. Also during a meeting inaugurating

a group of business leaders for immigration reform, each speaker emphasized the family ties, including their own, that tied them to this issue.

22. Reverend Walter L. Coleman, "What Kind of Immigration Reform Do We Want? A Response to Renee Saucedo," Familia Latina Unida Ministries, April 5, 2010, unpublished document.

23. Wences interview.

24. Rosi Carrasco, interview with author.

25. Passed on April 23, 2010, SB 1070, or the Support Our Law Enforcement and Safe Neighborhoods Act, is a strict anti-undocumented measure that, among other provisions, allows state police to ask for the papers of anybody they suspect of being undocumented, makes it a crime for undocumented people to look for work, and allows certain searches of undocumented immigrants without a warrant. The U.S. Supreme Court struck down many of these provisions in a June 2012 decision, but has allowed the "show me your papers" provision.

26. Wences interview.

27. Alaa Mukahhal, "Because We Are Human and We Demand Nothing Less," IYJL website, posted January 15, 2011, http://www.iyjl.org/because-we-are-human-and-we-demand-nothing -less/.

28. Wences interview.

29. Immigrant Youth Justice League website, http://www.iyjl.org/?p=2000.

30. Wences interview.

31. http://www.iyjl.org/were-not-cute-were-organized/.

32. Martin Unzueta, interview with author, March 29, 2012.

33. After the DREAM vote, youth from IYJL and other youth organizations left the UWD coalition and joined forces to create a new national organization called the National Immigrant Youth Alliance.

34. Immigrant Youth Justice League website, http://www.iyjl.org/?p=2392.

35. Immigrant Youth Justice League website, http://www.iyjl.org/?p=406.

36. Examples of parent organizations include Dreamer's Moms, which has chapters in nine states and is linked to UWD (for more, see http://voxxi.com/2013/07/13/dreamers-moms -immigration-reform/); and groups of parents within organizations, such as the New Orleans Center for Workers' Racial Justice.

CONCLUSION

1. Correspondence with Alma Silva, September 6, 2013.

2. "Elvira Arellano Returns to Chicago," video, Lincoln United Methodist Church Sunday Services, Chicago, March 23, 2014, https://www.youtube.com/watch?v=3aoYYlLZoSg. For more details on Arellano's return, see also http://voxxi.com/2014/03/18/elvira-arellano -bring-them-home-us-entry/.

REFERENCES

Abrego, Leisy. 2011. "Legal Consciousness of Undocumented Latinos: Fear and Stigma as Barriers to Claim-Making for First Generation and 1.5 Generation Immigrants." *Law and Society Review* 45, no. 2 (May): 337–370. doi: 10.1111/j.1540–5893.2011.00435.x.

Agosin, Marjorie. 1990. *The Mothers of the Plaza de Mayo: The Story of Renee Epelbaum.* Trenton, N.J.: Red Sea Press.

Ahmad, Muneer. 2011. "Developing Citizenship." *Issues in Legal Scholarship* 9, no. 1 (October): 1539–8323. doi: 10.2202/1539–8323.1129.

Amaya, Hector. 2007. "Dying American or the Violence of Citizenship: Latinos in Iraq." *Latino Studies* 5:3-24

Anzaldúa, Gloria. 1987. *Borderlands/La Frontera: The New Mestiza.* San Francisco: Aunt Lute Books.

Arendt, Hannah. 1958. *The Human Condition.* Chicago: University of Chicago Press.

Balibar, Etienne, and Immanuel Wallerstein. 1991. *Race Nation Class: Ambiguous Identities.* London: Verso.

Basch, Linda, Cristina Blanc-Szanton, and Nina Glick Schiller. 1992. "Towards a Transnational Perspective on Migration: Race, Class, Ethnicity, and Nationalism Reconsidered." *Annals of the New York Academy of Science* 645 (July): 1-24. doi: 10.1111/j.1749–6632.1992.tb33482.x.

Bau, Ignatius. 1985. *This Ground Is Holy: Church Sanctuary and Central American Refugees.* Mahwah, N.J.: Paulist Press.

Beltran, Cristina. 2009. "Going Public: Hannah Arendt, Immigrant Action, and the Space of Appearance." *Political Theory* 37, no. 5 (October): 591–622. http://www.jstor.org/stable/25655506.

Boehm, Deborah. 2011. "Out of Place: Youth and Deportation in the U.S.-Mexico Transnation." Paper presented at the Annual Meeting of Anthropology of Children and Youth Interest Group, Society for Cross-Cultural Research, and Society for Anthropological Sciences, Charleston, S.C., February 16–19.

Bonilla-Silva, Eduardo. 2012. "The Invisible Weight of Whiteness: The Racial Grammar of Contemporary Life in Everyday America." *Ethnic and Racial Studies* 35 (2): 173–194. doi:10.1080/01419870.2011.613997.

Bosco, Fernando. 2006. "The Madres de Plaza de Mayo and Three Decades of Human Rights' Activism: Embeddedness, Emotions, and Social Movements." *Annals of the Association of American Geographers* 96, no. 2 (June): 342–265. doi: 10.1111/j.1467–8306.2006.00481.x.

———. 2007. "Mother Activism and the Geographic Conundrum of Social Movements." *Urban Geography* 28 (5): 426–431. doi:10.2747/0272–3638.28.5.426.

Bosniak, Linda. 2008. *The Citizen and the Alien: Dilemmas of Contemporary Membership.* Princeton, N.J.: Princeton University Press.

Brotherton, David, and Luis Barrios. 2011. *Banished to the Homeland: Dominican Deportees and Their Stories of Exile.* New York: Columbia University Press.

Brown, Wendy. 2003. "Neo-liberalism and the End of Liberal Democracy." *Theory & Event* 7 (1). http://muse.jhu.edu/.

Capps, Randolph, and Fortuny Karina. 2006. "Immigration and Child and Family Policy." Washington, D.C.: Urban Institute. http://www.urban.org/publications/311362.html

Chaudry, Ajay, Randolph Capps, Juan Pedroza, Rosa Maria Castaneda, Robert Santos, and Molly M. Scott. 2010. "Facing Our Future: Children in the Aftermath of Immigration Enforcement." Washington, D.C.: Urban Institute. http://www.urban.org/publications/412020.html

Chavez, Leo. 1997. *Shadowed Lives: Undocumented Immigrants in American Society*. Independence, Ky.: Cengage Learning.

———. 2004. "A Glass Half Empty: Latina Reproduction and Political Discourse." *Human Organization* 63 (2): 173–188.

———. 2008. *The Latino Threat: Constructing Immigrants, Citizens, and the Nation*. Stanford, Calif.: Stanford University Press.

Chicago Reporter. 2003. "Terrorism Sting Busts Immigrants." March 1. http://www.highbeam.com/doc/1G1-99326227.html.

Cohen, Jean. 1985. "Strategy or Identity: New Theoretical Paradigms and Contemporary Social Movements. " *Social Research* 52 (4): 663–716. http://www.jstor.org/stable/40970395.

Coontz, Stephanie. 1993. *The Way We Never Were: American Families and the Nostalgia Trap*. New York: Basic Books.

———. 1998. *The Way We Really Are: Coming to Terms with America's Changing Families*. New York: Basic Books.

Coutin, Susan B. 2000a. "Denationalization, Inclusion, and Exclusion: Negotiating the Boundaries of Belonging." *Indiana Journal of Global Legal Studies* 7, no. 2, article 8. http://www.repository.law.indiana.edu/ijgls/vo17/iss2/8.

———. 2000b. *Legalizing Moves: Salvadoran Immigrants' Struggle for U.S. Residency*. Ann Arbor: University of Michigan Press.

———. 2003. "Illegality, Borders, and the Space of Non-existence." In *Globalization under Construction: Governmentality, Law, and Identity*, edited by Richard Warren Perry and Bill Maurer. Minneapolis: University of Minnesota Press.

Crittenden, Ann. 1988. *Sanctuary: A Story of American Conscience and the Law in Collision*. London: Weidenfeld & Nicolson.

Davidson, Neil. 2008. "Nationalism and Neoliberalism." *Variant* 32 (Summer). http://www.variant.org.uk/32texts/davidson32.html.

Davila, Arlene. 2008. *Latino Spin: Public Image and the Whitewashing of Race*. New York: New York University Press.

De Genova, Nicholas. 2005. *Working the Boundaries: Race, Space, and "Illegality" in Mexican Chicago*. Durham, N.C.: Duke University Press.

———. 2010. "The Deportation Regime: Sovereignty, Space, and the Freedom of Movement." In *The Deportation Regime: Sovereignty, Space, and the Freedom of Movement*, edited by Nicholas De Genova and Nathalie Peutz. Durham, N.C.: Duke University Press.

"Demonstrators Demand Amnesty for Illegal Immigrants." 2006. *People's Daily Online*, September 3. http://english.peopledaily.com.cn/200609/04/eng20060904_299243.html.

Department of Homeland Security. 2009. "Removals Involving Illegal Alien Parents of United States Citizen Children." http://www.oig.dhs.gov/assets/Mgmt/OIG_09-15_Jan09.pdf.

"Deportation Lawsuit Takes New Turn." 2006. *Chicago Tribune*, September 8. http://articles.chicagotribune.com/2006-09-08/news/0609080339_1_elvira-arellano—deportation-citizen-children.

Desmond, Matthew, and Ruth Lopez-Turley. 2009. "The Role of Familism in Explaining the Hispanic-White College Application Gap." *Social Problems* 56:311–334. http://scholar.harvard.edu/files/mdesmond/files/sp5602_05.pdf.

Dikec, Mustafa. 2013. "Beginners and Equals: Political Subjectivity in Arendt and Ranciere." *Transactions of the Institute of British Geographers* 38, no. 1 (January): 78–90. doi: 10.1111/j.1475–5661.2012.00508.x.

Dreby, Joanna. 2012. "How Today's Immigration Enforcement Policies Impact Children, Families, and Communities." Washington, D.C.: Center for American Progress. http://www.americanprogress.org/issues/immigration/report/2012/08/20/27082/how-todays-immigration-enforcement-policies-impact-children-families-and-communities/.

Flores-Gonzalez, Nilda, and Elena Gutierrez. 2010. "Taking the Public Square." In *Marcha: Latino Chicago and the Immigrant Rights Movement*, edited by Amalia Pallares and Nilda Flores-Gonzalez. Chicago: University of Illinois Press.

Fuligni, Andrew, Vivian Tseng, and May Lam. 1999. "Attitudes toward Family Obligations among American Adolescents with Asian, Latin American, and European Backgrounds." *Child Development* 70 (4): 1030–1044. doi: 10.1111/1467–8624.00075.

Gamson, Joshua. 1995. "Must Identity Movements Self-Destruct? A Queer Dilemma." *Social Problems* 42:390–407. http://links.jstor.org/sici?sici=0037- 7791%28199508%2942%3A3%3C390%3AMIMSAQ%3E2.0.CO%3B2-0.

Gerson, Kathleen. 2011. *The Unfinished Revolution: Coming of Age in a New Era of Gender, Work, and Family.* Oxford: Oxford University Press.

Gillis, John R. 1997. *A World of Their Own Making: Myth, Ritual, and the Quest for Family Values.* Cambridge, Mass.: Harvard University Press.

Golash-Boza, Tanya. 2012. *Immigration Nation: Raids, Detentions, and Deportations in Post-9/11 America.* Boulder, Colo.: Paradigm.

Golden, Renny, and Michael McConnell. 1986. *Sanctuary: The New Underground Railroad.* New York: Orbis Books.

Gomberg-Muñoz, Ruth. 2012. "Inequality in a 'Postracial' Era: Race, Immigration, and Criminalization of Low-Wage Labor." *DuBois Review* 9 (2): 339–353. http://works.bepress.com/ruth_gomberg-munoz/1.

Gonzales, Roberto, and Leo Chavez. 2012. "Awakening to a Nightmare: Abjectivity and Illegality in the Lives of Undocumented 1.5 Generation Latino Immigrants in the United States." *Current Anthropology* 53 (3): 253–281. doi: 10.1086/665414.

Grayzel, Susan R. 1999. *Women's Identities at War: Gender, Motherhood, and Politics in Britain and France during the First World War.* Chapel Hill: University of North Carolina Press.

Gutierrez, Elena. 2008. *Fertile Matters: The Politics of Mexican-Origin Women's Reproduction.* Austin: University of Texas Press.

Guzman Bouvard, Marguerite. 2002. *Revolutionizing Motherhood: The Mothers of the Plaza de Mayo.* Lanham, Md.: Rowman and Littlefield.

Hall, Stuart, and Paul du Gay. 1996. *Questions of Cultural Identity.* London: Sage Press.

Hartnett, Caroline S., and Emilio Parrado. 2012. "Hispanic Familism Reconsidered: Ethnic Differences in the Perceived Value of Children and Fertility Intentions." *Sociological Quarterly* 53 (4): 636–653. doi: 10.1111/j.1533–8525.2012.01252.x.

Harrison, Algea, Melvin N. Wilson, Charles J. Pine, Samuel Q. Chan, and Raymond Buriel. 1990. "Family Ecologies of Ethnic Minority Children." *Child Development* 61:347–362. http://www.jstor.org/stable/1131097.

Hawken, Paul. 2007. *Blessed Unrest: How the Largest Movement in the World Came into Being, and Why No One Saw It Coming.* New York: Viking Press.

Hawthorne, Monique Lee. 2007. "Family Unity in Immigration Law: Broadening the Scope of Family." *Lewis and Clark Law Review* 11: 809–833.

Hirsch, Jennifer S. 2003. *A Courtship after Marriage: Sexuality and Love in Mexican Transnational Marriages.* Berkeley: University of California Press.

Hondageneu-Sotelo, Pierrette, and Ernestine Avila. 1997. "I'm Here but I'm There: The Meanings of Latina Transnational Motherhood." *Gender and Society* 11, no. 5 (October): 548–571. doi: 10.1177/089124397011005003.

Honig, Bonnie. 2001. *Democracy and the Foreigner.* Princeton, N.J.: Princeton University Press.

Honohan, Iseult. 2009. "Rethinking the Claim to Family Reunification in Migration." *Political Studies* 57 (4): 768–787.

"Immigrant Mother Hurts Her Cause with Standoff." 2006. *Chicago Sun Times,* December 21. http://www.highbeam.com/doc/1P2-3695066.html.

Isin, Engin F. 2002. *Being Political: Genealogies of Citizenship.* Minneapolis: University of Minnesota Press.

Jakobsen, Janet R. 2000. "My Sexual Regulation? Family Values and Social Movements." In *God Forbid: Religion and Sex in American Public Life,* edited by Kathleen Sands. Oxford: Oxford University Press.

Jetter, Alexis, Anelisse Overleck, and Diana Taylor, eds. 1997. *The Politics of Motherhood: Activists' Voices from Left to Right.* Hanover, N.H.: University Press of New England.

Keely, Charles. 1971. "Effects of the Immigration Act of 1965 on Selected Population Characteristics of Immigrants to the United States." *Demography* 8, no. 2 (May): 157–169. doi:10.2307/2060606.

Kriesi, Hanspeter, Ruud Koopmans, Jan Willem Duyvendak, and Marco G. Giugni. 1995. *New Social Movements in Western Europe: A Comparative Analysis.* Minneapolis: University of Minnesota Press.

Lorentsen, Robin. 1991. *Women in the Sanctuary Movement.* Philadelphia: Temple University Press.

Lucero, Jose Antonio. 2008. *Struggles of Voice: The Politics of Indigenous Representation in the Andes.* Pittsburgh: University of Pittsburgh Press.

"Marking Up the Dream." 2010. Story six of *How Democracy Works Now.* Documentary series, directed by Michael Camerini and Sheri Robertson. DVD, 59 min.

Mascia-Lees, Frances, ed. 2011. *A Companion to the Anthropology of the Body and Embodiment.* Oxford: Wiley-Blackwell Press.

Massey, Douglas D., Jorge Durand, and Nolan J. Malone. 2003. *Beyond Smoke and Mirrors: Mexican Immigration in an Era of Economic Integration.* New York: Russell Sage Foundation.

McAdam, Doug, John McCarthy and Mayer Zald. 1996. *Comparative Perspectives on Social Movements.* Cambridge: Cambridge University Press.

Mendelson, Margot. 2010. "Constructing America: Mythmaking in U.S. Immigration Courts." *Yale Law Journal* 119. http://www.yalelawjournal.org/comment/constructing-america-mythmaking-in-us-immigration-courts.

Menjivar, Cecilia. 2006. "Liminal Legality: Salvadoran and Guatemalan Immigrants' Lives in the United States." *American Journal of Sociology* 111 (4): 999–1037. http://www.jstor.org/stable/10.1086/499509.

Meyer, David S. 2009. "How Social Movements Matter." In *The Social Movements Reader: Cases and Concepts,* 2nd ed., edited by Jeff Goodwin and James M. Jasper. Malden, Mass.: Wiley-Blackwell.

Meyer, David S., and Nancy Whittier. 1994. "Social Movement Spillover." *Social Problems* 41:277–298. https://webfiles.uci.edu/dmeyer/spillover.sp.pdf.

Mitchell, Mary. 2006. "Elvira Arellano Is No Rosa Parks." *Chicago Sun Times,* August 22. http://blogs.suntimes.com/mitchell/2006/08/arellano_is_no_rosa_parks.html.

Mothers Against Illegal Aliens. "Updates from Chicago." http://www.mothersagainstillegalaliens.org.

Ngai, Mae M. 2004. *Impossible Subjects: Illegal Aliens and the Making of Modern America*. Princeton, N.J.: Princeton University Press.

———. 2013. "Let's Get to the Root of the Immigration Problem." *Dallas News*, January 20. http://www.dallasnews.com/opinion/latest-columns/20130130-mae-m.-ngai-lets-get-to -the-root-of-the-immigration-problem.ece.

Niemman, Yolanda, Andrea Romero, and Consuelo Arbona. 2000. "Effects of Cultural Orientation on the Perception of Conflict between Relationship and Educational Goals for Mexican American College Students." *Hispanic Journal of Behavioral Sciences* 22(10): 46– 63. http://ird.crge.umd.edu/entry_display.php?id=332.

Nyers, Peter. 2010. "Abject Cosmopolitanism: The Politics of Protection in the Anti-Deportation Movement." In *The Deportation Regime: Sovereignty, Space, and the Freedom of Movement*, edited by Nicholas De Genova and Nathalie Peutz. Durham, N.C.: Duke University Press.

Oboler, Suzanne. 1995. *Ethnic Labels, Latino Lives: Identity and the Politics of Representation in the United States*. Minneapolis: University of Minnesota Press.

Okagaki, Lynn, and Peter French. 1998. "Parenting and Children's School Achievement: A Multiethnic Perspective." *American Educational Research Journal* 35:125–144. doi: 10.3102/00028312035001123.

Olivas, Michael. 2010. "The Political Economy of the DREAM Act and the Legislative Process: A Case Study of Comprehensive Immigration Reform." *Wayne Law Review* 55:1757– 1810. http://ssrn.com/abstract=1554032.

O'Reilley, Andrea, ed. 2007. *Maternal Theory: Essential Readings*. Toronto: Demeter Press.

Oyserman, Daphna, Heather Coon, and Markus Kemmelmeier. 2002. "Rethinking Individualism and Collectivism: Evaluation of Theoretical Assumptions and Meta-Analyses." *Psychological Bulletin* 128:3–72. doi: 10.1037//0033-2909.128.1.3.

Pallares, Amalia. 2010. "Representing La Familia: Family Separation and Immigrant Activism." In *Marcha: Latino Chicago and the Immigrant Rights Movement*, edited by Amalia Pallares and Nilda Flores-Gonzalez. Chicago: University of Illinois Press.

Pallares, Amalia, and Nilda Flores-Gonzalez, eds. 2010. *Marcha: Latino Chicago and the Immigrant Rights Movement*. Chicago: University of Illinois Press.

Passel, Jeffrey, and D'Vera Cohn. 2010. "U.S. Unauthorized Immigration Flows Are Down Sharply Since Mid-Decade." Washington, D.C.: Pew Hispanic Center. http://www .pewhispanic.org/2010/09/01/us-unauthorized-immigration-flows-are-down-sharply -since-middecade/.

Passel, Jeffrey, D'Vera Cohn, and Ana Gonzalez-Barrera. 2012. "Net Migration from Mexico Falls to Zero—and Perhaps Less." Washington, D.C.: Pew Hispanic Center. http://www .pewhispanic.org/2012/04/23/net-migration-from-mexico-falls-to-zero-and-perhaps-less/.

Perry, Tony. 2012. "Immigrant Marine in Life, U.S. Citizen in Death." *Los Angeles Times*, December 7. http://articles.latimes.com/2012/dec/07/local/la-me-citizen-posthumous- 20121207.

Ranciere, Jacques. 1999. *Dis-agreement: Politics and Philosophy*. Minneapolis: University of Minnesota Press.

Sabogal, Fabio, Gerardo Marin, Regina Otero-Sabogal, Barbara Banoss Marin, and Eliseo Perez-Stable. 1987. "Hispanic Familism and Acculturation: What Changes and What Doesn't?" *Hispanic Journal of Behavioral Sciences* 9:297–412. doi: 10.1177/07399863870094003.

"Sanctuary for Now: One Illegal Immigrant Battles in the Public Eye." 2007. *Milwaukee Journal Sentinel*, February 9. http://milwaukee-journal-sentinel.vlex.com/vid/sanctuary-illegal -immigrant-battles-74395461.

Santa Ana, Otto. 2002. *Brown Tide Rising: Metaphors of Latinos in Contemporary American Public Discourse*. Austin: University of Texas Press.

Sarkisian, Natalia, and Naomi Gerstei. 2012. *Nuclear Family Values, Extended Family Lives: The Power of Race, Class, and Gender*. New York: Routledge.

Sarkisian, Natalia, Mariana Gerena, and Naomi Gerstel. 2006. "Extended Family Ties among Mexicans, Puerto Ricans, and Whites: Superintegration or Disintegration?" *Family Relations* 55:331–344. http://eric.ed.gov/?id=EJ738176.

Schwartz, Seth. 2007. "The Applicability of Familism to Diverse Ethnic Groups: A Preliminary Study." *Journal of Social Psychology* 147 (2): 101–118. doi:10.3200/SOCP.147.2.101–118.

Self, Robert. 2012. *All in the Family: The Realignment of American Democracy since the 1960s*. New York: Hill and Wang.

Stacy, Judith. 1997. *In the Name of the Family: Rethinking Family Values in the Postmodern Age*. Boston: Beacon Press.

Stephen, Lynn. 2007. *Transborder Lives: Oaxacan Indigenous Migrants in the U.S. and Mexico*. Durham, N.C.: Duke University Press.

Swedlow, Amy. 1993. *Women Strike for Peace: Traditional Motherhood and Radical Politics in the 1960s*. Chicago: University of Chicago Press.

Tarrow, Sidney. 1994. *Power in Movement: Social Movements, Collective Action, and Politics*. Cambridge: Cambridge University Press.

Telles, Edward, and Vilma Ortiz. 2007. *Generations of Exclusion: Mexican Americans, Assimilation, and Race*. Durham, N.C.: Duke University Press.

Thronsonn, David B. 2008. "Custody and Contradictions. Exploring Immigration Law as Federal Family Law in the Context of Child Custody." *Hastings Law Journal* 59. http://ssrn.com/abstract=1155223.

Tomsho, Robert. 1987. *The American Sanctuary Movement*. Austin: Texas Monthly Press.

Touraine, Alain. 1988. *Return of the Actor: Social Theory in a Post-Industrial Society*. Minneapolis: University of Minnesota Press.

Valenzuela, Angela, and Sanford Dornbusch. 1994. "Familism and Social Capital in the Academic Achievement of Mexican Origin and Anglo Adolescents." *Social Science Quarterly* 75:18–36. http://psycnet.apa.org/psycinfo/1995–15273–001.

Van der Klein, Marian, Rebecca Jo Plant, Nichole Sanders, and Lori Weintrop, eds. 2012. *Maternalism Reconsidered: Motherhood, Welfare, and Social Policy in the Twentieth Century*. New York: Oxford: Berghahn Books.

Warren, Kay B., and Jean E. Jackson. 2003. *Indigenous Movement, Self-Representation, and the State in Latin America*. Austin: University of Texas Press.

Wessler, Seth F. 2011. *Shattered Families: The Perilous Intersection of Immigration Enforcement and the Child Welfare System*. Washington, D.C.: Applied Research Center. http://www.annarbor.com/ARC_Report_Shattered_Families_FULL_REPORT.pdf.

———. 2012. "Nearly 205K Deportations of Parents of U.S. Citizens in Just Over Two Years." *Colorlines*, December 17. http://colorlines.com/archives/2012/12/us_deports_more_than_200k_parents.html.

Willen, Sarah. 2007. *Transnational Migration to Israel in a Global Comparative Context*. Lanham, Md.: Lexington Books.

Wright, Melissa. 2001. "Feminine Villains, Masculine Heroes, and the Reproduction of Ciudad Juarez." *Social Text* 19 (4): 93–113. http://muse.jhu.edu/login?auth=0&type=summary&url=/journals/social_text/v019/19.4wright.html.

Yoshikawa, Hirokazu. 2011. *Immigrants Raising Citizens: Undocumented Parents and Their Young Children*. New York: Russell Sage Foundation.

Zavella, Pat. 2011. *I'm Neither Here nor There: Mexicans' Quotidian Struggles with Migration and Poverty*. Durham, N.C.: Duke University Press.

————. 2012. *Why Are Immigrant Families Different Now?* Policy Brief. Center for Latino Policy Research University of California. http://escholarship.org/uc/item/77k1morm#page-4.

Zorn, Eric. 2006. "Deportation Standoff Not Helping Cause." *Chicago Tribune*, August 17. http://articles.chicagotribune.com/2006–08–17/news/0608170077_1_elvira-arellano -arrest-and-deportation-rosa-parks.

Zuñiga, Victor, and Edmund T. Hamman. 2006. "Going Home? Schooling in Mexico of Trans-national Children." *Confinesde Relaciones Internacionales y Ciencia Politica* 2 (4). http:// digitalcommons.unl.edu/cgi/viewcontent.cgi?article=1043&context=teachlearnfacpub.

INDEX

drug cartels, 32, 138
drug convictions, 29, 34
Duncan, Arne, 107–108
DuPage County (Ill.), 98, 125
Durand, Jorge, 23–24
Durbin, Dick, 39–40, 64, 104–
105, 108, 114, 119, 122

economics: and Crisóstomo, 54–59, 61;
and displacement, 50, 54, 56, 58–59,
61; and DREAM Act, 98–103, 105–
109, 111–112, 119–120, 127; economic
justice, 8; and financial crises, 27, 107;
and financial deregulation, 101; and
FU national campaign, 85–86; global
political economy, 57–58, 99, 101–102,
106–107, 112, 127; and immigration laws,
25, 27–30, 35–37; and LFLU, 68–69,
71; and neoliberal frame, 98, 100–103;
and reproductive threats, 29–30
Ecuador, 45
education: and DREAM Act, 103–111,
128; and familism, 11; and immigration
laws, 29, 36; and learning disabilities, 36,
39; and LFLU, 70–71; and Proposition
187 (Calif.), 29; and STEM, 107–108
egalitarianism, 4, 69
elections, Mexican, 50
elections, U.S., 41, 82–83, 88–
89, 132, 145n12
El Paso (Tex.), 102, 127
El Salvador, 38, 143n1
Emanuel, Rahm, 130
embassies, U.S., 54, 141n2
employers: of domestic workers, 57; and sanctions, 27
enforcement, 132, 139; and DREAM Act,
113, 115; and expedited removal, 32;
external enforcement, 29–30, 32; and
immigration laws, 24, 29–32, 37; and
immigration reform bills, 41; intensification of, 35; internal enforcement, 29–30,
32, 35; and raids, 32, 54, 65, 75–76, 81,
89, 145n6. See also border enforcement;
Immigration and Customs Enforcement
English language, 111–112
entrepreneurship, 100, 102, 107–108, 130
Esparza, Hugo, 127
essentialized visions of family, 11

ethnic boundaries: and intersecting, 18; and "transborder," 15
eugenics, 8, 30
Evangelicals, 56, 79, 82–85, 88–90, 145n9
exclusions, 5–7, 12–14, 16–17, 22, 133–
34, 137, 139; and Arellano, 60; and
Crisóstomo, 60; and DREAM Act, 18,
101, 105–106, 116, 123, 126, 133; and
immigration laws, 24, 29–30; and Jiménez,
Raquel, 62–63; and LFLU, 69–70, 73–74,
96; from state services/resources, 29–30
expedited removal, 32
extended families, 25
extreme hardship, 1, 32–33, 74

Facebook, 125, 132, 136
fairness, 26–27, 90, 143n6; and
DREAM Act, 104, 108–109
Familias Unidas (FU), 20, 63, 129, 135;
and agency, 91–92, 96; and collective identity/action as theme, 81–87,
91–92, 94–95, 135; and family frame,
21, 56, 90–91, 94–96; and Golden Rule,
86–87, 91; and higher law as theme,
79–81, 86, 91; and national campaign,
21, 75–93; and oppressed people,
immigrants as, 79, 81–82, 84–86; and
responsible leadership as theme, 87–90;
significance of national campaign, 90–93;
structure/themes of rallies, 78–90
Families for Freedom (New York), 72–74
familism, 11–12
family as political subject, 1–3, 7–12, 17,
21–22, 62–96, 133–135, 138–140; and
citizen children/relatives, 48, 62–74, 79,
85, 91–93; as collective/valuable, 93–96;
and cultural constructions of family,
25–26; and essentialized vision, 11; and
familial love/responsibility, 66–69; and
FU national campaign, 21, 75–96; and
immigration laws, 25–26, 37; and Jiménez,
Raquel, 62–63, 91; and LFLU, 64–74,
95–96, 126; and political subjectivities,
17, 19–20; and visits to ailing/dying
relatives, 66–67. See also family frame
family as social institution, 2, 7, 11–12
family frame, 3, 11, 17, 19–22; and
Arellano, 38, 48, 52–53, 59–61;
and Crisóstomo, 56, 58–61;

Institutional Revolutionary Party. *See* PRI
intersecting, 2, 17–19, 135, 138
intersectionality, 9, 47–48, 59, 126
Iraq veterans, 47–48
IRCA. *See* Immigration Reform
and Control Act
Isin, Engin, 14
IYJL. *See* Immigrant Youth Justice League

Jackson, Jean, 45
Jakobsen, Janet, 7–8, 70
Jefferson, Thomas, 78, 90
Jesucristo es mi Refugio (Evangeli-
cal) Church (Dallas, Tex.), 77
Jews, 84, 89
Jimenez, Marta, 70
Jiménez, Raquel, 62–63, 91
Johnson, Lyndon B., 8
Joliet (Ill.), 77, 79–80, 89, 92
Juarez, Mexico, 143n8
judicial system. *See* courts of law,
U.S.; immigration laws

Keely, Charles, 24–25
Kennedy, John F., 26
kidnapping, 138

labor systems, 136; and agricultural jobs,
116; and bracero program, 24; and cheap/
flexible labor, 57–58, 68–69, 112; and
DREAM Act, 104, 106–107, 120; and
immigration laws, 25; and labor history,
42; labor issues, 56; and labor migration,
51, 68–69, 104; and labor movement, 2,
41, 95, 124; protections for, 4, 25; temporary guest worker programs, 29, 104,
112; and "transborder," 15; and unemployment relief, 36; and work permits, 124
La Familia Latina Unida (LFLU), 19–20,
62–63, 66, 93–95, 116; and Arellano,
20–21, 38–40, 44, 46, 48, 52, 64–65,
135, 138; background of, 64–65; and
Barrios, Martin, 43–44; and citizen
children, 48, 66, 69–73, 144n3, 145n4;
and DREAM Act, 126; and familial
love/responsibility, 66–69, 73, 85; and
family frame, 21, 63–64, 94–96, 126;
and family values, 66–67, 69–73, 94,
96; and mixed-status family as political

subject, 65–66; and national campaign,
63, 75–78; and online photo album, 46,
66, 70; and private bill, 64–65; strategies of, 73–75. *See also* Familias Unidas
Latin Americans, 3; and cultural constructions of family, 25–26; depictions of, 6;
as domestic workers, 57; and economic
displacement, 58; and LFLU, 69
Latino Action Youth League
(LOYAL), 98, 121, 126
Latinos, 2–3, 21; and DREAM Act,
127–128; and familism, 11–12; and
FU national campaign, 76–78, 81–85,
88–92, 94–95, 145n12; and immigration laws, 37; and "Latino threat," 6;
racialization of as foreigners, 5–6; and
representativity, 45–46, 49; second- /
third-generation, 45–46, 56, 83, 145n12
legal permanent residents (LPRs), 5;
and DREAM Act, 106, 112, 117;
and FU national campaign, 85, 91;
and immigration laws, 27–28, 31–
32, 34, 141n2, 142n11; and LFLU,
65, 73; and NACARA, 145n8
legal status, 1–5, 16–17; and DREAM Act,
114, 116–117, 123, 125, 128–130; and
FU national campaign, 77, 84–85, 91,
146n13; and immigration laws, 23–24,
26, 30–32, 34, 36–37; and LFLU, 69,
73; and political subjectivities, 16–17;
and theorization of noncitizenship,
3–7. *See also* legal permanent residents; undocumented immigrants
LFLU. *See* La Familia Latina Unida
liberal democracies, 3–4, 13, 100
liminality, 14, 16, 130; and LFLU,
72; liminal legality, 16
Lincoln, Abraham, 90
Lipinski, Dan, 136–137
lobbying, 18, 48, 64–65, 72, 109
Lopez, Fanny, 126, 137
Lopez-Turley, Ruth, 11
Los Angeles, 41–42, 46; Homies
Unidos, 72–74
LOYAL. *See* Latino Action Youth League
Lozano, Emma, 39, 55, 63
LPRs. *See* legal permanent residents
Lucero, Jose Antonio, 45
Lutherans, 83

ABOUT THE AUTHOR

AMALIA PALLARES is an associate professor of political science and Latin American and Latino Studies and the director of Latin American and Latino Studies at the University of Illinois at Chicago. She received a B.A. from the University of Houston and a Ph.D. in government from the University of Texas at Austin. She is the author of *From Peasant Struggles to Indian Resistance: The Ecuadorian Andes in the Late Twentieth Century* and the coeditor of *Marcha: Latino Chicago and the Immigrant Rights Movement*.

AVAILABLE TITLES IN THE LATINIDAD: TRANSNATIONAL CULTURES IN THE UNITED STATES SERIES

CPSIA information can be obtained at www.ICGtesting.com
Printed in the USA
BVOW01s1203270215

389388BV00023B/5/P